HERMANN...GOERTZ

CRET

ENCL.... *repub*

INSPECTOR GENERAL'S OFFICE

REF........

Belfast 25421.

F...44446./BIH/JS

S..37./440/39

Royal Ulster Constabulary,

BELFAST.

...12th.......January.,.........1942...

1060

iddell,

have got some information about GOER~

the Spring of 1940 Stephen
ssion for the I.R.A. '
got there he wa~
by the I.P
t whe~

H/1357
(5 pages)

MOST SECRET

e below water level would
freeboard). Towing t
azardous and almost
ade in Russia the product
ntil the late Spring and
efore June or July

WORLD WAR II PLANS
THAT NEVER HAPPENED
1939–45

WORLD WAR II PLANS
THAT NEVER HAPPENED
1939–45

MICHAEL KERRIGAN

amber
BOOKS

This edition first published in 2011

Published by
Amber Books Ltd
74–77 White Lion Street
London N1 9PF
United Kingdom
www.amberbooks.co.uk

ISBN: 978-1-907446-64-1

Printed in China

Project Editor: Sarah Uttridge
Designer: Jerry Williams
Picture Research: Terry Forshaw

Contents

Introduction

We naturally see World War II as one of the great historic dramas of modern times: a terrible, titanic struggle between good and evil. On the ground, a heroic epic of arms, it was a tragedy for the millions of soldiers and civilians who suffered and lost their lives, from the streets of London to the Burmese forests and the Russian steppe. This was truly a world war, pitching submarines against merchant shipping in the deep Atlantic; guerrillas against Japanese army units in the Philippines. Iceland was occupied; Australia was threatened with invasion; the North African desert became a theatre of war.

But behind the scenes a more mundane struggle was taking place as the combatant powers attempted to direct the drama. While commanding officers looked for the feints and moves that would win them the edge in battle, back home their political masters sought the strategic initiatives that would bring victory. In support, civil servants, intelligence agents and officials of every kind frantically pulled

MacArthur lands at Leyte (20 October 1944), on the brink of completing his quest to liberate the Philippines.

strings and set up schemes, seeking to stage-manage the action as it unfolded. They certainly had an impact – though by no means necessarily the one they anticipated. Their decisions (or, sometimes, indecision) played themselves out in the field of combat, nudging the narrative in a new direction here; tipping the balance infinitesimally there.

Plan of Action

The opening up of key archives over the last few years has enabled us to look backstage and see in unprecedented detail how planners on both sides tried to shape events. Intelligence reports, directives, memos, minutes of cabinets and committees: a vast array of sources has become available, affording vivid insights into their thinking. Churchill rides a hobby-horse here; Eisenhower expresses impatience there; a Japanese industrialist gloats over the capabilities of the new super-bomber he hopes to build...

A vast array of sources, but also a potentially bewildering one. This book sets out to consider how rear-echelon planning influenced frontline action in a series of specific operations. That way, we can get a focus: chronological distance from the war, far from obscuring things, has brought perspective.

On Paper

The catch, of course, is that the best-laid schemes proverbially go awry. The contempt of the frontline soldiery for their headquarters staff and their political masters back home is legendary – and has been in every conflict in every age. But then the hierarchy's hopelessness just highlights the eternal gap between theory and practice, between plan and reality: the 'SNAFU' may be a military concept, but its applicability is universal. It's become a cliché: when we say that this or that plan looks good 'on paper', we're implicitly suggesting that it won't work.

Hence the – on the face of it, perhaps, perverse – decision to deal here with plans that didn't actually take place. What can be the value of a history of what hasn't happened? As this book sets out to show, it can in fact be immense. In part as an ironic commentary on actual events. So clear does the historic outline of what happened become that it has easily forgotten how very nearly it didn't; it quickly comes to seem inevitable, when it was actually anything but.

And that's an important thing to lose sight of. When we see World War II as following a single triumphant trajectory, disregarding the provisional plans, the false starts, the improvisatory execution, the bright ideas that came to nothing, we're actually forgetting the very stuff of war.

Fantasy Fighting

It's easy to conclude indeed that, the more obviously and ingeniously 'planned' an operation is, the more likely it is not to come to fruition. It's

Hitler feeds a fawn. The leader's personal quirks influenced the progress of the conflict profoundly yet unpredictably.

It is a characteristic of military problems that they yield to nothing but harsh reality.
General Dwight D. Eisenhower, recalling wartime challenges in 1949.

The story of the war was set down in triplicate. Or at least one side of the war was: each combatant's decision-making was meticulously recorded day by day – sometimes even hour by hour. Researchers in the archives of the combatant nations now have access to an enormous wealth of information: the challenge is to see the narrative wood for so many documentary trees.

DEPARTMENT OF DEFENCE CO-ORDINATION

MINUTE PAPER

6875.

SUBJECT : JAPANESE PLAN FOR INVASION OF AUSTRALIA.

SECRET

CHIEF OF THE NAVAL STAFF

CHIEF OF THE GENERAL STAFF

CHIEF OF THE AIR STAFF

from th...

(NAVAL BRITISH MOST-SECRET)

SECRET - BIGOT   BIGOT

ALLIED FORCE HEADQUARTERS

C-3 SECTION   COPY NO. 33

7 May 1943.

MEMORANDUM FOR: Chief of Staff.

SUBJECT : Plan for Operation BRIMSTONE.

1. Attached is an Appreciation and Outline Plan for Operation BRIMSTONE together with a draft directive for issue to the Force Commanders. Although this operation has not yet been approved by the Combined Chiefs of Staff it is considered that Force Commanders should be appointed and planning should start now, so that, if the operation has to be undertaken, an agreed plan will be ready and time will not be lost.

2. It is not possible at present to detail the forces to be made available for this operation but it appears that:

a. The naval forces required can be made available from those which will be in the MEDITERRANEAN after HUSKY, provided that no other major operation is undertaken simultaneously.

b. The air forces required can be made available as soon as the situation in HUSKY allows them to be diverted from that operation.

c. The military forces can be provided as follows:

(1) If the operation is to be undertaken as soon as possible after HUSKY and before any action on the mainland of ITALY is taken:

II Corps US   34th and 36th Inf Divs
                     1st Armd Div

5th Corps Br   1st, 4th, 46th Inf Divs
                     6th Armd Div

(2) If the operation is to be undertaken after action against the Toe of ITALY;

II Corps US   34th and 36th Inf Divs
                     1st Armd Div

VI Corps US   Three Inf Divs US from HUSKY

d. The shipping and landing craft available in the MEDITERRANEAN after Operation HUSKY would, it is estimated, be sufficient to meet the requirements of this operation, provided no major withdrawal of landing craft from the MEDITERRANEAN has meanwhile taken place. It should be noted, however, that orders have been issued for the US shipping and landing craft now in the MEDITERRANEAN to be withdrawn after HUSKY. Reallocation of these or similar craft sufficient to meet the military plan will be necessary if this operation is to be undertaken.

3. In the Draft Directive the target date for the operation has been set as mid-September. Unless Operation HUSKY is concluded with unexpected rapidity, it is considered that this is the earliest date which could be achieved in view of the facts that:

SECRET - BIGOT

- 1 -

SECRET
(NAVAL BRITISH MOST SECRET)

...tober, 1942
...ich was
...which is
...strating
...telligence
...ernal

...retary
...Committee.

...OCUMENT IS THE PROPERTY OF HIS BRITANNIC MAJESTY'S GOVERNMENT   66

Printed for the War Cabinet. October 1942.

...ECRET.

...483.

...1942.

TO BE KEPT UNDER LOCK AND KEY.

It is requested that special care may be taken to ensure the secrecy of this document.

WAR CABINET.

...OLICY FOR THE CONDUCT OF THE WAR.

Memorandum by the Minister of Defence.

...arbour and the entry of the United States into the war on one ...broke out upon us on the other, opened an entirely new phase ...oceeded with professional advisers to Washington in order to ...ion with President Roosevelt. We were all agreed that the ...er was the prime objective, both in magnitude and in time, ...ust be held as far as possible until the defeat of Germany and ...hole force to be turned upon her.

...ne the President showed himself already deeply interested in ...rican intervention in French North Africa by landings at ...ngier. This operation was called "Gymnast." General ...en advancing towards Benghazi and Agedabia and we had the ...ation, called "Crusader," would be followed by "Acrobat." ...e of our Desert Army to Tripoli. "Gymnast" was explored ...ut before any definite decision could be taken General ...s were thrown back to the Gazala position. All prospects of ...closed and "Gymnast" faded a good deal. However, both ...dent and I continued to regard it as the main and most attractive form of the first American impact upon the Western theatre of war.

[24533]

Copy No. 14

Eire.

17.   In her present attitude Eire constitutes a serious liability.   Although the Government of Eire would probably call instantly for our help in the event of a German attack on Eire territory, they would undoubtedly resist any attempt Eire in advance of a German attack.

TOP SECRET.

BE KEPT UNDER LOCK AND KEY : NEVER TO BE REMOVED FROM THE OFFICE.

SPANISH MINISTER, ANGORA, REPORTS MR. EARLE'S

APPOINTMENT TO GERMANY.

No: 139197

Date: 9th December, 194

From: Spanish Minister, ANGORA.

To: Minister for Foreign Affairs, MADRID.

No: 315-6.

Date: 5th December, 1944.

[Cable: I B].

Mr. EARLE, the personal delegate of the President of the UNITED STATES, tells me th he has received instructions to be ready to undertake a journey to GERMANY, without details to the place or method of getting there.   It is his wish to go to AMERICA first for a thorough exchange of views.

He informed me that the anti-Russian party in the UNITED STATES grows daily, and th the President himself bears in mind the Soviet danger even if —— necessities of the war for to temporize and not dispense with help that valuable for the moment.   A French doctor who knows de GAULLE personally said that this pr —— [I was due to him].

me informer who, a month in advan —— raids, now assure

him
V.3
bef

Director-General
F.O.(3).
Admiralty (2)
War Office-(4
Air Ministry
M.I.5. (2).
Colonel Vick
Major Morton
Sir E. Brid

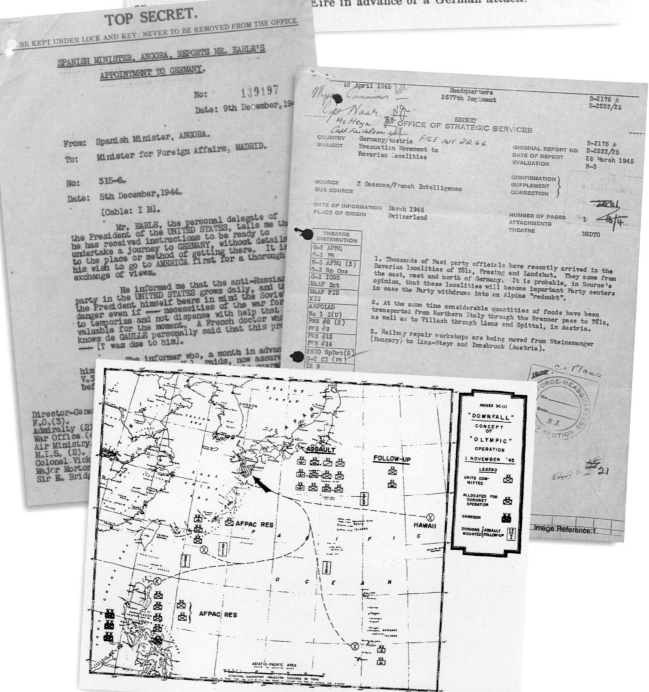

12 April 1945

Headquarters
2677th Regiment

B-2175 &
B-2222/25

SECRET

OFFICE OF STRATEGIC SERVICES

COUNTRY   Germany/Austria
SUBJECT   Evacuation Movement to
           Bavarian Localities

FILE INF 2266

ORIGINAL REPORT NO.   B-2175 &
                      B-2222/25
DATE OF REPORT   28 March 1945
EVALUATION   B-3

SOURCE   Z Cezanne/French Intelligence
SUB SOURCE

CONFIRMATION
SUPPLEMENT
CORRECTION

DATE OF INFORMATION   March 1945
PLACE OF ORIGIN   Switzerland

NUMBER OF PAGES
ATTACHMENTS
THEATRE   MEDTO

THEATRE
DISTRIBUTION
G-2 AFHQ
G-2 PB
G-5 AFHQ (3)
G-3 Sp Ops
G-2 IOSS
MAAF Int
MAAF FIU
NIU
AMFOLAD
No 1 I(U)
PWB #8 (2)
PWB #9
PWB #12
PWB #14
2600 SpDet(5)
G-2 CI (PI)
IS 9

1. Thousands of Nazi party officials have recently arrived in the Bavarian localities of Tölz, Freising and Landshut. They come from the east, west and north of Germany. It is probable, in Source's opinion, that these localities will become important Party centers in case the Party withdraws into an Alpine "redoubt".

2. At the same time considerable quantities of foods have been transported from Northern Italy through the Brenner pass to Tölz, as well as to Villach through Lienz and Spittal, in Austria.

3. Railway repair workshops are being moved from Steinamanger (Hungary) to Linz-Steyr and Innsbruck (Austria).

Image Reference:1

Grand strategy was experienced at street level in the London of the Blitz.

Martin', dumped off the coast of Spain, was washed up, recovered and the documents read – helping to distract the Germans in advance of 'Husky', the invasion of Sicily.

Reality Checks

Improbability, then, need not in itself be an insuperable obstacle to success. But backroom brainstorming, unimpeded by anything too rigorous in the way of a concern for the realities of action, is always liable to come up with imaginatively arresting yet extravagantly fantastical strategies.

Otherwise quite reasonable plans can come unstuck as well, however, foundering (like Operation Handcuff, Operation Culverin, or Bulldozer, on a lack of available tactical or logistical support. A fleet, an army in the wrong place at the wrong time; a shortage of transport or covering artillery: any one thing can turn a winning formula into a lost cause. Timing is of course crucial, the factor that made a non-starter out of Sledgehammer and ruled out Roundup, whilst Operation Overlord went ahead with ultimate success.

Wishful Thinking

Easy as it is to sneer at the staff and politicians, frontline warriors are no more immune to quixotic zeal. General Douglas MacArthur made a personal mission of his drive to regain ground and ultimately recover the Philippines. His heroic enthusiasm is evident in every detail of Operation

tempting even to suspect that military planning is inherently self-indulgent. What else are we to make of an Allied plan to make an aircraft carrier out of ice or a Nazi scheme to stage a wholesale abduction of the 'Big Three' Allied leaders? Could anyone seriously have contemplated taking out Mussolini in a targeted bombing raid? Or making a hostage of His Holiness the Pope?

Well, perhaps the kind of person who seriously contemplated 'Operation Mincemeat', the plan to trick out the dead body of a London down-and-out found on the streets as a high-level Allied agent, bearing plans of an imaginary invasion of Greece and Sardinia scheduled for 1943. That plan didn't just go ahead: it worked triumphantly. Famously, the body of 'Major

Tulsa. Fortunately, naval chiefs were able to cast a colder eye on his plans – and cold water on the operation. US General Lucian Truscott summed up Eisenhower's audacious plans for Operation Satin by saying that it would be 'logistically sound if everything is one hundred percent'. The same might be said for several more of the contemplated-but-cancelled operations covered here.

In some cases, it is clear the planners were looking for a 'silver bullet' of some kind; some inspired breakthrough that would secure victory at a stroke. It might be the assassination of some key personage (they didn't come much more key than Adolf Hitler, target for Britain's Operation Foxley,) or some miraculous machine of war. Japan's Sen-Toku *I-400* submersible aircraft carrier was one such; Germany's Amerika bomber another: either might – at least in theory – have changed the outcome of the war.

Military Mights

This, then, is the story of the World War II that might have been. In some ways should been, perhaps – it certainly must have seemed that way to the strategists as this or that pet plan foundered on the rocks of a rapidly-shifting reality. It is a narrative full of ironies, but full of insight as well: into the ways of military thinking and the realities of war.

The Stars and Stripes flies over Iwo Jima, March 1945 – a triumphant conclusion to a chaotic campaign.

Chapter One
1939–1941

There was to be no 'Phoney War' for the military planners – though plenty of operations didn't come off, whether because they were found to be misconceived or impracticable – or were simply overtaken by fast and furious events.

From the conventional historical perspective, one inescapable reality defined and directed the course of the war in its early stages: Germany's superiority, in men and equipment, in preparedness – and in the advantage of surprise. And that perspective may well have been a just one: behind the scenes, however, things appeared to be a great deal less clear-cut. Allied optimism underwrote audacious plans; whilst the Nazis experienced immense frustration at their failure to 'follow through' on early victories.

Far from feeling deflated after Dunkirk, a Britain belaboured by the bombing of the Blitz was full of ideas for taking the War to Germany. Some of its schemes were defensive, including plans to pre-empt potential German interventions from Iceland to the Azores. Neutral Ireland became a veritable battleground – at least in the imagination of the intelligence officers of either side. Meanwhile, Hitler chafed as the months went by and his plans for a cross-Channel invasion remained hopelessly stalled.

German troops move through Trondheim in April 1940: the sheer pace of the German advance in Norway took the Allies by surprise.

Operation Stratford

A plan to pre-empt a German invasion of Scandinavia by occupying the Swedish orefields was far too ambitious to have had any real prospect of success.

The Anglo-French Supreme War Council gave the go-ahead for Operation Stratford as early as its Paris meeting of 5 February 1940: by this time, German intentions in Scandinavia were already becoming clear. The plan was for 100,000 troops to be installed in central Sweden – fully equipped with all the weaponry and other equipment they would need – to receive the Nazi invaders when they arrived. Churchill was behind the plan, just as he was behind so

many operations during which the Allies overreached themselves: his can-do eagerness involved them in a fair few can'ts.

Winston's War Games

Even in hindsight, with the knowledge that (finally, after five years) he prevailed, the optimism he was showing during the Allies' darkest hour beggars belief. If generals are said to fail because they are trying to fight the previous war, Churchill was unabashed about taking a second crack at ideas he'd tried as First Lord of the Admiralty from 1914 to 1915. His tenure in that post had come to a disastrous end with the failure of the Gallipoli

Above: Winston Churchill. The elder statesman's dignified deportment masked a boyish love of adventure.

Below: Sweden's miners never knew how close to the wartime action they very nearly came.

German anti-aircraft gunners guard an installation on the coast of the Gulf of Finland.

Campaign – and there were arguably echoes of that venture in what he was proposing now.

Naval power was, he insisted, key:

The great question for 1940, as for 1915, is whether and how the Navy can make its surplus force tell in shortening the war.

He went on to entertain options he scarcely had:

If I had to see an extension of the war to Scandinavia or the Balkans, I would choose the former every time. It is nearer to us, better adapted to sea-power (which might even be brought to bear with air-power in the Baltic); Germany herself has to cross the sea to reach Scandinavia; and the Scandinavians are real live he-men to have as allies.

A Scandinavian Sideshow?

Even if Britain and a hard-pressed France could have come up with the manpower and coped with the logistics – and that's a very big question – it's hard to see how the expending of so much effort in what was always likely to be a peripheral theatre in the conflict could have been justified. In later years, Churchill would exasperate the Americans with his unfailing instinct for choosing the indirect approach – his suggestion in 1942 that the Allies approach Germany through Europe's 'soft underbelly' rather than attacking directly through France; his preference for a strategy he likened to drawing a noose round the enemy's neck. It's a vivid image, but it suggests a man who is not thinking in terms of a fast kill. He was, of course, an unusual character in many ways, but in nothing more so than this strange combination of gung-ho enthusiasm and elaborate indirectness.

In the end, events overtook the Allies and Churchill was forced first to scale down his plans for Stratford and then quietly to let it go. Yet Scandinavia remained important: it was never quite a sideshow. If only as a source of resources for the Reich, it remained an important prize, so it continued to have a place in Allied calculations.

As far as Churchill was concerned, Britannia's destroyers ruled the waves.

Operation Wilfred/Plan R4

A plan to invade Norway with a view to cutting off a strategic source of iron ore from the Nazis in neutral Sweden was all too rapidly overtaken by events.

Since the time of Bismarck, 'Blood and Iron' had been the chief ingredients of German foreign policy. The 'young German', said Hitler, should be 'as hard as Krupp's steel.' But metals were of much more than symbolic importance for a country setting out to pursue a strategy of *blitzkrieg*: the Nazi war effort would be anaemic without abundant supplies of steel. Yet Germany's home-produced ore supplies were scant. As of the beginning of 1940, the French fields of Lorraine looked likely to be out of bounds (no one could have guessed how quickly France would fall when the time came). Germany already imported ore from Sweden's Arctic Kiruna and Malmberget regions, some of it coming east and south across the Baltic, but much came via the Norwegian port of Narvik.

The Allies too had their eye on Sweden's ore – though less for their own sakes than for that of denying it to Germany. The outbreak of the Winter War in November 1939 was opportune. Finland's plight seemed the perfect pretext for an expedition through Norway and Sweden, ostensibly in support of the Finns, which would enable them to

occupy the vital orefields and supply-lines. But the Scandinavian states saw straight through this pretended mercy-dash, and refused permission to send troops across their territory.

Shadow Boxing
Winston Churchill then came up with an alternative plan – or, rather, two. The first, named Operation Wilfred, was to involve the mining of Norwegian ports. The hope was that this would provoke a German reaction which

The Norwegian port of Narvik was strategically vital – and guarded accordingly.

The *Altmark* was the centre of a diplomatic incident in 1940.

I reported by telephone to the War Cabinet, who were agreed that Wilfred should go forward.

Winston Churchill, April 1940.

could in turn be used to justify an Allied invasion of Norway, codenamed R4. In its wake, British and French forces would quickly be in a position to push on into northern Sweden. Anglo-French plans were well afoot by late March, in anticipation of a German invasion.

Ironically, this came on 9 April 1940 with the German launch of Operation Weserübung – which was justified by the widespread (and by no means misplaced) belief that the Allies had themselves been planning to take Norway. Led by Nikolaus von Falkenhorst, under Hitler's direction, the invaders came at Norway up through Denmark and from the North Sea: Sweden, though still unoccupied, was virtually encircled.

Plan R4 was redundant now, of course, but with so many men mobilized and transport and equipment marshalled, the Allies were at least in a position to help

Norway defend itself. The signs were hopeful at first, but the Anglo-French forces had to be whisked away within weeks to assist in the defence of France.

The *Altmark* Incident
Norwegian neutrality had been viewed with suspicion by both sides from the start. Winston Churchill, always sceptical, was outraged in February 1940, when Norwegian patrol boats let a naval supply ship, the *Altmark*, sail through their country's waters with only the most token checks, on the pretence that it was voyaging on civil business. This despite the fact that several British prisoners of war were captive in the hold. On 16 February, a party from HMS *Cossack* boarded the *Altmark* to free the men. Norway's protests were swept aside. The incident served to lift British morale: so swashbuckling was the boarding that cutlasses were used!

Nikolaus von Falkenhorst commanded Operation Weserübung, reporting straight to Hitler.

Plan W

If Germany was preparing plans for an invasion of Ireland, Britain had to have its own, officials felt. Perhaps surprisingly, the Irish government agreed.

As critics of Switzerland have long suspected, some neutral nations are more neutral than others. Many in Britain believed that the Irish Free State was giving Germany its discreet support. Prime Minister Neville Chamberlain had held out the possibility of a united Ireland in return for Irish enlistment in the Allied cause, but this had been turned down by a suspicious Dáil.

Anti-English feeling undoubtedly ran high in some sections of the population. Eamon De Valera was notoriously to sign the condolence book at Germany's Dublin embassy when Hitler died in 1945; and there's no doubt that many diehard Republicans took the view that 'my enemy's enemy is my friend'. Churchill felt almost personally affronted by the Dáil's decision to uphold Irish neutrality at the outbreak of the conflict, viewing with disdain a posture of non-alignment that implied some sort of equivalence between the Allied and Axis sides.

Ports and Pre-emption
From a more pragmatic point of view, there was the issue of the Treaty Ports. The Anglo-Irish Treaty that had established the Free State in 1922 had allowed

Britain still had rights in Treaty Ports, including Queenstown (known today as Cobh).

for Britain to continue having rights over deep-water anchorages on the Atlantic coast. These were at Queenstown (now Cobh, in Co. Cork); not far away at Berehaven, in Bantry Bay; and further north at Lough Swilly, in Donegal. At a time when it was already clear that supplies brought in from the United States and the wider world were going to be vitally important, would Britain have to invade the Free State to ensure access to these ports?

And then, through the summer of 1940, increasing amounts of intelligence chatter were intercepted, suggesting that the Germans were themselves considering an attack on Ireland, in Operation Green. Should some pre-emptive strike be launched? Indeed, should the British make

sure that Germany couldn't take Ireland by occupying the country for themselves?

Common Ground
Britain chose instead to open talks with Irish statesmen and intelligence officials. For political and tactical reasons, these were held in secret. They were also held with different parties: while De Valera's Fianna Fáil was stridently anti-English (at least in rhetoric), the opposition Fine Gael party was more amenable. Britain began by establishing contact with Richard Mulcahy, the Fine Gael leader, to explore the possibility of a joint Anglo-Irish command for the island of Ireland as a whole. The hope was that, with Mulcahy on board, De Valera would feel he had no alternative but to agree.

142. The establishment of enemy forces in Eire would further threaten the vital supply line of our Western ports. On the other hand an enemy attack upon Eire would put us in a position to establish naval and air bases there with the consent of the Eire Government; and once the enemy attack was repelled we should have gained considerable advantage in the defence of our Western and Northern approaches.

At present it is clear that Eire is determined to maintain her neutrality at all costs and will not permit British forces to enter the country, unless the enemy had previously invaded it. In view of the time factor involved, we must retain forces in Northern Ireland and in the United Kingdom ready for immediate entry into Eire at the moment the Eire Government are prepared to permit our entry —both to deny bases to the enemy and to occupy them for our own use.

Password 'Pumpkins'

And so, with more or less reluctance, he did. His Secretary of External Affairs, Joseph Walshe, went to London with Colonel Liam Archer of the Free State's military intelligence agency, G2. On 24 May, they met senior officers from British intelligence and the armed services. At follow-up meetings in Belfast and Dublin, Brigadier Dudley Clarke – most famous today as the founder of Britain's Commandos – talked through tactics with General Officer Commanding Sir Hubert Huddleston, his senior staff, and their equivalents from the Free State Army.

Army Chief of Staff General Daniel McKenna made it clear that De Valera drew the line at allowing British forces into the Free State in advance of any German invasion, but the Irish were ready to make available any information that would help him to make his plans. Further talks were held with Frank Aitken who, as Minister for the Co-ordination of Defensive Measures, had overall charge of the preparations made by the Free State.

The codename 'Plan W' was agreed on for the British invasion, which was to take place if – and only if – the Irish called for help, following an attack by Germany. In that event, Britain's representative in Dublin, John Maffey, was to contact Sir Hubert Huddleston in Belfast, with the one-word message 'Pumpkins'; that would be the signal for Huddleston to head southward with his troops. In the event, Operation Green withered away, and the signal was never sent.

This note from the War Cabinet states: 'At present it is clear that Eire is determined to maintain her neutrality at all costs and will not permit British forces to enter the country, unless the enemy had previously invaded it.'

Left: Eamon De Valera discreetly did what he could to help the British, despite the hostile rhetoric he used.

Plan Kathleen

Another plan for an Irish invasion – this one, though, was dreamed up by the patriots of the IRA. But the Germans concluded that Kathleen could never have worked.

The history books insist that World War II started on 1 September 1939, with Germany's invasion of Poland. There's a case, though, for saying that it started sooner. After all, it had been eight months earlier on 1 January that the IRA (Irish Republican Army) formally declared war with Britain.

Cruel Comedy
A joke? Not quite. There had already been a bitter War of Independence with Britain

(1919–21), which was itself followed by fighting (1922–3) between those Free Staters who were prepared to settle for the 26 counties that would eventually become the Irish Republic we know today and those out-and-out Republicans who would accept nothing less than an end to British rule across the whole of Ireland. This was why the IRA still existed, despite the achievement of Independence – and why it was proscribed in what was supposed to be its homeland.

To the IRA, Ulster represented unfinished liberationist business: one last push, and Ireland would be a nation. To the Germans, the North of Ireland was both its British enemy's most vulnerable

Could the IRA really serve as Germany's secret weapon?

TRANSCRIPT OF KEY PARAGRAPHS

Top:
Subject: Hermann Goertz
As is known, GOERTZ arrived by parachute and landed in County Westmeath. He parachuted his wireless set and equipment separately. His intention was to land in County Tyrone.

Having collected himself, after his descent, he went to, or near, the local 'village idiot', who was very perturbed and upset at seeing such as person coming out of what is known as a 'Dry Ditch' by the side of the road shouting "Hi. Hi. I want you". In order to soothe the 'Village Idiot' GOERTZ gave him a hundred dollar note.

Bottom:
While at Held's house, GOERTZ met, for the first time, Stephen Hayes, Acting Commander in Chief of the I.R.A., vice Sean Russell, absent. Goertz was unfavourably impressed, not only by Hayes, himself, but by the organization of his alleged Irish Republican Army. However, Held, Hayes and 'Another' (known unofficially, and not to me at all) schemed, devised and concocted the famous "PLAN KATHLEEN" in Held's own house, and written in Goertz's own handwriting.

Subject.....HERMANN...GOERTZ..

INSPECTOR GENERAL'S OFFICE.

Telephone No.: Belfast 25421.

Your Reference..PF.44446/BIH/JS

Our Reference...CS.37/440/39

Royal Ulster Constabulary,

BELFAST.

...12th.......January,.........1942...

Dear Liddell,

    I have got some information about GOERTZ and what he said.

    In the Spring of 1940 Stephen HELD went over to Belgium on a mission for the I.R.A.; the mission being to buy arms. When he got there he was apparently unsuccessful and was ordered by the I.R.A. to go on to Germany.   He went on to Frankfurt where it is believed he met STEWART, husband of Mrs Stewart of Laragh, and possibly GOERTZ.   The latter denies he met HELD but there is reason to believe that he at least saw him. *P.F.48339*

    HELD painted a rosy picture of a powerful I.R.A., numbering about 5,000, ready in Southern Ireland to give the Germans immediate assistance, provided they procured arms.   The plan of campaign was that the Germans should land 50,000 troops at about five different points-Larne, Coleraine, Derry and Sligo were mentioned.   This appealed to the Germans in a minor degree, and so GOERTZ was despatched to survey the land before the Germans committed themselves to the supply of arms.

    As is known, GOERTZ arrived by parachute and landed in County Westmeath.   He parachuted his wireless set and equipment separately.   His intention was to land in County Tyrone.

    Having collected himself, after his descent, he went to , or near, the local village (name unknown) and just outside he met the 'Village Idiot' who was very perturbed and upset at seeing such a person coming out of what is known as a 'Dry Ditch' by the side of the road, shouting "Hi. Hi. I want you".   In order to soothe the 'Village Idiot' GOERTZ gave him a hundred dollar note.(100%).   However, he found that this did not produce any more intelligence than had at first appeared and seeing a man ploughing in the distance GOERTZ decided to introduce himself to the ploughman.   The conversation between them is not forthcoming, other than the fact that the ploughman told GOERTZ that he had been a 'damned fool' to have given the "Idiot" a hundred dollars, and on that advice GOERTZ took the dollar note back and gave the 'Idiot' a pound note instead.   The parting was mutual.   At this stage GOERTZ was put wise to the fact that he had not landed in Northern Ireland and was left in rather a quandry as to what line of action he would take.   He had previously obtained Mrs.STEWART's address from her husband in Germany and so decided to make for her house at Laragh, Co.Wicklow.

    When GOERTZ made his landing he was dressed in a German Officer's uniform, including greatcoat, hat and pack, the idea being that should he be taken prisoner he would be treated as a prisoner of war.

    GOERTZ moved only by night.   At one stage he got to what is believed to be the river Boyne, where he thought he saw two policemen, in the moonlight, and he became alarmed.

Immediate/

    While at Held's house, GOERTZ met, for the first time, Stephen HAYES, Acting Commander in Chief of the I.R.A., vice Sean RUSSELL, absent.   GOERTZ WAS UNFAVOURABLY IMPRESSED, NOT ONLY BY HAYES, HIMSELF, BUT BY THE ORGANISATION OF HIS ALLEGED IRISH REPUBLICAN ARMY.   However, HELD, HAYES and 'Another'(known unofficially, and not to me at all) schemed, devised and concocted the famous " PLAN KATHLEEN" in HELD's own house, and written in GOERTZ's own handwriting.

province and a potential platform from which to launch future air raids – even an invasion.

Spy from the Sky

Abwehr agent Hermann Goertz was parachuted into Ireland in the summer of 1940, and immediately set about establishing contacts with the IRA with the help of German-descended Stephen Carroll Held. Generally known as Stephen Carroll, he had no record as an IRA sympathizer; indeed, his main sympathies were with his mother's Fatherland. Goertz was quickly disillusioned by his dealings with Ireland's Republicans. Stephen Hayes was out of his depth; the IRA hopelessly disorganized and ill-equipped. He himself was hopelessly compromised when police raided Carroll's home and found secret papers; Goertz went on the run, but was captured in November 1941. In 1945, on hearing that he was to be sent back to Germany, he took cyanide since he apparently feared falling into Soviet hands.

Rising Hopes

The Germans had given some thought themselves to the possibility of an Irish invasion.

Germans are known to be taking soundings at Cobh harbour and in the Kerry bays ...

TD (MP) Richard Mulcahy, letter to Gerald Boland just min, 8 jun

Ireland's War of Independence had left unfinished business between Free Staters and Republicans.

Hermann Goertz is grim-faced for his photo by the Irish Special Branch.

What made Plan Kathleen different was that it was originated by the IRA. Substantially drafted by April 1940, it was devised by Belfast Volunteer Liam Gaynor, who in another life was a civil servant in Ulster's Unionist Stormont state. Stephen Hayes, IRA chief in the absence of Sean Russell (then in the United States), gave the plan his approval. It entailed a German landing, either outside Derry in the northwest or at Carlingford Lough on the east coast, and a coordinated IRA uprising along both sides of the Border.

In fairness, the logic appears to have been not so much that the IRA would take Ulster by military force or even that a German expeditionary force would physically occupy the province. Rather, the plan assumed that the German landings would bounce the Britain into hasty and irrevocable steps that were likely to violate the neutrality of the Free State, and that this provocation would be enough to bring the whole of Ireland into the fight for Ulster.

Naval Nonsense
As far as it goes, this makes a degree of sense. What made the Germans despair was Gaynor and Hayes's complete failure to address the practicalities of the plan from the German perspective. After all, the suggested action in Ireland was dependent on large numbers of men and large amounts of equipment being transported some considerable distance by sea – through waters that were effectively controlled by the Royal Navy.

WHALE OR SEA EAGLE?
German agent Helmut Clissmann spent several years in Ireland before the war, before being whisked away once hostilities broke out. He had established strong contacts with a number of leading Republicans – not just far-right figures like the writer Francis Stuart but ideological leftists like *An Phoblacht* editor and IRA leader Frank Ryan.

Clissmann was to be a passenger in the seaplane which would put down discreetly on Lough Key, Co. Roscommon. He would bring with him £40,000 and a radio transmitter so that he could stay in touch with the Fatherland. The renewed relationship between him and Ryan was to be the cornerstone of the scheme.

Under Clissmann's direction, the IRA would carry out acts of sabotage in the North while he and Ryan intervened with De Valera's government on their behalf. But with the plan so vague – and Canaris uncooperative – the weeks went by and Whale was effectively beached. It was resurrected in the summer of 1941 as Operation Sea Eagle, but fared no better under this new name. The *Abwehr* Chief vetoed it completely before it could commence.

Operation Tannenbaum

Hitler had no intention of respecting the neutrality of the Swiss, it seems. But the Swiss had no intention of giving up without a fight.

Good fences … Switzerland was taking no chances with its Nazi neighbours.

'The Battle of France is over,' Churchill told Britain's House of Commons on 18 June 1940. 'I expect the Battle of Britain is about to begin.' Wasn't he forgetting something? The Battle of Switzerland? Some took the possibility very seriously indeed. Within a week of Winston Churchill's speech, Hitler had given the order for a plan to be drawn up for the invasion of Switzerland: the *Oberkommando des Heeres* (Army High Command) was hard at work.

The German dictator felt deep anger towards the Swiss. He had seen them as kindred spirits, and expected them to respond to his rise with an *Anschluss*, just as Austria had done in 1938. But many Swiss were of French and Italian background, and even those who did speak German identified strongly with an independent Switzerland.

Neutral or Not?

Was Switzerland more valuable to Nazi Germany as a neutral state? Swiss bankers, it's been claimed, were the launderers of Nazi gold. Some historians have suggested that Swiss neutrality was bogus; that the country was effectively an ally of Germany – if not by its own

choice then by the fact that, from the time of the Fall of France, it was boxed in by hostile states. Others, however, have held Switzerland up as a heroic example of patriotic self-sufficiency – even of the need for Americans to have the right to carry guns! An often-emotional, inevitably partisan debate still rages over whether Hitler left Switzerland alone because it suited him to do so or, rather, because he feared to strike.

Not So Peaceful

The historic presence of the Red Cross and a host of other humanitarian organizations in more recent times may easily mislead. Swiss neutrality was never about pacifism. No nation has been more preoccupied with the need to defend itself than the 'violent rabble' who sent the Burgundians of Charles the Bold

packing in 1476. Subsequently, the Swiss had spent several centuries as the European mercenaries of choice. In 1939, as now, neutrality was a proud tradition to be fiercely defended. All had to do their duty when called upon; within three days of the outbreak of war, 400,000 Swiss had indeed been mobilized.

General Henri Guisan, their commander, didn't expect the Germans to be promptly put to flight or for his homeland to be left inviolate: what he did hope was that he could make the prospect of invasion an uninviting one. Failing that, he wanted his countrymen to make its conquest as difficult and dirty a job as they possibly could. Rather than envisaging a heroic stand at his country's frontier, then, Guisan made plans for fighters to fall back in good order, slip away and hole up in a *Réduit* – a remote

TRANSCRIPT OF KEY PARAGRAPHS

I understand that some of the captured Archives of the German War Ministry are now accessible in this country. I should be very much interested to have an opportunity of seeing the German plans, entitled "Plan Tannenbaum", drawn up for the invasion of Switzerland during the last war. I am particularly interested in the political considerations (rather than the military ones), which are part of the Memorandum.

As I spent the whole of the last war in Switzerland in the capacity of a voluntary refugee in Lausanne and was at that time in touch with the Swiss Federal Department for Foreign Affairs in Berne, this document would be of especial interest to me.

I should be very grateful indeed if you could kindly let me know, whether I could have access to the said document.

Believe me, dear Mr. Passant,

Yours sincerely

Austrian Ambassador

and formidably fortified retreat high up in the Alps. This would subsequently be their base for a long and determined guerrilla war that would cost the occupier dear in resources and in lives. The Swiss themselves would pay dearly too: the majority of their country, including cities and major towns, would have to be abandoned to the mercies of the Germans.

Alpine Assault

The initial assumption was that 21 divisions would sweep in from newly conquered central France, where two million troops were essentially idle. After an infantry feint over the Jura Mountains had lured the Swiss Army out, the Germans would cut in behind them from the west, while an Italian army invaded from the south. The plan was scaled down in subsequent revisions: not till October 1940 was it finalized under the name Tannenbaum (Fir Tree). And it then gathered dust on a shelf – to this day we don't know why.

Operation Ikarus

In Greek mythology, high-flying Icarus was too ambitious and came crashing down into the Aegean. Operation Ikarus came unstuck over colder waters.

Operation Only-Too-Thinkable as far as the Germans were concerned, Operation Fork had gone ahead on 10 May. Within a week, the British had taken over Iceland. The move was frankly pre-emptive. Germany had occupied Denmark and Norway in April, and the island nation would have been a logical next-step.

Iceland was officially neutral but, since nobody expected the Germans to respect this status, the British saw no reason why they should respect it either. They'd moved even more swiftly to take the Faroe Islands, a Danish possession just a stone's-throw from the Shetlands – not just part of Britain but a vital naval base.

A Daunting Prospect
Ironically, the evidence suggests that the idea of invading Iceland

MOST SECRET.

TO BE KEPT UNDER LOCK AND KEY : NEVER TO BE REMOVED FROM THE OFFICE. THIS FORM IS TO BE USED FOR AIR INTELLIGENCE MESSAGES ONLY.

CX/MSS/946/T21.

ATLANTIC.
AIR OPERATIONS.

SOURCE SAW REPORT OF VISUAL RECONNAISSANCE CARRIED OUT BETWEEN 0645 AND 0710 HRS 2/5/42 BY A/C A6 + EH OF 1(F) 120 WHICH GAVE THE FOLLOWING INFORMATION :-

REYKJAVIK HARBOUR - ABOUT 15 MEDIUM SIZED MERCHANT VESSELS.
REYKJAVIK AERODROME - RUNWAYS CONSTRUCTED, AERODROME OCCUPIED.
EYRABAKKI AERODROME - OCCUPIED.
HJAFSFJORD - ABOUT 12-15 MERCHANT VESSELS AND ONE VESSEL APPARENTLY A LIGHT CRUISER.
SEAPLANE BASE TINGVELIR - WHAT APPEAR TO BE TAXI TRACKS ON THE ICE. NO AERODROME INSTALLATIONS OBSERVED.

REPORT WAS ADDRESSED TO FLIEGERFUEHRER NORTH (WEST) AT TRONDJHEM.

B/A   HSM/IWT   2335/3/5/42.
RD NG.

TRANSCRIPT OF KEY PARAGRAPHS

Source saw report of visual reconnaissance carried out between 6:45am and 7:10am 2/5/42 by a/c A6 + EH OF 1 (F) 120 of which gave the following information:-

Reykjavik harbour – about 15 medium sized merchant vessels.
Reykjavik aerodrome – runways constructed, aerodrome occupied.
Eyrabakki aerodrome – occupied
Hjafpfjord – about 12–15 merchant vessels and one vessel apparently a light cruiser.
Seaplane base Tingvelir – what appear to be taxi tracks on the ice.

The Royal Navy was firmly in charge in the waters around Iceland.

hadn't crossed Hitler's mind. Inevitably, however, it did now. Operation Ikarus was the result: troops of the 163rd Infantry Division were to embark on the converted liners *Bremen* and *Europa* at the Norwegian port of Tromso. Backed by a Panzer battalion and an armoured reconnaissance company, with some mobile artillery, they would land on the northern coast, outside Akureyri, and in the east near Reykjavik.

But the British by now had settled in and were formidably well-established on the island. The few hundred marines who had mounted the original invasion had been replaced by regular army troops – 4000, with more arriving all the time.

Counting the Cost

Operation Weserübung had been a triumph for the Germans, as bold and swashbuckling as it had been ruthlessly effective – but this victory for *blitzkrieg* had still come at quite a heavy cost. Particularly to the navy: the heavy cruiser *Blücher* had been lost, the *Scharnhorst* and the *Gneisenhau* badly damaged; the cruiser *Admiral Hipper* was suffering chronic engine problems; the light cruiser *Königsberg* had been shot up by coastal batteries, as had the artillery training ship *Bremse*. And so the list went on. Nothing was more certain than that further losses and damage would be inflicted by the Royal Navy as the Ikarus invasion force made its fateful voyage.

Deep Waters

It wasn't really this that daunted the Germans, though: indeed the officers of the intended invasion-force weren't really daunted at all. It was their intended escorts who

British troops were well-dug in, in readiness for any German invasion of Iceland.

were blenching at the prospect. Air Force chiefs shook their heads at the thought of sending bomber crews out so far across the stormy vastness of the North Atlantic. Naval high-ups were, if anything, less convinced: simply getting the expedition to Iceland was going to take a four-day voyage across seas that were at best unpredictable, at worst atrocious.

And this would be true not just for the initial invasion but for every time an attempt was made to resupply any occupying force on the island. Or indeed to come to its defence, should the Allies decide to try to take the island back. Whatever the other calls on its men and ships in a war that seemed to be deepening by the week, a hard-pressed *Kriegsmarine* would have to run the gauntlet of the Royal Navy. By June the idea had been dropped.

Operation Hammer

A plan to take Trondheim, setting up a bridgehead there for a counter-offensive against Norway's invaders, had to be abandoned in the face of overwhelming German force.

Despite the fact that the Allies had lost Norway, hopes remained that a naval operation might work the miracle they needed. The *Altmark* Incident had been a bit of rare good news. The practicalities apart, it was natural that the authorities should think in terms of a seaborne assault.

Trondheim was the obvious target. Deep and sheltered, the Trondheimsfjord also extended far enough inland to cut a long, thin country almost in half. Even now, the greatest concentration of German forces was in the south – those in the north around Narvik were meeting stiff resistance. An Anglo-French landing backed by a naval assault might enable the Allies to isolate this northern force, not to mention the orefields that were the reason for the German occupation.

Assault from the Sea
From the moment when Trondheim had been taken on 9 April, the MP and retired Admiral Sir Roger Keyes had been badgering Churchill about the importance of retaking the city – even offering to command an assault, using any old vessels the Navy might be able to rustle up. Captured coastal

Adrian Carton de Wiart, head of Hammer.

batteries along the Trondheimsfjord could be put out of action by bombardment from the sea. Churchill – always up for an operation with a suggestion of improbability and daring – appeared to be enthusiastic about Keyes's plan.

Questionable
And yet, as the days went by, there was a continuing vagueness about the naval component of this operation, which is thrown into relief by the crispness of General Adrian Carton de Wiart's communication:
Capture of Trondheim considered essential. Plan proposed is as follows:
Intend landing 600 marines at Aandalsnes (not Aalesund), 17th April, to be reinforced, if possible, at earliest opportunity. Propose you should exploit from Namsos,

while force from Aandalsnes will also threaten Trondheim in conjunction with Norwegian forces. Meanwhile combined operation for direct attack on Trondheim will be developed ? to take advantage of your pressure …

That '?' is eloquent, though the reality is that this is pretty much as close as we get to a description of Hammer – at least in the first instance. Carton de Wiart's landings, supposed to be subsidiary to the main seaborne event, ended up going ahead on their own as the Operation Sickle to a Hammer that had been quietly dropped.

Moving On
In fairness, the apparent indecision has to be seen in the context of a fluid and fast-developing situation. Landings by British marines and French Alpine troops went so well, at least initially, that Hammer was back on the agenda for discussion by the War Cabinet on 19 April. This revised operation, the memorandum shows, was to involve a beefed-up land attack, whilst His Majesty's ships were to attack the coastal gun-emplacements, feinting at an all-out assault but really just imposing a longer-term blockade. In the event, this Hammer too was returned to the toolbox, while Sickle became bogged down, the Allied troops evacuated as attention turned to France.

TRANSCRIPT OF KEY PARAGRAPHS

In view of the success of the landings at Namsos and Andalsnes the Chiefs of Staff have thought it right to re-consider the plan for Operation "Hammer" as a matter of urgency.

The Chiefs of Staff have always realised that Operation "Hammer", as originally conceived, was open to very considerable risks. A combined operation involving an opposed landing has at all times proved to be one of the most difficult and hazardous operations of war.

The revised plan, in brief, is as follows:-

(a) Push in the maximum forces possible at Namsos and more particularly at Andalsnes.

(b) Get control of the road and rail communications running as quickly as possible through Dombaas.

(c) The force from Namsos to invest Trondheim from the North and the force from Andalsnes to advance on the port from the South.

(d) A bombardment of the outer forts by H.M ships, with a view to deluding the enemy into thinking a direct assault is about to take place just before the main landings at (a) above.

105

ANNEX II.

I.C.(40) 81
Also C.O.S.(40)297(S))
19TH APRIL, 1940.

WAR CABINET.
MILITARY CO-ORDINATION COMMITTEE.

OPERATION "HAMMER".

Aide Memoire prepared for the Chiefs of Staff.

In view of the success of the landings at Namsos and Andalsnes the Chiefs of Staff have thought it right to re-consider the plan for Operation "Hammer" as a matter of urgency.

2. In the first place, the Chiefs of Staff have always realised that Operation "Hammer", as originally conceived, was open to very considerable risks. A combined operation involving an opposed landing has at all times proved to be one of the most difficult and hazardous operations of war, for which the most detailed and careful preparation is necessary.

3. They have appreciated that the plan had the following disadvantages:-

(a) The concentration of almost the whole of the Home Fleet in an area where it could be subjected to heavy air attack.

(b) In the absence of previous reconnaissance and of air photographs, the plan has been worked out from maps and charts.

(c) Owing to the urgency of carrying out the operations at the earliest possible date, insufficient time has been available for that detailed and meticulous preparation which is so necessary in operations of this character and magnitude.

-1-

106

... still holds.

8. The revised plan, in brief, is as follows:-

(a) Push in the maximum forces possible at Namsos and more particularly at Andalsnes.

(b) Get control of the road and rail communications running as quickly as possible through Dombaas.

(c) The force from Namsos to invest Trondheim from the North and the force from Andalsnes to advance on the port from the South.

(d) A bombardment of the outer forts by H.M. ships, with a view to deluding the enemy into thinking a direct assault is about to take place just before the main landings at (a) above.

-2-

Operation Sealion

Hitler's plan for invading Britain appeared at first glance to be as elaborately worked-out as it was massively ambitious. Considered more closely, though, it starts to seem more sketchy.

By the summer of 1940, there were only two countries left to fall to the Germans: Switzerland and Britain. There was real doubt in German minds about Switzerland: did it offer more as a conquest or as a (not altogether uncooperative) neutral neighbour. Britain, though, was both the more prestigious prize and, potentially, the most real and present danger. Along with an industrial base out of all proportion to its size and the resources of a world empire – in supplies and manpower – it had a formidable tradition of waging war by land and sea.

An Irrelevant Army?
That said, Hitler's *Wehrmacht* had by now made clear its mastery on land. Having taken much of western Europe in a matter of weeks, it had trounced the British Expeditionary Force (BEF) in France so comprehensively that there was widespread disbelief that it had survived. Operation Sickle Cut had so swiftly cut the British off that II Corps' Commander, General Alan Brooke, wrote, 'Nothing but a miracle can save the BEF now.'

A miracle of sorts occured. More than a quarter of a million

For Official Use Only

German Invasion Plans for the British Isles 1940

Military High Command
Department for War Maps and Communications
BERLIN

The German invasion plans were captured and translated by the Allies in 1944.

soldiers – French as well as British – were extricated between 26 May and 4 June. In failing to eliminate these fighting men, the Germans had made a serious mistake. In the long run, this was an omission that would come back to haunt them. For the moment, though, Britain's land forces were to all intents and purposes an irrelevance. Hitler found it easy to overlook them.

Hitler had good reason to write off Britain's land forces after Dunkirk. Less excusable was his failure to take account of the episode's morale-raising power. Britons speak of the Dunkirk Spirit to this day. The BEF's evacuation had been led by the Royal Navy, but hundreds of 'little ships' had given their assistance too. Ferries and fishing boats; freighters, tugs and even sailing yachts and cabin cruisers had all helped carry soldiers to safety, crewed entirely by their civilian volunteers.

The excitement of the experience had produced a national adrenaline-rush. Britons were exhilarated by its skin-of-the-teeth success.

An Amphibious Attack

Hitler's plans for Operation Sealion, as recorded in his Directive No. 16, were issued on 16 July. Said the *Führer*,

Since Britain shows no sign of being prepared to come to an agreement despite her desperate military situation, I have resolved to prepare – and, should it be necessary, pursue – an amphibious operation against England.

The point of this operation will be to prevent the English homeland from being used as a base for the continuation of the war against Germany. If need be, the whole island might be occupied.

An amphibious force was to move in along a 'broad front', he said, stretching 'from the area of Ramsgate to that of the Isle of Wight'. This far from the continent, the *Luftwaffe* would have to do duty as artillery; the navy as engineers. The different branches of the German military should think things through from their own perspectives, said Hitler. If any advance operations ('such as the occupation of the Isle of Wight or the county of Cornwall') were going to be needed to make the landing possible, then this was the time to plan them – though

the final decision to proceed would rest with him.

The Aryan Angle

'Since Britain shows no sign of being prepared to come to an agreement …' – is there a hint of wistfulness in the *Führer's* tone? Had Hitler been hoping that the Anglo-Saxons would rethink their position?

There certainly seems to have been a hint of that in the Last Appeal to Reason he made in the Reichstag on 19 July 1940. Copies of this were showered

Dunkirk had been a disaster – true. But, longer-term, it had been a morale-booster for Britain.

The Early Plan, July to end of August 1940.

1. On 1 July, Halder, Chief of Staff of the German Army, started serious discussions on preparations for the invasion of Britain, and on the 9th he noted in his diary:- "during afternoon:work on draft operational plans for invasion of Britain". Brauchitsch then approved this draft, and, at the Berghof conference on 13 July, a report was made to Hitler on the planned execution of the assault on Britain (to be carried out like a river crossing). The OKH recommendations were approved as a basis for practical preparations, and the first OKH invasion order was issued on 17 July. +

2. Before examining this order, which contained the germ of the early plan, it is convenient here to point out the distinctive characteristics of the early plan and the generals involved. In brief, the distinctive features were:-

a) A broad-front landing on three sections of the South coast of England:-

    i)   Margate to Hastings (16 Army) under Army Group A)
    ii) Brighton to Portsmouth (9 Army)
    iii) either side of Weymouth (6 Army under Army Group B). This soon became Lyme Bay with only a subsidiary landing near Weymouth.

b) Use of 39 divisions in four waves.

For the purpose of military preparations, this basic idea, virtually unaltered, continued in force until the end of August. It involved a formidable array of military personalities. Von Rundstedt and Von Bock were commanding the same army groups with which they had achieved such spectacular successes in the French campaign. As might be expected, Rundstedt had the major rôle: under him, Busch and Strauss were commanding 16 and 9 Armies, Reinhardt and von Hoth had the same panzer corps (XXXXI and XV Corps) which had contributed so effectively to the execution of the new mobile form of operations, and Manstein was leading one of the first-wave corps (XXXVIII). Under von Bock, von Reichenau was the C-in-C of the same 6 Army with which he had fought the B.E.F. in Belgium, and von Kleist, who had commanded the famous armoured group during the Meuse breakthrough, was apparently intended to participate with XXII (Panzer) Corps. The whole operation was under the personal direction of the C-in-C of the German Army, von Brauchitsch, and his Chief of Staff, Halder.

+ Source: Halder's diary.

* Considerably reorganised.

TRANSCRIPT OF KEY PARAGRAPHS

On 1 July, Halder, Chief of Staff of the German Army, started serious discussions on preparations for the invasion of Britain, and on the 9th he noted in his diary: 'during afternoon: worked on draft operational plans for invasion of Britain'. Brauchitsch then approved this draft, and, at the Berghof conference on 13 July, a report was made to Hitler on the planned execution of the assault on Britain (to be carried out like a river crossing).

Before examining this order, which contained the germ of the early plan and the generals involved. In brief, the distinctive features were:

a) A broad-front landing on three sections of the South coast of England ...

b) Use of 39 divisions in four waves.

For the purpose of military preparations, this basic idea virtually unaltered, continued in force until the end of August. It involved a formidable array of military personalities.

Aircraft of the *Luftwaffe* were going to give cover to the invasion fleet.

over southeastern England from German planes. The Nazis, he insisted, had only ever wanted to free their country from the unfair penalties laid upon it by the Versailles Treaty – and from the 'fetters of a small substratum of Jewish-capitalist and pluto-democratic profiteers'. Right-thinking Englishmen and -women would surely see the justice in this fight.

Hitler was, if not an Anglophile, then an admirer of the British imperial achievement, as the English historian Andrew Roberts reminds us in his 2009 study *The Storm of War*. Even while the fight for France was raging, he points out, the German leader was talking in flattering terms of the 'civilization' Britain had brought to the world. What Roberts describes as the 'slapdash' nature of the Nazi invasion-plan can be easily explained, he argues: Hitler's heart simply wasn't in it;

and ultimately, that was why the Sealion didn't swim.

Preparations were to be completed by the middle of August – some four weeks off. In that time, the *Führer* noted, key conditions had to be met:
a) The English air force must be so far neutralized, both physically and in morale, that it will be able to put up no significant resistance to the German invasion.
b) Sea lanes must be cleared of mines.
c) Both entrances to the Straits of Dover, and the western approach to the Channel in a line roughly from Alderney to Portland, are to be closed off by minefields.
d) Landing zones must be covered by heavy artillery on the continental coast.
e) British naval forces should be kept occupied, both in the North Sea and (by the Italians)

in the Mediterranean for the period before the invasion. All these conditions came down to the same thing really: the English Channel had to be a German pond for troops in vast numbers to make their way across safely; its shores too had to be under German control.

Disembarkation Dilemmas

This was all the more important because the Germans had as yet no purpose-built landing craft to call upon: Hitler was hoping to do the whole thing using canal- and river-barges. Of the 2000- odd craft his *Kriegsmarine* managed to commandeer in Germany and the conquered

Benelux countries, only about a third were engine-powered – and their engines were designed for use in sheltered inland waterways. The remainder would have to be towed across the Channel by tugs and other powered vessels. When they reached their destination, moreover, they would have to be painstakingly and precisely moved into position so that the troops on board could be discharged in safety; the tanks, trucks, heavy equipment and materiel of every kind unloaded without loss.

These are not the kind of manoeuvres that can be conducted under heavy fire. Or, for that

SEALION PLANS

Apart from a thrust to the southwest, with an essentially diversionary landing at Lyme Bay, Dorset, the German assault was going to be closely concentrated on the coasts of Kent and Sussex. Once this southeastern bridgehead had been secured, the occupation of Britain as a whole would be straightforward.

Invasion training – but Germany had hardly any purpose-designed landing craft.

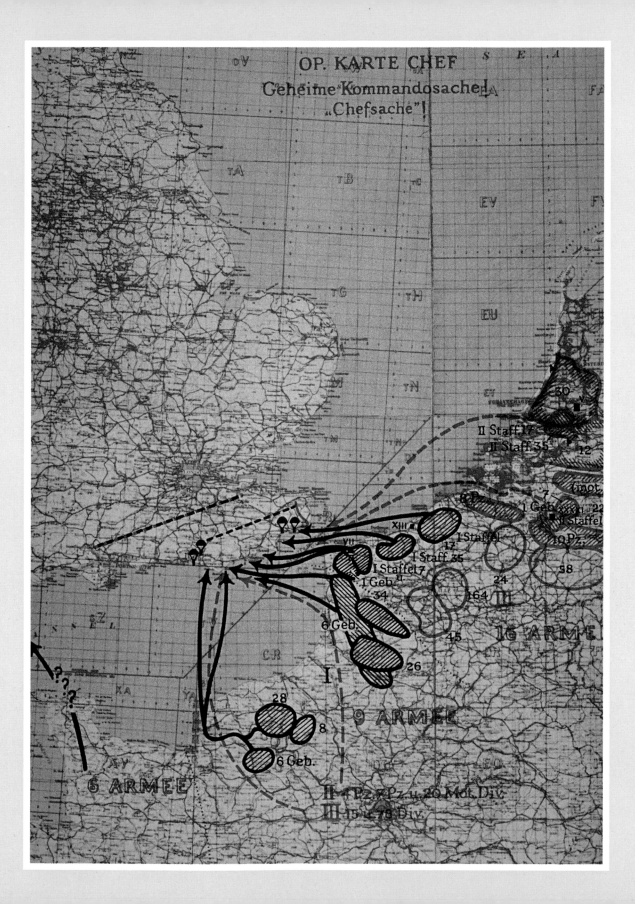

PROJECTED LANDINGS

Sealion was so long in the planning that it was inevitable the British would get wind of it. Comparing this map with the one on the previous page shows how closely they had been following German thinking. What neither map can show is the situation in the air, where the RAF's dominance was destined to render Germany's plans null and void.

Operation "SeaLion": Projected Landing of the 1st Wave Divisions, mid-September 1940.

Legend

Boundary between 16 and 9 Armies

Main bridgehead to be won by 16 and 9 Armies

Dropping zone for 7 Parachute Division.

Direction of divisional thrusts.

The Germans were relying on river barges for the Channel crossing.

matter, in heavy seas. It wasn't that Operation Sealion was impractical as such – it *might* have worked, in the right conditions; had the conditions have been just so.

The difficulties facing Sealion had been identified at the end of 1939, when army chiefs drew up their own plans for an amphibious invasion of England in the study document *Nordwest*. They had identified a starting point in Belgium and a landing site much further north, along the East Anglian coast, but this received a scornful rejection from *Reichsmarschall* Hermann Göring.

So pessimistic was he about the prospects for any such amphibious invasion that he had said it 'could only be the final conclusion of an already victorious war with Britain'. Any resistance would be too much resistance, he felt, for what was bound to be a slow and cumbersome and substantially defenceless seaborne force.

Firepower

In some respects, it should be acknowledged, circumstances actually favoured the Germans. Now that they had occupied the Pas de Calais coast of northern France, it was easy enough to bring up big guns that could pound British shipping in the Channel – and even to some extent the southern English coast. The largest of several railway guns, the K12 had a 21cm (8.3in) barrel and a range of 115km (71 miles). Four permanent batteries, fortified with concrete, were placed in positions that commanded the Channel waters. Several mobile batteries were also brought into play: German gunners could pick off British vessels more or less at will. Further mobile batteries were made ready for installation on the English side just as soon as a successful landing had taken place.

The 'broad front' was quickly narrowed: landing men in meaningful numbers along more than 190km (120 miles) of coast would have required a force of over 160,000. It was decided that the landing area would extend from Rottingdean, just east of Brighton, to Hythe, in southern Kent. Even this would require a force of 67,000 troops.

The *Kriegsmarine* would provide an escort, but the emphasis would be on creating diversions in the days before the attack took place. For all the ferocity of its U-boat war, Germany's surface navy was small and weak. Particularly by comparison with that of an island nation which, however beleaguered now, had been able to boast that it 'ruled the waves' since the eighteenth century. There was nothing to be gained from taking on the Royal Navy in a straight fight. So it was hoped that diversionary sorties of the type

that the cruiser *Admiral Hipper* was to undertake in the North Atlantic, between Iceland and the Faeroes, would have the effect of drawing away British naval vessels.

Foiled by Fighters

The *Führer* can be congratulated on having spotted the central weakness of his own scheme: the need to neutralize the RAF had been his point 'a', of course. In the event, the 'Few' of the RAF's fighter force famously took to the air that July in response to wave after relentless wave of German attacks. Several dramatic weeks later, they had driven the *Luftwaffe* from England's skies. The rest is history; and Operation Sealion isn't. In late September, it was quietly dropped.

As England, in spite of her hopeless military situation, still shows no willingness to come to terms, I have decided to prepare, and if necessary, to carry out, a landing operation against her.

Adolf Hitler, 16 July 1940.

Shipping heavy guns such as these across to Britain would be a huge logistical effort.

Operation Green

> *Eire.*
>
> **17.** In her present attitude Eire constitutes a serious liability. Although the Government of Eire would probably call instantly for our help in the event of a German attack on Eire territory, they would undoubtedly resist any attempt on our part to land forces in Eire in advance of a German attack.

Ireland became a focus for the strategic planners of both sides in 1940: its possibilities as a base for attacking England were all too clear.

Through the summer of 1940, the Irish Free State was an object of English suspicion. The sense of betrayal many felt at the Free State's secession was crowned by the new nation's decision to sit out what it described as the 'Emergency'. This fed the mood of public paranoia.

Ireland's Opportunity?

And it was true that those Republicans who had reacted to World War I by observing that 'England's difficulty is Ireland's opportunity' hadn't missed the opportunity potentially afforded by this new war. With the six counties of the North still to be 'freed' from the Union with Britain, some elements in the IRA were indeed looking to Berlin for help – though how much they were actually finding must be doubtful. Ireland *was* in Germany's sights, however, if only as a convenient base from which

bombing raids or amphibious expeditions might be mounted on mainland Britain. At the very least, a German presence in the Emerald Isle would pin down British troops in Ulster, preventing their involvement in the defence of the mainland.

Fact or Feint?

Field Marshal Theodor von Bock is believed to have come up with the scheme in August 1940, just weeks after Operation Sealion was first mooted. It has often been thought that Operation Green was no more than a fiction, a feint designed to distract the British from Operation Sealion, and that it was never actually intended to take place.

Reality, and Realism

It seems, though, that *Generalleutnant* Leonhard Kaupitsch, Commander IV and VII Army Corps, was indeed given the task of drawing up a plan for invading Ireland.

Preparations were nothing if not thorough. An army of agents delved into everything from economics journals to tourist

The British were in no doubt of the dangers Ireland represented:
'In her present attitude Eire constitutes a serious liability. Although the Government of Eire would probably call instantly for our help in the event of a German attack on Eire territory, they would undoubtedly reist any attempt on our part to land forces in Eire in advance of a German attack.'

Theodor von Bock is thought to have conceived Operation Green.

guidebooks, providing notes on over 200 towns and villages. Reconnaissance planes crisscrossed the countryside, photographing harbours and landing-grounds. The Germans were to set off with 50,000 men from French ports such as Lorient, St Nazaire and Nantes, coming ashore between Dungarvan and Waterford. Mobile artillery and engineer units would be among the first to arrive, to set in motion the rapid conquest of a nation that was regarded as negligible in military terms.

That assessment was justifiable, yet Green still faced formidable challenges, as Grand Admiral Raeder pointed out in his review. Germany's naval resources were scanty enough: with all available craft likely to be needed for Operation Sealion, there would be none left to shepherd tens of thousands of troops on this lengthy voyage across open sea, or to escort them around England's Cornish coast. Even if the invasion succeeded, supplies and communications would subsequently have to be guaranteed if German forces were not to find themselves stranded like sitting ducks. In the event, once Sealion had been abandoned, there could be no green light for Green.

Above: Leonhardt Kaupitsch was entrusted with the task of preparing plans for an invasion of Ireland.

Left: German planes made a systematic photo-survey of Ireland, its towns, its harbours and airfields.

Ireland ... is known to have low clouds and consequently very frequent damp and foggy weather.

German Naval Staff rule out effective air support for Operation Green.

The US and the Azores

US fears in the Atlantic focused for a time on the Azores – a potential base from which attacks on America might be launched.

Long before it was a combatant – long before there was a war, indeed – America was making preparations. In 1939, with global conflict fast becoming a reality, a series of colour-coded documents its intelligence agencies had been drawing up since the 1920s were cancelled, in favour of a new generation of 'Rainbow Plans'.

Not until 1941 did Rainbow 5 condescend to take notice of the Azores – an island group almost 1500km (930 miles) to the west of Portugal, whose territorial possession it had long been. At 3900km (2400 miles) from America's eastern coast, it was hardly in the front line of the war.

Mid-Atlantic

Neither was it by any normal standards an important place, with a total land area of just a few hundred square miles and a population significantly less than Winston-Salem or South Bend. Those few Americans who had heard of the Azores (or the still fewer who had actually been there) knew of them only as a rest-and-refuelling stop for transatlantic liners and flying boats.

This was precisely the problem. What could be done by a Cunard liner could also be done by a German cruiser; what was good for Pan Am was good for the

A staging stop for flying boats: the Azores in 1930.

TRANSCRIPT OF KEY PARAGRAPHS

As the War Cabinet are aware, we have for some time been examining the question of seizing strategic points in the Cape Verde island and the Azores.

2. The object in seizing these islands would be:-
(a) to deny their use to the enemy and to secure the cable stations.
(b) to secure for our own use in the Azores an air base and a refuelling base if Gibraltar were to become unusable.

Advantages of securing the Islands for our own use.
4. If Gibraltar becomes unusable as a naval base it would be desirable that we should secure for ourselves a base in the Azores, since otherwise we should have no base between Plymouth and Freetown. Naval forces operating from the Azores would be in a better position to fill the gap in our patrol line surrounding Europe than they would if they were to operate from Freetown or Plymouth. Similarly, flying boats could operate from these islands, although it will be a long time before we shall have the requisite number of these aircraft.

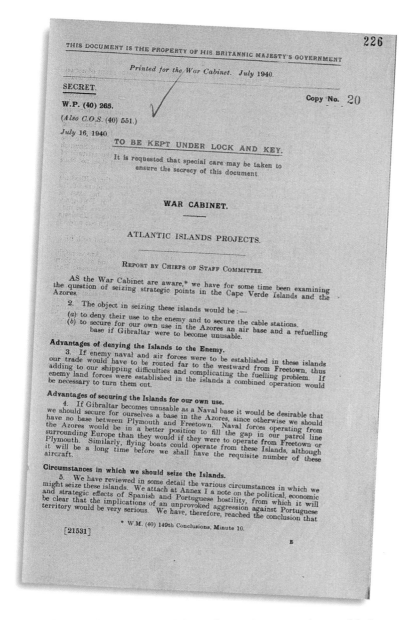

Luftwaffe too. The Azores had the potential to become a vital strategic staging post. And not just that, given the generally improving capabilities of aircraft – and specific hints let slip by the German leadership about a long-range bomber project (Project Amerika) – it was suddenly becoming not only possible but easy to envisage the Azores becoming the base from which the Germans might launch an aerial assault upon the United States.

Wireless Warning

President Roosevelt himself warned of the danger in a radio address to the American people on 27 May 1941:

The Azores and the Cape Verde Islands, if occupied or controlled by Germany, would directly endanger the freedom of the Atlantic and our own American physical safety … Old-fashioned common sense calls for the use of strategy that will prevent such an enemy from gaining a foothold in the first place.

But such a strategy was harder to devise than it might be expected. US troops were not yet considered battle-ready in any great number, and with contingency plans already afoot, logistical and transport provision was already overstretched. Once ashore, US occupiers would be sitting ducks for German attacks from Iberia and Africa. Even so, plans were made for an expedition by the 1st Division and the 1st Marine Division, involving 28,000 men, with 11,000 in reserve.

Salazar Says Yes

The President was listening to his military advisers, though. Portugal, for its part, warned that it would resist with all its strength – not only for the sake of its patriotic pride but for the troops and civilians who would be exposed if the islands should become a battleground. In the end, a difficult operation didn't seem to be worth the candle. When Salazar responded favourably to an offer of American support in the event of an attack by Germany, this was deemed an acceptable compromise, and plans for occupation were quietly shelved.

Operation Felix

Spain was a bystander in World War II, and of marginal interest to the combatants of either side. But the Rock of Gibraltar, connected to the Spanish mainland, was another matter.

The *Führer* and the Generalissimo had rather less in common than we might expect – except for their low opinion of one another. 'That fat sergeant,' Hitler said of Spanish dictator Francisco Franco after their railway-carriage conference at Hendaye, France, in October 1940; Franco likened him to a 'stage actor'.

No matter. Though in principle allies, their two nations weren't closely involved. Franco wasn't a joiner: he wanted what he could get out of Hitler's war (chiefly French Morocco) but, as the *Führer* didn't fail to see, he wasn't interested in doing any of the heavy lifting. Spain had, in fairness, been left utterly exhausted by its Civil War.

Destination Gibraltar
To some extent, however, the two countries were already working together – and had been for several months, getting up plans for a major assault that would take Gibraltar. The merest speck on the map, Gibraltar has always loomed large strategically because of its position that enables it to

The Royal Navy's oldest aircraft carrier in service, HMS *Eagle*, patrols the waters off Gibraltar.

control traffic in and out of the Mediterranean Sea.

At Hendaye, Hitler formally asked Franco for his permission to mount an attack through Spain. The Rock, he promised, would be handed over to Spain once the Allies had been defeated. Franco remained noncommittal, but Hitler was determined to pursue the project. In November, in *Führer* Directive No. 18, he outlined his plan for Operation Felix: General Ludwig Kübler would bring one army corps streaming south across the Pyrenees and down through Spain; Rudolf Schmidt's 2nd Panzer Army would provide protection in the rear; and fighters and dive-bombers would fly from Spanish airfields in support.

Besieging Britain

With the Battle of Britain already lost, Hitler could see the focus of the fighting shifting. If the country couldn't be taken, it could be put to siege.

The *Kriegsmarine* had from the first been doing its best to isolate Britain. U-Boats were wreaking havoc on transatlantic shipping. Hitler now intended to turn the screw. The fighting for North Africa was not (or not entirely) about oil, as is frequently assumed. It is important to remember that the countries along the southern shore of the Mediterranean control the approaches to the Suez Canal. A strong Italian presence in the region already, and the fact that French Morocco and Algeria were now under Axis control, made it seem possible to cut Britain off completely from its eastern empire.

A Lukewarm Response

Franco again cast cold water on the plans: with most of its population barely on the bread line, Spain couldn't possibly sustain a major military offensive.

General Ludwig Kübler was in the frame for Felix as commander of Germany's invasion force for Spain.

General Franco and Nazi officials discuss plans for a Blue Division of Spanish volunteers to support the *Wehrmacht*.

OPERATION "FELIX"

FOREWORD.

1.   The GERMAN documents on Operation "FELIX", sent to us in photostatic form, appear to be a set of rough notes of reconnaissances, reports of conferences, and appreciations collected over a number of years – probably from about 1938 to 1941 – from which detailed operation orders might have been written.

       A List of Dates against references is given in Appendix "A" (attached) from which it will be seen that no attempt has been made to put these documents in chronological order.   There is no system of cross reference.

       The views in many of these documents conflict and, without dates, it is difficult to know what the final decisions on many points would have been.

2.   The most definite information as to INTENTION comes from the High Command Operation Instruction at 1694/170, the Instruction addressed to H.Q. 49th Army Corps at 1694/180, the Instructions for Commander-in-Chief SIXTH ARMY at 1694/215 and "Instructions for the Preparation and carrying out of the Operation "FELIX" (presumably by Commander-in-Chief VI Army) at 1694/220.

       These give a good idea of the general Plan of Campaign and from other documents an idea of the tactical plan for the attack on GIBRALTAR may be gathered.

       There is a very comprehensive description of the ground from the R. GUADIARO to TARIFA from the besieging artillery point of view at extracts 1694/420 to 436.

3.   The information extracted from these documents has been dealt with under the following headings:-

/(a).........

TRANSCRIPT OF KEY PARAGRAPHS

Left: The German documents on Operation "FELIX", sent to us in photostatic form, appear to be a set of rough notes of reconnaissances, reports of conferences, and appreciations collected over a number of years – probably from about 1938–1941 from which detailed operation orders might have been written.

The most definite information as to intention come from the High Command Operation Instruction at 1694/175, the Instruction addressed to H.Q 49th Army Corps at 1694/180, the Instructions for Commander-in-Chief Sixth Army at 1694/215 and Instructions for the Preparation and carrying out of the Operation "FELIX" (presumably by Commander-in-Chief VI Army) at 1694/220.

Right:
Arsenal Tunnel: This leads to Admiralty Magazine
North Front Galleries: Described as "being shown to tourists and with shelter for 16,000 people".
Tunnel of San Miguel: Described as protected room and as possessing cistern.

In any case, he asked insultingly, how could he be sure that Hitler would ever be in the position to give him Gibraltar? He was all too clearly unconvinced that Germany was going to win the war.

Weeks passed, and the Spanish dictator brushed off repeated requests by Germany and Italy alike. Hitler was ready to proceed without his permission – and to take the country's colonies in North Africa to use as bases for his U-Boats. In June 1941, however, Operation Barbarossa began and his priorities changed. Operation Felix was stored on the shelf.

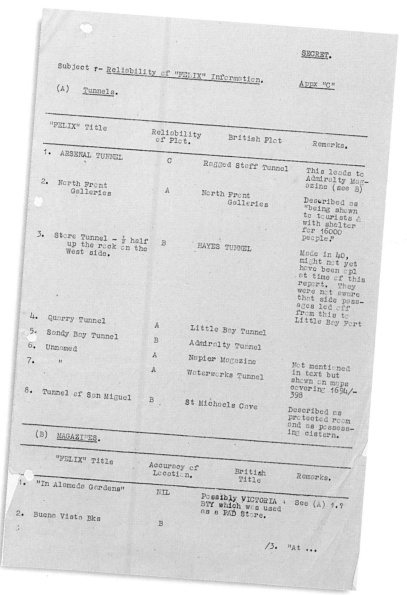

Operation Shrapnel

A plan to occupy the Cape Verde Islands involved a surprising number of risks. Fortunately, it did not have to be pursued.

Neither Spain nor Portugal was fighting in World War II, but that does not mean they played no part. Both sides wooed them, both sides threatened them – for the most part implicitly, since neither side wanted them to join the other.

That said, America's Rainbow 5 plan did not beat about the bush.

It envisaged an occupation of the Cape Verde Islands in conjunction with an assault on the Azores, even though the strategic significance of the two archipelagos was different. Where the Azores offered a mid-Atlantic staging post for an attack on the United States, the Cape Verde group – 570km (350 miles) off Cap Vert, on the coast of Senegal – mattered more in reference to the mainland of western Africa and control of its offshore shipping lanes.

SECRET

W.P. (41) 190 (E)   COPY NO.   12

C.O.S. (41) 164.

WAR CABINET

JOINT PLANNING STAFF.

OPERATION "SHRAPNEL"

On February 22nd a telegram was sent by the Chiefs of Staff to C.-in-C. South Atlantic and G.O.C. West Africa, stating that it was proposed to carry out operation "Shrapnel" with troops drawn from the garrison of Sierra Leone.

At Annex "A" is a copy of the reply which has been received from G.O.C. West Africa.

We attach at Annex "B" a draft signal to C.-in-C. South Atlantic and G.O.C. West Africa for the approval of the Chiefs of Staff.

TRANSCRIPT OF KEY PARAGRAPHS

Left: On February 22nd a telegram was sent by the Chiefs of Staff to C.-in-C. South Atlantic and G.O.C West Africa, stating that it was proposed to carry out Operation Shrapnel with troops taken from the garrison of Sierra Leone.

Right: 1. In accordance with the instructions of the Chief's of Staff orders have been issued for the return of Force Shrapnel to this country.

3. A decision is required regarding the notice at which the force is to be held, and the amount of leave that may be granted.

4. We recommend:-
(a) that the force should be placed at 96 hours' notice, as in the case of Operation "Truck".
(b) That 14 days leave, with free railway travel, should be granted subject to recall at 24 hours' notice. The possibility of the Force being unable to sail within 96 hours during this period should be accepted.
(c) That the Ministry of Shipping should be invited to make similar arrangements as regards the crews of the ships.

WAR CABINET

JOINT PLANNING STAFF

OPERATION "SHRAPNEL"

Note by the Joint Planning Staff.

1.   In accordance with the instructions * of the Chiefs of Staff orders have been issued for the return of Force Shrapnel to this country, and it should arrive about the end of the first week of February.

2.   Arrangements are being made for the Force to be accommodated in the Glasgow area. The necessary security measures are under consideration by the Inter Service Security Board.

3.   A decision is required regarding the notice at which the Force is to be held, and the amount of leave that may be granted.

4.   WE RECOMMEND:-

(a) That the Force should be placed at 96 hours' notice, as in the case of Operation "Truck".

(b) That 14 days' leave, with free railway travel, should be granted subject to recall at 24 hours' notice. The possibility of the Force being unable to sail within 96 hours during this period should be accepted.

(c) That the Ministry of Shipping should be invited to make similar arrangements as regards the crews of the ships.

(Signed) C.S. DANIEL

I.S.O. PLAYFAIR

C.E.H. MEDHURST

Cabinet War Room.

22nd January, 1941.

* C.O.S. (41) 18th Meeting, held on 15th January, 1941.

Coastal Control

Given the risks to the Suez Canal, the route around the Cape was crucial. Whoever occupied the islands was able to control the passage of shipping. The clear danger was that, if the Allies delayed, the Germans would step in; and there were signs that they were doing so already. Intelligence reports suggested that U-boats were infiltrating island waters, using them for a sheltered rendezvous.

Island Jumper

Hitler was singing from the same hymn sheet. His *Führer* Directive No. 18 (12 November 1940) decreed that 'Gibraltar is to be captured and the Straits closed'.

The English … *are to be prevented from gaining a footing at any other point on the Iberian peninsula or the Iberian islands … The* Atlantic Islands *(especially the Canaries and Cape Verde Islands) will assume additional naval*

importance after the operations for Gibraltar, both for the British and for ourselves …

Despite his call for special measures to be taken to 'limit the numbers of those working on these plans', Hitler's Atlantic Islands *idée fixe* was the talk of his staff officers, who jokingly referred to the *Führer* as the 'Island Jumper'.

So, on the face of it, did it make sense for the Allies to get to the islands first? That's how it struck the Americans, and Churchill. Were Spain to join the Axis or – more likely now – were Germany to invade the country to take Gibraltar, the occupation of the islands would become not only permissible but essential. Operation Shrapnel was provisionally drawn up with this contingency in mind, to be launched by troops then stationed in Sierra Leone.

Churchill's advisers advised caution, though.

Operation Inadvisable

The operation shouldn't be the option of first resort, they warned. It was unlikely to be the formality the leadership imagined. And if, as appeared inevitable, an invasion stampeded the Portuguese and Spanish dictators into the Axis camp, the Germans would be given use of the Canaries. In the event, as time went on, Spain stayed clear of the conflict and Germany became bogged down in Russia, the moment passed. By the beginning of 1941, the order was going out for the recall of the Shrapnel force.

Operation Isabella

Spain's status in the war was ambiguous. In one sense it was clearly a spectator, standing on the sidelines; yet its strategic significance was potentially enormous.

As Europe spiralled into war through the summer of 1939, the status of Spain was something of a riddle. Its natural sympathies appeared to be with the Axis powers. After all, Franco was a dictator, and a sworn enemy of communism and all its works. For all his (often brutal) authoritarianism, however, he had little patience with the world-changing rhetoric or the totalitarian philosophies of Fascist Italy or Nazi Germany. A simple soul ideologically, he supported the old institutions of Church and state. In diplomatic terms too, he liked to do things his own way.

An Aggravating Ally

Franco may have been a monster, but he was nobody's fool – and nobody's puppet. Hence Hitler's exasperation, and eventually anger. For all his sympathy with German aspirations, Franco – a seasoned soldier – was sceptical about Hitler's power to achieve them. Put brutally, he believed he might well lose the war. Spain had much to lose as well: specifically, the Canary Islands. The British Navy would make short work of seizing them. Hence his hesitancy, and his temporizing. In the end,

Spain's most serious contribution was the service of several thousand volunteers in the German cause. Many in this so-called Blue Division fell on the Russian Front. But Franco was to prove a frustrating partner: for all the warm words he offered, he thought only of himself and Spain, never giving the Nazi leader the wholehearted support that Hitler had believed to be his right.

An Iberian Irrelevance?

Up to a point, it didn't matter where the Spanish dictator's loyalties lay. It was centuries since Spain had been a superpower, and now the country had been left broken by three ferocious years of civil war. Its starving people had no fight left in them; its economy was shattered. Hitler himself had been wary of acquiring an ally who would cost him much more in

Recruits to the Spanish Blue Division bid 'adios'. Few were to return from the Russian Front.

assistance than it could conceivably supply him in support. Yet he had hoped for more cooperation from General Franco than he seemed to be receiving in October 1940 at the meeting they had together on a train in southern France.

Spain still mattered, Hitler believed – and not just because British Gibraltar might be attacked from its territory and control established over the entrance to the Mediterranean. As was the case with Ireland, German strategic thinking saw not only offensive opportunities but defensive dangers: what if the Allies came up through Spain to open a southern front in France?

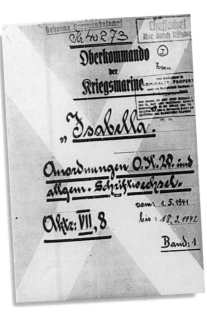

TRANSCRIPT OF KEY PARAGRAPHS

'Isabella' arrangements
Begun: 1.5.1941
Closed: 18.3.42

A brief contents of each section:

Attack preparations against the Iberian peninsular and Gibraltar p1–4 (instruction Gr. West and Adm. Frkr) p5–7

Arrangements for the provision of undertaking 'Isabella' p8–10

Installation of the Navy for 'Atilla' and 'Isabella' p11

Coast reinforcements of Portugal p28–35

Likewise Gr. West p41

Battery provision for 'Isabella' p42

Personnel provision for special enterprise 'Isabella'

No direction over extending navy organization 'isabella' p53–55

Inhalts-Verzeichnis

CASE GE 44

zu den Akten: "Isabella": Anordnungen OKW und allgem. Schriftwechsel.
Akts: VII.8 Band: 1.
√ = Briefbuchführer hat Kts.
Begonnen: 1. 5. 1941
Geschlossen: 18.3.42

Eigene B.Nr.	Frf Nr.	Fremde B.Nr.	Kurzer Jnhalt:	Blatt:
585/41.Chefs	3 E+Vfg.	OKW 44640	Angriffsvorbereitungen gegen die Iberische Halbinsel und Gibraltar. (Unterrichtung Gr.West u. Adm.Frkr.)	1–4
634/41.Chefs	4	OKH I/0486	Anordnungen für die Versorgung für das Unternehmen "Isabella".	5–7
624/41.Chefs	E+ Vfg	Gr.West 1867	Einsetzung Marineorganisation "Atilla für "Isabella".	8–10
639/41.Chefs	E+ Vfg	" 1874	Unterrichtung über "Atilla" und "Isabella" an Gr.West.	11
11634/41.Gkds	E+ Vfg	H.Gr.A KVO	Entsendung Kapt.z.S.Wagner nach Bordeaux zur Besprechung	12–16
11804/41.Gkds	Vfg.	--	Desgleichen.	
25459/41.Geh.	Vfg.	--	Desgleichen.	
9+17/41.Gkds	3	A.VI 2363	Seetransporte von Groß nach Portugal oder Spanien.	
970/41.Chefs	2	AOK 7 J.42	Aktennotiz über Besprechung 7.AOK am 10.6.41	21–27
751/41.Chefs 3 Anl.	2	1.Skl. KM b	Küstenbefestigungen Portugal, Tejo-Mündung (Lissabon) und bei Setubal (1 Pilsstreifen).	28–35
697/41.Chefs	1 E+Vfg.	OKH 916	Stellungnahme zu einzelnen Punkten "Isabella"-Unternehmen.	36–40
989/41.Chefs	Vfg	--	Desgleichen an Gr. West.	
12381/41.Gkds	4	Qu.AId 2950	Batterie-Bereitstellung f.Isabella	41
970/41.Chefs	1	AOK 7 J.42	Aktennotiz über Besprechung mit 7.AOK am 10.6.41	42
970/41.Chefs	Vfg.		Personalbereitstellung für Sonderunternehmung "Isabella".	43–46
992/41.Chefs	E+ Vfg.	Gr.West 1959	Eintreffen der Marine-Sondergruppen an den einzelnen Tagen.	47–48
1006/41.Chefs	-	Gr.West 1959	Vereinbarung über Einsatz der Marinegruppen mit AOK 7.	49–50
979/41.Chefs	E+ Vfg.	Gr.West 1961	Keine Weisung über Ausbau Marine-organisation Isabella.	51–52
1063/41.Chefs	5	Qu.AII	Bereitstellung Marinesondergruppe Dora und Fritz u.Mar.Art.	53–55
13200/41.Gkds	Vfg.		Bereitstellung eines PKW für Kpt.z.S. Wagner mit AOK.7	56–57

Sketchy Strategy

From the German point of view, then, Spain wasn't as peripheral as Franco chose to believe. The *Caudillo*'s prevarications over Operation Felix infuriated Hitler, who decided to take action, with or without consent. He set out his plan for Operation Isabella in June 1941: it was back-of-an-envelope stuff, not much more than the hastiest of outlines – though Hitler tended to believe his roughest sketch was law. He did, however, appreciate that, with a new front about to open in the Soviet Union, Isabella would have to wait.

In the event, the plan did indeed wait and wait, and wait … as Operation Barbarossa first flagged and then failed.

Ricin Rain

Late in 1941, an ambitious (if improbable) plan was devised by the British to use millions of needles to sow death across Germany.

'We are afraid we do not understand your requirements,' says the letter from the Singer Sewing Machine Company, dated Christmas Eve 1941: 'From your remarks it seems the needles are required for some other purpose, other than sewing machines.'

You might say that. The request from Britain's Chemical Defence Research Department, though vague in its terms, had been vast in the quantities concerned. Briefly the Department was working on a plan to have millions of needles envenomed by being dipped in ricin (or, perhaps, in anthrax), then dropped from planes over Germany's armies in Europe.

Released in such huge numbers that they would look like

rainclouds, they would be falling fast enough by the time they reached earth to pass through at least two layers of clothing and penetrate deep beneath the skin. The planners were certain of this because unfortunate sheep and goats at a secret research station in Canada had been clad in battledress and exposed to the poison darts. The results had apparently been most satisfactory. Rather than simply being allowed to rain freely from the heavens, the needles could also be packed into explosive cluster bombs – 30,000 at a time. When the bombs went off, the darts would be sent shooting off in all directions with devastating speed and force.

A Biological Bludgeon

By this stage in the war, the threat of a German invasion of Britain had receded (though it had not, of course, been banished altogether). Whitehall and Porton Down planners were thinking more about softening up enemy forces in advance of an Allied attack – for the Nazi war machine was still frighteningly strong. Germ warfare wasn't cricket, but then nor was war – as the British had long since discovered. Biological toxins offered possibilities that couldn't be ignored.

Scientists experiment with deadly toxins: anthrax remains a huge threat in warfare and is still considered by many as a weapon.

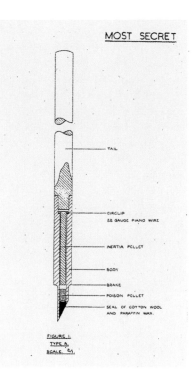

MOST SECRET

TAIL

CIRCLIP
22 GAUGE PIANO WIRE

INERTIA PELLET

BODY

BRAKE

POISON PELLET

SEAL OF COTTON WOOL
AND PARAFFIN WAX.

FIGURE I.
TYPE A.
SCALE. ⅔/I.

And what possibilities! The merest jab with a poisoned needle of this kind could potentially cause disablement; if the victim wasn't able to pluck out the poisoned dart within 30 seconds, an agonizing death was just about inevitable. Diarrhoea, vomiting and seizures are just a few of the symptoms of ricin poisoning. Such spectacular sufferings would not just kill the victim but also throw the military medical system into paralysis – and demoralize those personnel who hadn't actually been hit.

Personnel, Not Property
Another, and still more controversial, advantage of a weapon of this sort was that – like the later 'neutron bomb' – it would kill people without

The plan was to manufacture Ricin darts like this in their millions and for them to wreak havoc on the enemy.

destroying structures. So it was possible to imagine cutting a swathe through German forces in Western Europe without tearing the heart out of the cities they were occupying.

Yet this advantage immediately underlined the weapon's obvious downside: anyone indoors would be protected from the poison 'rain'. Any German in a tank, truck or car, or perhaps just behind a wall, would be protected – even a helmet might be enough, with a bit of luck. And so, the needle-darts were dropped – or, rather, they weren't: the British decided that they were too 'uneconomical' as a weapon. The project as developed was put on the shelf.

The symptoms produced are: twitching of the muscles, profuse salivation and sweating, acute defecation, micturition and retching. The pulse becomes very slow and the blood pressure falls.

British researcher into ricin, strain T1123, 1945.

Porton Down in Wiltshire remains an important centre for the research and development of secret weapons.

THE USE OF POISONED DARTS FROM THE AIR.

Reference Ptn. 3156 (U.2903) dated 9.3.44, Suffield's comments F.E.S. S.7011 dated 31.3.44, and your new appreciation of the subject, the writing of which was postponed in June owing to other committments.

Canada has been pursuing the problem actively in the meantime, and the following interim remarks have been forwarded for our information.   Since the problem is largely a C.W. one we feel that the appreciation should be delayed no longer since it will obviously have an effect on Canada's future programme of work. It is understood from Lord Stamp and Lt. Col. Flood that Canada is awaiting this appreciation.

MS 1.   "7 Sept. 1944. - Although the original design of dart withstood breakup on discharge from a cluster projectile, the straw tail was insufficiently strong.   A stronger tail and a more uniform dart has now been obtained although the original design is basically unchanged.   Mass production of this new unit is practical, at reasonable cost."

MS 2.   "7 Sept. 1944. - A ballistically stable cluster projectile which fits the British 500-lb. A/C stowage has been designed. This projectile holds a total of approximately 30,000 darts in 9 containers - over 95% of the darts fall stably, when declustering occurs.   Some difficulty has been experienced in getting all nine containers to open, but it is believed that this problem is now solved."

MS 3.   "7 Sept. 1944. - Recent work by the Toxicity Laboratories at the University of Chicago has shown that for larger animals, such as the goat, sheep and monkey, the compounds N-methyl urethane of m-diethylamino-phenol methiodide T.1123, (American code TL.1217) and the corresponding methochloride (TL.1299) are much more lethal than T.1708.   Subsequent examination of these two materials has shown that the overall performance, that is the effect on small and large animals, appears to be better than T.1708 in that there seems to be the less species variation.   Therefore, the work done up to the present has been chiefly on the compound T.1123, which was more available than TL.1299.

Some approximate LD 50 values are as follows:

Compound	Species	LD 50 (γ/Kg) (approx).
T.1123	goat	100
T.1123	goat	60
T.1123	Sheep	75
TL.1299	Sheep	70

(not Vaccurate)

On the basis of the above figures, darts have been coated with various quantities of T.1123-adhesive mixture representing 1, 2, 3, 4 LD 50 doses, inserted into goats for different periods of time, and the dart then removed.   The following is a brief summary of the results.

I.

Document page 2

Dose	Time in Tissues	No. of Goats	% Mortality
1 x LD 50	left in	10	0
2 x "	" "	9	33
3 x "	2 min.	5	60
3 x "	1 min.	5	40
4 x "	1 min.	5	100
4 x "	30 secs.	10	100
4 x "	15 secs.	8	75
4 x "	10 secs.	10	60
4 x "	5 secs.	10	50

Another trial was carried out in which T.1123 was incorporated in a new type of paste and applied to the darts. These darts were inserted subcutaneously into sheep for different time intervals. In this experiment, the amount of toxic material on each dart was equivalent to 4 times the LD 50 dose, as was estimated by subcutaneous injection of T.1123 solutions.

No. of Sheep	Time in Tissues	% Mortality	Remarks
9	15 secs.	44	All collapsed.
9	10 secs.	44	" "
9	5 secs.	22	" "
9	momentarily	0	" "
9	"	0	8 LD 50 dose used, all collapsed.

Trials are being carried out to test the stability of T.1123 and TL.1299 when incorporated in a paste and placed on darts. The toxic material was made up as described in MS 4.

The following are the sets of conditions under which the coated darts are being tested, and the results obtained to date:

Test	Temp.(°C)	Relative Humidity(%)	Time (Days)	Remarks
1	25	20 - 30	72	Material still retains toxicity. LD 50 approximately 60 γ/Kg.
2	50	20 - 30	72	Material still retains toxicity. LD 50 approximately 50-65 γ/Kg.
3	25	90	1	Material runs off the dart in liquid form.
4	50	90	1	Material runs off the dart in liquid form.

Attempts are being made to overcome this property of the dart coatings and are still in progress.

The hygroscopic properties of several compounds similar to T.1708 are being investigated. To date the compounds most resistant to moisture are T.1708 and TL.1327 (American code).

The effect of high humidity on coatings made from all these compounds using two different adhesives has also been

Document page 3

investigated. Results similar to those above were recorded.

The stability to heat of the compounds mentioned above is being investigated."

MS 4. "7 Sept. 1944. - Solvars 404 and 357 have been used as adhesives for the coating of MS 1 devices, with T.1708, and have been found to be superior to 545 in that the coating appears to be dissolved off more rapidly. The adhesive qualities are about the same.

When attempts were made to coat MS1 devices with T.1123 and TL.1299 (American code), using the Solvars 545, 404 and 357, the materials would not form a good paste which could be applied to the MS 1.

A mixture prepared using a procedure obtained from Capt. A. Ames of C.W. Laboratories appeared quite satisfactory and was used in subsequent work. It consists of the following ingredients:

8.14 gms.		T.1123
1.0 "		Cellosize WS (Hydroxethyl cellulose 10% soln. in water).
0.1 "		Carbowax 4000
0.1 "		Citric acid.

A machine has been constructed for coating the MS 1 devices semi-mechanically. It has been shown to be capable of coating an average of 10 MS 1 per minute. With an expert operator this rate could be increased. Essentially it is a spinning die (shaped to fit exactly about the MS 1 head) into which is fed the coating material under slight pressure (about 3-5 lbs/sq.in.). The method of coating simply involves inserting the MS 1 into the die and removing it coated. It is proposed to coat 70,000 MS 1 devices at Suffield."

MS 5. "7 Sept. 1944. - One successful trial has been carried out in which the new cluster projectile charged with 30,000 darts was released from 7000 ft. and declustered at 3500 ft. Penetrating hits were attained on 16 out of 36 goats and sheep disposed on the area. The contamination was remarkably uniform. Although only 7 out of 9 containers in the cluster discharged their contents, 10,000 sq. yds. were contaminated to a density of about 2 sq. yd. and 7000 sq. yds. to a density of about one per two sq. yds. It is believed the problem of attaining complete opening of the dart containers has now been solved".

Biology Section,
Porton.
13th November, 1944.

Chapter Two
1942

By 1942, the war looked very different. Not only were the original combatants getting one another's measure, but the Japanese and Americans had joined the fray, and the Russians were putting up ferocious resistance to the Germans.

The great challenge for America in its early months at war had been that of recovering its equilibrium after the sheer shock of Japan's attack on Pearl Harbor on 7 December 1941. Victory at Midway secured the initiative for America in the Pacific, 4–7 June, whilst in the months that followed the British would defeat Rommel's army at the Second Battle of El Alamein, whilst the Soviets would hold the Germans at Stalingrad.

In the East, the Allies were desperate to get their forces on to the offensive – though still fearful of Japanese attacks, from Australia to Madagascar and Ceylon. In the West, the pressure was on to open up a 'Second Front' for an insistent Stalin, whose Red Army was still struggling hard to hold on in Russia. Within the Western high command there was – if not division, at least disagreement – over what sort of action it was appropriate to take: an invasion of France or a more indirect approach.

The conflict unfolded against an enormous range of environmental backdrops. Here Signal Corps cameramen ford a river in the rainforest of New Guinea.

Operation Tulsa

Flush with victory after Midway, MacArthur made plans to launch a lightning advance through New Guinea and the Solomon Islands to the Japanese base at Rabaul.

The US Navy's triumph at Midway (May–June 1942) had marked a pivotal point in the Pacific War: even at the time, that much was clear. At last, the balance knocked so badly awry at the time of the Pearl Harbor raid had been corrected. The United States was back on its feet, and ready to march on.

A Personal Matter
Specifically, General Douglas MacArthur wanted to advance upon Rabaul. He believed it barred his way to the Philippines.

Having been forced out of the Philippines a few months before, he had made a personal pledge to come back to free them: 'I came out of Bataan and I shall return.' MacArthur was, for all his professionalism, that kind of emotionally driven man; he took his fighting personally.

Operation Tulsa for taking Rabaul was a case in point – starting with the target, which itself was something of a mirage. The main Japanese base in the southwest Pacific, Rabaul lay at the eastern end of New Britain, the largest island of the Bismarck group. Here had been marshalled some 60 Zero fighters and a similar number of twin-engine bombers along with seaplanes for reconnaissance. There were also warehouses and workshops.

General Douglas MacArthur made it a personal target after Midway – Rabaul or bust.

Rabaul was heavily attacked from the air by the Americans, but not until November 1943.

It was an important airbase, then, but it was no more. It certainly didn't have any of the elaborate fortifications or big guns the Allies believed it had. Nor, despite MacArthur's romantic resolution, did it really have to be taken before an attack could be launched against the Philippines.

An Ambitious Plan

No matter. His thinking reflected that of the Allies at the time – though the idea that a two-pronged advance might be made eastward along the northern coast of New Guinea on the one hand and northwest up the Solomon Islands on the other to take Rabaul (and all in the space of a fortnight) was all his own.

The plan was especially unrealistic given the absence of adequate airfields to support the heavy bombers he saw as providing aerial cover for the advances from either side. Along with his own army (three divisions), he wanted a two-carrier task force and a Marine division for the final, climactic amphibious assault on Rabaul itself.

Air Force Commander George Brett insisted that he would need 12 new airfields fit for heavy bombers in New Guinea alone. Particularly important would be Buna, located on the island's northeast coast.

Unfortunately, by the time the Corps of Engineers was organized, the Japanese had taken Buna. The Americans started building at Milne Bay instead, but reality spoiled the plans in other ways too. Admiral Nimitz, on the

The US Navy and Marine Corps took the Solomon Islands one by one.

Navy's behalf, nixed the amphibious grand finale. In such closely confined waters, he argued, the fleet would meet certain destruction.

Gone, But not Forgotten

But if Tulsa never quite went ahead, it wasn't quite abandoned either: the outline of MacArthur's plan is clearly recognizable in what ultimately transpired. While MacArthur and his men pushed east across New Guinea, the Navy and Marine Corps island-hopped their way up the Solomons – in a series of separate operations that were agonizingly protracted and shockingly bloody, rather than the single sweeping pincer movement that MacArthur had imagined to be possible.

The balance of power at that moment was too delicate to make wise the attempted seizure of a position so exposed to enemy counterattack.

Fleet Admiral Ernest Joseph King, Commander in Chief US Fleet and Chief of Naval Operations.

Operation Herkules

It was supposed to be the culminating action of the two-year Siege of Malta, but the right moment never quite came, and the initiative was lost.

A major British naval base, just 93km (57 miles) from the Sicilian coast, Malta was always going to be a target in the event of a war with Italy. Surprisingly, given that its strategic significance had been acknowledged since ancient times, the island had very little in the way of fortification. The British had passed up the chance of improving its defences in the pre-war years, despairing of it as completely undefendable.

An arid outcrop in mid-Mediterranean, Malta had no real prospect of being able to sustain itself with food; most essential supplies – including oil – had to be shipped in. Making the island militarily impregnable would only postpone the inevitable, prolonging the agony for defenders who stood no real chance of getting through a determined siege. The decision had already been taken that, when war broke out and the island came under attack, the British would cut their losses and let it go. Alexandria, on the coast of Egypt, would replace it as their main base.

Islands Under Siege

So much for the power of foresight. In the event, when hostilities began, events followed a completely different course. The expected onslaught wasn't slow in coming: with the RAF engrossed in the Battle of Britain, few planes or pilots could be spared for Malta's air defences, so Mussolini's bombers were able to ply back and forth at will. Valletta, with its dockyard, suffered heavy damage. The island was buffeted by bombs for weeks on end.

The good news for the Maltese was that, relentless as the bombing might have been, there was no attempt to follow through at ground-level with an amphibious attack. Their island would have been very vulnerable in this case, but since Mussolini had chosen to commit the vast majority of his troops to the invasion of Greece, the strategy of aerial bombardment was maintained. Yet Malta could take this sort of punishment as long as its supplies held out. For, if the island had few fortifications, it had natural air-raid shelters in the form of caves, cushioned from

The British were determined to hang on to Malta at any cost.

shocks by the soft sandstone through which they ran. Casualties among the islanders were accordingly low, and spirits high – even if the longer-term outlook wasn't quite so rosy.

Whatever Italy's priorities, the strategy of the Germans was being decided by events on quite a different island. By November 1940, the Battle of Britain had run its course. The *Luftwaffe* had thrown just about everything it had at the Royal Air Force, the British people and at UK industry and commerce. Britons had come through in what Winston Churchill called 'their finest hour'. But the *Luftwaffe* had lost more than 1500 aircraft in what had been the first real check for their *blitzkrieg* tactics: the Germans had to retire to lick their wounds.

Into Africa

Not, of course, that their efforts to quell British resistance were at an end – but it was clear that a new approach would be required. The focus now shifted to the south: Hitler's hopes of taking Gibraltar were part of a broader strategy of isolating the British from their empire.

In this context, Malta took on a new importance: an imperial possession, it had an historic role as a waystation on the route to Suez and the East. North Africa was significant in this scheme since whoever occupied its coast was in a position to control access to the Suez Canal.

Running the Gauntlet

Egypt itself had been an informal colony of Britain since the nineteenth century, but the rest of the Maghreb was now in Axis hands. The victim of a one-sided war of conquest by Fascist Italy in 1934, Libya belonged to Italy. Other countries, including Tunisia, Algeria and eastern Morocco, were under the control of (Vichy) France. Western Morocco was Spanish-ruled, and while Hitler may have had his difficulties with General Franco, he was certainly no friend of the Allied powers. British shipping in the Mediterranean already had to steer a careful course as it ran the gauntlet of forces from Axis-held southern Europe on the one hand and North Africa on the other. If the Axis held Malta, they would have the British in a stranglehold.

The people of Malta bore their sufferings so stoically that the island was awarded the George Cross.

Ugo Cavallero converses here with Erwin Rommel.

For Britain, it suddenly seemed that Malta had to be held at all costs; for the Axis powers, the island was a prize that simply had to be seized. For both sides, it was as vital to deny Malta to the other as it was to have the facilities it offered for themselves. From the British perspective, the possession of the island made possible the passage of ships through the Mediterranean; it was also the platform from which attacks on Axis aircraft and shipping assisting in the build-up of forces in North Africa could be made. Italy's Supreme Commander Ugo Cavallero was in no doubt about Malta's strategic importance:

The assault on Malta will cost us many casualties, but I consider it absolutely essential for the future development of the war. If we take Malta, Libya will be safe.

Straight From the Fox's Mouth

Destined to go down in history for the flair and imagination with which he fought, Field Marshal Erwin Rommel nonetheless had a quick enough eye for the more mundane. As early as May 1941, the 'Desert Fox' was warning that his swashbuckling attacks and his men's heroics were all going to be in vain if they couldn't receive the equipment and supplies they needed. 'Without Malta,' he said frankly, 'the Axis will lose control of North Africa.'

Kurt Student talks tactics with his men in Crete; Malta should have been a walkover after that ferocious struggle.

A Major Undertaking

Field Marshal Albert Kesselring had overall responsibility for Herkules, though Generalmajor Kurt Student was to take charge of the airborne assault. As commander at the Battle of Crete, he'd had a tough grounding in this very specialized sort of operation. This time round, though, he had time to do do some serious homework. Some 500 German Junkers Ju52 transport planes (plus some 200 transporters of the *Regia Aeronautica*, the Italian Air Force) and 500 gliders of assorted size. Student and his staff worked out where every drop was to be made, where every aircraft was to come to land, and exactly what 29,000 airborne troops were to required to do.

The operation would have an amphibious component too, though this wasn't expected to arrive in Malta before the airborne troops had made it safe to land. Italian forces were to make the attack, which was to come in two waves: first, some 25,000 shock troops – including marines and commandos – with mobile artillery and light tanks; these would be followed by more than 30,000 regular troops bringing with them heavy artillery and tanks. In preparation, landing craft were specially built by the Italians – about 50 in all; the plan assumed that these would be supplemented by craft brought in by the Germans.

The Moment Passes

A big operation then, with huge numbers of men and vast amounts of materiel involved, considering the tiny island they were trying to take. And frantic resistance was pretty much guaranteed, so dramatically had Malta's military value soared since the North Africa campaign got under way in earnest.

Ironically, its preparations were to be undercut by the demands of that campaign as it continued. Rommel, who had done so much to sell the cause of Operation Herkules to a sceptical *Führer*, was faring better than expected in his Libyan offensive: scenting victory, he was desperate to push on towards Alexandria and Suez. As time went on and more and more men and resources were channelled into his campaign, it became clear to Kesselring that the chances of Herkules being successfully carried through were receding fast. Hitler, who had never been fully behind the plan, now became unsympathetic, and in the spring of 1942, the idea was dropped.

Hitler ended the interview by grasping me by the arm and telling me in his Austrian dialect: 'Keep your shirt on, Field Marshal Kesselring! I'm going to do it.'

Albert Kesselring on his efforts to save Herkules.

Germany was dogged by its shortage of the specialized landing craft needed for amphibious operations.

Anthrax by Air

The British overreached themselves when they decided to deploy this biological weapon against the Germans. Not because it wouldn't work but because it would work too well.

Gruinard, a lovely island, lies off Scotland's western coast, as beautiful a spot as any in the Hebrides. Till recently, though, it had a fearful reputation as the 'Typhoid Mary' of the Isles.

For it was here that, in 1942, the British government began its experimental anthrax programme. Oxford University's Professor R.L. Vollum produced a particularly nasty strain of anthrax, named Vollum 14578 in his honour. Sheep were exposed to spores, scattered from small explosive devices. They were filmed while, over the next few days, they died.

On the One Hand ...

Emboldened by this success, the Allies prepared a project named (with macabre irony) Operation Vegetarian. Anthrax spores would be packed into five million linseed cakes for dropping by bombers over Germany's pastureland.

Cattle would eat them, before being slaughtered for consumption by civilians: soon the country would have a mass-outbreak on its hands.

The symptoms would start with mouth- and throat ulcers; vomiting and fever would quickly follow before pains were felt in the abdomen as the bacillus ate away at the tissue of the digestive tract. The patient's diarrhoea and vomiting would be bloody now.

Gruinard Island was not considered to be fully safe until it was cleaned up in the 1990s.

TRANSCRIPT OF KEY PARAGRAPHS

<u>Appendix 1</u>
<u>Bomb A/C 4-lb. Type F charged N</u>

From actual field trials and experiments on monkeys, it is estimated that an unprotected man will be subjected to a 50% risk of death from 1 clustered projectile (+ 25% for ineffectiveness) containing 106 4-lb. Type F bombs charged N over the following areas:-
Mild exercise in the open = 250,000 sq. yds. (1000 downwind)
Mild exercise in built-up area = 50,000 sq. yds.

Thus for effective use, and assuming man undergoing mild exercise, 12 clustered projectiles per square mile (or 640 acres) will be required in open country, or 60 clustered projectiles per square mile in built-up areas (plus, in each case, 25% for ineffective bombs).

According to BW(44)30, the American plant is capable of charging 500,000 4-lb bombs per month. Thus the 4,277,100 bombs required for 6 German cities could be charged in 8½ months.

Within four or five days, the patient would be dead.

In the meantime, Germany's surviving cattle herd would largely have succumbed to the disease, producing a food crisis for those who'd escaped the anthrax.

Dead to the nth Degree

A secret Allied laboratory was meanwhile mass-producing anthrax for another operation. This large-scale attack would cut out the cattle stage: spores were to be dispersed by bombs directly over German cities. The technicians at Grosse Ile, in the St Lawrence just outside Quebec City, Canada, believed they could make 300lb (135 kg) of spores a week, enough to arm 1500 bombs. It was hoped eventually to have five million bombs in all.

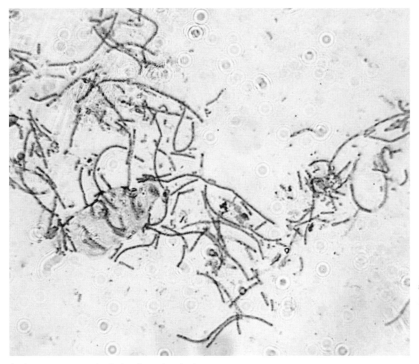

Anthrax spores are both deadly and enduring.

Studies of the bombing density needed to saturate specific centres in spores were made – and so excited were Allied planners, apparently, that these continued for some time after the war's end.

Overkill

The Grosse Ile centre was closed after a series of accidents, but not before its technicians had manufactured 70 billion doses of anthrax – enough to kill the whole world 30 times over. But then, that was the problem. How was anthrax possibly to be contained? And it wasn't just the range of its toxicity or the ease of its manufacture: anthrax spores are astoundingly persistent. Gruinard wasn't safe for humans until the present century –

decades after the experiments, and then only after a prolonged and systematic decontamination programme.

A table prepared at Porton Down in 1944 compares the performance of the anthrax ('N') with a more conventional poison gas CG (Phosgene). The case for anthrax is made with gruesomely compelling logic. One category is telling, however: for 'Availability of terrain for occupation after use', the official's comment for anthrax is, quite simply, 'None'.

It was all very well destroying the German people's capacity to resist. What, however, would be achieved by ensuring that their country would be to all intents and purposes uninhabitable for generations after?

TRANSCRIPT OF KEY PARAGRAPHS

The enemy is known to have experimented before the war with bombs filled with the same agent, and if he has developed it satisfactorily and uses it against us we shall suffer from the affects already noted. We could only retaliate with the same weapon, hoping that united resources and opportunities were greater than those of the enemy.

Scheme for comparison of **N** with **CG**.

Immediate effect:
N = Nil.
CG = Lachrymation and coughing.

Persistent effect:
N = Secondary inhalation deaths. Cutaneous casualties and deaths persisting for weeks, months or years, according to terrain.
CG = Nil.

Manufacture:
N = not established. Pilot plants now functioning successfully.
CG: Established.

Immediate recognition:
N = Impossible. **CG** = Easy.

Retaliation by the enemy.

22.
    The enemy is known to have experimented before the war with bombs filled with the same agent, and if he has developed it satisfactorily and uses it against us we shall suffer from the effects already noted. We could only retaliate with the same weapon, hoping that united resources and opportunities were greater than those of the enemy.

    On the other hand, if the enemy initiated B.W. with some other form of agent and we found it desirable to retaliate with the present project, the resources of Germany would be quite inadequate to develop a similar project in time to be effective in this war. This opinion is based on knowledge of the scale of the plans projected in U.S.A. and on the assumption that the economic resources of the enemy are already fully employed.

Scheme for comparison of N with CG.

23.
    Although a comparison between the effect of this project and that of phosgene is not valid, the following scheme is given:-

	N	CG
Immediate effect:	Nil	Lachrymation and coughing.
Delayed effect:	2-7 days or sometimes later. Deaths.	About 6 hrs. Casualties with few deaths.
Persistent effect:	Secondary inhalation deaths. Cutaneous casualties and deaths persisting for weeks, months or years, according to terrain.	Nil
Manufacture:	Not established. Pilot plants now functioning successfully.	Established.
Supplies:	Limited for special operations.	Unlimited.
Stability:	Unproved over periods greater than 6 months in temperate climates. Probably limited in tropics.	Satisfactory.
Immediate recognition:	Impossible.	Easy
Protection (respirator)	Good, but only if worn continuously in presence of hostile aircraft.	Easy
Availability of terrain for occupation after use	None	Unlimited
Operational requirement to produce these effects over equal areas	1 A/C	20 A/C

Biology Section,
Porton.
March 25rd 1944.

P. FILDES.

Operation Sledgehammer

Too much, too soon in a conflict still spiralling out of control at a terrifying rate, an ambitious invasion of Normandy planned for 1942 was quickly shelved.

In retrospect, the battle lines of World War II seem clearly drawn, yet since its start the situation had been subject to changes at dizzying speed. The Soviet Union had begun as an ally (however uncomfortable) of Nazi Germany. The United States had not been involved at all. France, on the other hand, had seemed the staunchest and strongest of allies: Germany's own generals appear to have feared the worst when they invaded the country.

All Change

What a difference the months had made. France had fallen in no time flat: its quick collapse seems to have been the result of a wholesale failure of intelligence, not just in Paris but in London. And then, on 22 June 1941, Hitler had 'kicked in the door' of what he saw as a ramshackle Soviet Union. Operation Barbarossa had

We are making preparations for a landing on the Continent in August or September 1942 ... provided that it appears sound and sensible.

Winston Churchill, memo to Molotov, April 1942.

The German invasion of the Soviet Union in July 1941 meant that Germany was now fighting on two fronts.

British prisoners of war are paraded through the streets of Dieppe.

begun. The Germans had irrupted into the Soviet Union with what's believed to have been the biggest fighting force ever deployed: 4.5 million men. The USSR was now fighting for its survival.

For Britain, arguably, things were looking up. The Soviets were hardly friends, but they were now functioning as allies; they were certainly doing some seriously heavy lifting. Casualties were fearful on this Eastern Front, where Hitler's armies were engaged in a race war, attempting to clear the steppe of Slavs. If truth be told, the Soviets were losing badly, but – more important from the perspective of the Western allies – they were soaking up an enormous amount of Axis pressure.

Not that the Germans were having things all their own way. Their statistics don't tell an especially happy story either. Though light by Soviet standards, their casualties were by any normal standards grim indeed. Whilst they didn't take anything like as many fatalities as the Soviets did, more than 100,000 died – and 700,000 or so were wounded. They had somehow to be carried along and cared for. No fewer than 14,000 Axis soldiers had to have limbs amputated owing to frostbite in the winter of 1941–2. They became a further drag on an army that was already bogged down in hostile territory. Literally so: the invading army was just 150km (90 miles) from Moscow in October 1941, when its advance was stalled by the onset of the *Rasputitsa*, the torrential autumn rains.

Regaining the Initiative

By the beginning of 1942, moreover, the United States was at Britain's side. The year to come could be faced with a bit more confidence. Even so, Britain still felt bloodied from its experiences at Dunkirk. It comes as no

---

EASTERN FRONT ARITHMETIC

3,000,000 Number of soldiers (German, Romanian, Hungarian) who invaded the Soviet Union on 22 June 1941.

2270 Number of aircraft accompanying invasion force.

3350 Number of invading tanks (there were 625,000 horses too).

1200 Number of Soviet planes lost in the first day's fighting (almost the entire Soviet Air Force was destroyed).

300,000 Number of Soviet prisoners taken by Germans after just one battle – at Smolensk, July 1941.

3000 Number of Soviet tanks lost at Smolensk.

600,000 Number of soldiers captured after taking of Kiev, mid-September.

3,000,000 Number of Red Army soldiers taken prisoner by the end of 1941.

650,000 Number of Soviet soldiers killed in the course of the Battle of Moscow, October 1941–January 1942.

2,663,000 Total number of Red Army soldiers killed by February 1942 – believed to be 20 times the figure for the Axis forces.

90m Number of civilians now in enemy territory.

[C.O.S. (42) 192 (O).
June 30, 1942.]

ANNEX I.

Operation "Sledgehammer."

Note by Minister of War Transport.

AT a meeting* of the Chiefs of Staff Committee on the 24th June, I was invited to circulate a memorandum for consideration by the Chiefs of Staff on the 1st July showing the implications of taking up the shipping required for "Sledgehammer."

2. My Department has been informed orally that the "lift" required by C.C.O. is the same as that notified last May, namely—

(*a*) 100 medium and large coasters (for an average of 30 M.T. vehicles each).†
(*b*) 100 small coasters (for stores—total lift 20,000 tons).
(*c*) 30 ocean-going cargo ships (for an average of 100 M.T. vehicles each).
(*d*) 1,000 dumb-barges (for an average of 2¼ M.T. vehicles each).
(*e*) 30 Cross-Channel type passenger vessels‡ (12 as Auxiliary Infantry Assault ships and 18 as personnel carriers—average 800 men each).
(*f*) 500 deep-draught towing craft.
(*g*) 250 shallow-draught towing craft.

3. With reference to requirement at 2 (*b*) above, although the demand is for 100 small coasters with a total lift of 20,000 tons, it is necessary for reasons of reliability of winches and engines that vessels of an average of 400 tons capacity should be allotted; 50 vessels of this type can lift 20,000 tons on the required draught. It is, therefore, suggested that if only 200 tons per ship can be discharged on one tide the vessels should remain on the beach for two tides; the eventual risk under these circumstances might be less than if a 100 vessels were used for one tide each.

4. The withdrawal of 30 ocean-going ships—paragraph 2 (*c*)—means in terms of imports a loss of about 500,000 tons per annum. For reasons of carrying efficiency, it would be necessary to employ—as part of these 30 ships—some 20 vessels now engaged in carrying war supplies from the United Kingdom and United States to overseas destinations; this would involve an annual reduction in the movement of these supplies of about 200,000 tons. Firm notice of the requirements for ocean-going ships must be given at least six weeks before the date of the operation, if wasteful delays are to be avoided.

5. The 1,000 dumb-barges—paragraph 2 (*d*)—have been taken up and are now being converted by the Admiralty.

6. The required number of cross-channel passenger ships—paragraph 2 (*e*)—can be made available, though some curtailment of the civilian sailings between the United Kingdom and the Isle of Man, Northern Ireland and Eire is inevitable. The 12 vessels required as Auxiliary Infantry Assault ships have already been taken up for conversion, and the 18 personnel carriers are earmarked.

7. It is understood that the Admiralty will provide the 500 deep-draught towing craft—paragraph 2 (*f*).

8. The Admiralty will also provide as many as possible of the 250 shallow-draught towing craft—paragraph 2 (*g*). We will furnish the remainder.

9. The effect of removing the 200 coasters required under 2 (*a*) and 2 (*b*) would be to throw upon internal transport 500,000 tons a month of additional freight, 70 per cent. of which would be coal. It is considered that inland transport could accept a large part of this burden during the summer but, in order to ease the strain (i) it would be necessary to make greater use of the East Coast

---

* C.O.S. (42). 188th Meeting, Minute 3.
† Originally 150 coasters for an average of 20 vehicles each.
‡ These are exclusive of 10 similar vessels already on C.C.O.'s service.

ports (including London) for ocean-going vessels, and (ii) it might be necessary to use a certain number of ocean-going steamers on coastal service, with a consequent loss of imports at the rate of about 450,000 tons per annum. Meanwhile, suitable coasting vessels are being earmarked and action is being taken to improve the loading and discharging gear of those required to lift M.T. vehicles, as six weeks* will be required to prepare and move to their loading ports the full number of ships indicated.

The strain on internal transport will be increased by the concurrent demands of "Bolero." The continuance of the strain during the winter will create a serious deficiency of internal transport.

10. Although these initial demands can be met it is essential that careful consideration should be given to subsequent developments and to the shipping requirements they would involve. At present we are asked to assume that over a period of two or three weeks the wastage of merchant ships and craft employed may amount to 50 per cent. and that the remaining 50 per cent. would suffice for the maintenance of the Forces landed. If, however, the operation is to develop into a major invasion, it seems that indefinite and much greater liabilities upon our shipping resources would be entailed. I wish to press that fuller consideration should be given to this point at once.

11. It should also be borne in mind that if casualties to craft approximate to the figure given, cross-channel type passenger steamers could not be provided for a similar operation on the same scale either this year or next.

12. It is assumed that the Chief of Combined Operations has satisfied himself that beaching operations of the magnitude contemplated, and with commercial craft of the type to be employed, are, in fact, practicable under the conditions likely to be encountered. Certain trials have been held but not on a large scale, nor with loaded vehicles. Further trials with the new gear now being fitted in the coasters are essential. It is problematical whether cargoes of loaded M.T. vehicles could be successfully discharged and handled on the beach. In any event, the beaching of large ocean-going ships might well lead to the loss of the ships. It is considered that ships of this type should not be used until harbour facilities are available.

13. No insuperable difficulties are anticipated in regard to port facilities on the South Coast to provide for an operation of the size envisaged, provided that T.L.Cs. and barges are all loaded at hards or on beaches and not at berths.

Great George Street, S.W. 1,
June 30, 1942.
* Subject to delivery of blocks and trunnions.

[C.O.S. (42) 194 (O)
June 30, 1942.]

ANNEX II.

CERTAIN IMPLICATIONS OF MOUNTING OPERATION "SLEDGEHAMMER."

Memorandum by Chief of Combined Operations.

IN accordance with C.O.S. (42) 61st meeting (O), Minute 2, I forward, for the information of the Chiefs of Staff Committee, the following notes on the implications of mounting operation "Sledgehammer."

Landing Craft Implications.

2. By hypothesis the operation would employ all the landing craft in the United Kingdom that are operationally fit. The movement to assemble these landing craft on the south coast must begin forthwith, and from now onwards they will have to be employed exclusively on training the "Sledgehammer" force, and subsequently on waiting at their final assembly positions for the operation.

2.

Effect on Army Training.

3. Since the troops to be employed on "Sledgehammer" must be chiefly drawn from units which have already completed preliminary combined operation training, it follows that the training programme for further units of Home Forces will come to a complete and immediate standstill. This interruption will continue until after the operation is carried out or cancelled, say, for a period of two to three months. Furthermore, the concentration of training efforts on the "Sledgehammer" force will occupy the time of all training instructors, &c., and thus delay the opening of the new C.T.Cs. on which the combined operational training of the United States Forces largely depends when they arrive in this country.

Effect on Naval Training.

4. The effect on naval training will also be most unfavourable. Although a limited number of landing craft which are not operationally fit will be left up north, and could be used for the training of naval personnel, the need to employ instructors for the "Sledgehammer" force will prejudice their use for this purpose.

Effect on 1943 Operations.

5. The present training programme (i.e., not allowing for "Sledgehammer") can only just meet the training requirements for "Round-Up" by the late spring of 1943. It therefore follows that the interruption referred to above cannot fail, either to delay the date by which the operation could be launched next year, or to reduce the size of the assault force available by the present target date. While it is difficult to give precise figures, I estimate, very roughly, that the delay would amount to approximately three months, or, alternatively, that the operation would have to be launched with a trained assault force amounting only to 5 divisions, as opposed to the 8 at present visualised.

Shipping.

6. The effects of taking up the large volume of shipping required for "Sledgehammer" have already been brought to the notice of the Chiefs of Staff.

Effect on Raiding Operations.

7. It would obviously be impossible to mount any large-scale raid during the period we were preparing for "Sledgehammer" unless they could be carried out by switching a part of the "Sledgehammer" force to carry them out as an alternative. While this is a possibility which should not be excluded, there is very real danger that it would result in the raiding force being inadequately trained either for "Sledgehammer" or for the raid.

Conclusion.

8. It will be seen from the foregoing that the implications of mounting an operation on the scale of "Sledgehammer" at the present juncture would be most serious, and in my judgment they should not be accepted unless there is a firm intention of actually carrying out the operation.

(Signed) LOUIS MOUNTBATTEN,
Chief of Combined Operations.

Great George Street, S.W. 1,
June 30, 1942.

3.

TRANSCRIPT OF KEY PARAGRAPHS

1. At a meeting of the Chiefs of Staff committee on the 24th June. I was invited to circulate a memorandum for consideration by the Chiefs of Staff on the 1st July showing the implications of taking up the shipping required for 'Sledgehammer'.

2. By hypothesis the operation would employ all the landing craft in the United Kingdom that are operationally fit. The movement to assemble these landing craft on the south coast must begin forthwith and from now onwards they will have to be employed exclusively on training the 'Sledgehammer' force, and subsequently on waiting at their final assembly positions for the operation.

3. The effect on naval training will also be most unfavourable. Although a limited number of landing craft which are not operationally fit will be left up north, and could be used for the training of naval personnel, the need to employ instructors for the 'Sledgehammer' force will prejudice their use for this purpose.

Conclusion. It will be seen from the foregoing that the implications of mounting an operation on the scale of 'Sledgehammer' at the present juncture would be most serious and in my judgment they should not be accepted unless there is a firm internation of actually carrying out the operation.

Louis Mountbatten
Chief of Combined Operations

surprise, therefore, that Britain should have shown some scepticism about Sledgehammer – an operation that might easily prove as disastrous as the defeat of the British Expeditionary Force (BEF) in France.

Neither, on the other hand, is it so remarkable that an 'Up and at 'em' tactic of taking the fighting to the Germans should have appealed to the can-do strategists on the US side. Though British staff scoffed at their naivety, there were good reasons for mounting an invasion of France – or even just a major raid – at this stage of the war.

First, and maybe most important, Stalin was clamouring for a 'second front' to be opened.

And it was hard to deny that Soviet forces were entitled to support. Then there was the craftier calculation: what if the Red Army's resistance crumbled? Or, for that matter, if – by some as yet inconceivable fortune – the Soviets won? Either way, it made sense for the Western Allies to take back the initiative any way they could.

A Positive Precedent

If the British didn't instantly dismiss the idea of Sledgehammer out of hand, this was due in part to their recent success at St Nazaire. This naval base stands on the northern banks of the Loire where it enters the Bay of Biscay. It was vital for its dry dock

facilities and its fortified U-boat pens. Three destroyers set off with a small flotilla. One of them, HMS *Campbeltown*, was laden with explosive and stripped of heavy fittings to reduce her draft so that (with the help of an unusually high spring tide) she could clear the sandbanks of the estuary. She was also specially armoured round the bows. The idea was that she could be used as a battering ram to penetrate the heavy dock gates, opening the way for the motor launches and patrol boats that were carrying in all some 700 commando troops.

The attacking convoy was spotted as it approached, but it had the advantages of surprise and speed – and the skill and

The St Nazaire Raid was an unusual combination of heroic daring and success.

A momentous meeting in which we accepted their proposals for offensive action in Europe in 1942 perhaps and 1943 for certain.

Diary of General Sir Alan Brooke, after meeting with the Americans, 8 April 1942.

Left: Troops attend an MG34 machine gun in one of the fortifications which made up the Germans' 'Atlantic Wall'.

Below: The St Nazaire Raid inflicted considerable damage on that port's U-Boat pens.

courage of the commandos, who quickly seized control and set explosives around key installations. The *Campbeltown* sailed right into the dry dock before the men on board abandoned ship and detonated the charges. The raid was an extraordinary success: the dry dock remained unusable until after the war. There'd been no thought of the raiders lingering, however, to establish themselves permanently in the port – and even so, it had been very costly in lives.

Mixed Feelings

A smash-and-grab raid on some key port would raise morale, American strategists suggested, and send the right sort of signal to Stalin and his forces in the east. The more so if an invasion force could establish itself there for the longer term. Cherbourg or Brest might then be the bridgehead for a more sustained assault on mainland Europe, clawing back the conquests of Germany over time.

The British couldn't feel quite so gung-ho, though. With the fate of the BEF so fresh in their minds, they wondered whether the Sledgehammer wasn't actually going to end up as the nut, caught in a crushing counter-attack by German forces. By July 1942, their uneasiness had prevailed. Pointing to the lack of landing craft, they persuaded the Americans to give up on the idea. Stalin was to get his second front a few months later, but it was to be far to the south, in Africa.

Australia ... or Not?

Plans for a Japanese invasion of Australia never quite reached the stage where the operation needed a name, but discussions were serious – and surprisingly specific – for a while.

A monotonous hum disturbed the peace of the Darwin morning of 19 February 1942. It rose gradually to reach a strident cacophony as waves of aircraft came screaming out of the sky, attacking not just ships but warehouses and offices, dock installations, cranes and quays.

This first wave of about 180 carrier-based attackers were followed by heavy bombers from Sulawesi, Indonesia.

Sounding the Alarm

When the smoke had cleared, it was time to count the cost. Along with port installations, eight ships had been sunk, including a US destroyer and troop transport. Even today the number of casualties is unclear (estimates range from 240 to about 1100 killed), but no one disputes the damage done to the port of

Right: Australians knew that a Japanese invasion was a real – and terrifying – threat.

Below: The air raid of 19 February 1942 damaged Darwin extensively.

DEPARTMENT OF DEFENCE CO-ORDINATION

MINUTE PAPER

SECRET

SUBJECT: JAPANESE PLAN FOR INVASION OF AUSTRALIA.

CHIEF OF THE NAVAL STAFF

CHIEF OF THE GENERAL STAFF

CHIEF OF THE AIR STAFF

    I refer to cablegram No.274 of 2nd October, 1942 from the Australian Legation, Chungking, a copy of which was forwarded to you on 5th October and a further copy of which is attached. Herewith are forwarded copies of a map illustrating the Japanese plan and commentary thereon by Chinese Intelligence together with a copy of memo from the Department of External Affairs in regard to this matter.

           Secretary
           Defence Committee.

DEPARTMENT OF EXTERNAL AFFAIRS.

CABLEGRAM. 3391.

SECRET

Date sent: 1/10/42.
Time 1.30 p.m.
Date Recd.: 2/10/42.

DECYPHER FROM:-

AUSTRALIAN LEGATION,
C H U N G K I N G.

No.274.

    The Director of Intelligence on Japanese Affairs told Australian Journalists here that documents captured on Japanese soldiers show definitely that the intention last July was to invade Australia. Heavy attack was to be launched on September 15th, coupled with feint attack on Darwin. Losses in Midway and Coral Sea prevented this. I understand that Army Headquarters Melbourne received similar information from the British Military Attache here some time ago.

              EGGLESTON.

Copy to - War Cabinet.
     Advisory War Council.
     Dept. of Defence.

2/10/42.

TRANSCRIPT OF KEY PARAGRAPHS

To: Chief of Naval/General and Air Staff.

I refer to cablegram No.274 of 2nd October, 1942 from the Australian Legation, Chunking, a copy of which was forwarded to you on 5th October and a further copy of which is attached. Herewith are forwarded copies of a map illustrating the Japanese plan and commentary thereon by Chinese Intelligence together with a copy of memo from the Department of External Affairs in regard to this matter.

Bottom: The Director of Intelligence on Japanese Affairs told Australian Journalists here that documents captured on Japanese soldiers show definitely that the intention last July was to invade Australia. Heavy attack was to be launched on September 15th, coupled with feint attack on Darwin. Losses in Midway and Coral Sea prevented this. I understand that Army Headquarters Melbourne received similar information from the British Military Attaché here some time ago.

Darwin. Or to morale in a nation plunged into panic about the possibility of invasion.

It's often assumed that, since no invasion took place, this scare can be dismissed as hysteria. The reality, however, is less clear-cut. Japan needed no persuasion of Australia's strategic importance as the obvious base for any Allied fightback. The question was whether it made more sense to attempt an invasion or simply to cut the country off from its main sources of supply.

On the One Hand ...

The Navy brought forward plans for an invasion of Australia's northern coast at a General Headquarters meeting on 4 March 1942. Commanders of the Fourth Fleet, based at Truk, requested soldiers for such a venture. Along with removing Australia from the war, it would allow access to country's resources – from wool and wheat to minerals. The Army immediately objected that occupying a country the size of a continent was unrealistic; advocates of the plan countered that this was an advantage. A firm bridgehead could be established in the tropical north, long before resistance could be mobilized in the southern population centres.

... on the Other

Yet it wasn't just Australia's size, said the generals: it was the extent to which an invasion would stretch the Japanese armed forces' overall operating perimeter in the Pacific. Surely to breaking-point, they reasoned. It made more sense

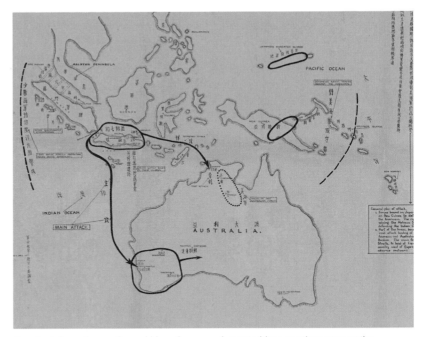

An attack from the north would have been supplemented by a southwestern strike.

to take control of islands further to the north so that air and sea communications between Australia and the war zone could be cut off that way, while the fight against America and its Pacific Fleet continued. In the end, opinion swung emphatically against the invaders. Admiral Isoku Yamamoto's plan for a showdown at Midway was instead adopted. The option of invading Australia remained open, in theory at least – but losses at Midway were to make it unrealistic.

Points of View

Just a captain at the time, but on the fast-track to becoming a rear-admiral, Baron Sadatoshi Tomioka was an influential advocate of invasion:

If we take Australia now, we can bring about the defeat of

Great Britain. With only a token force, we can reach our aim!

Another voice in favour was that of Admiral Takasumi Oka of the General Staff in Tokyo:

We need to actively move our forces to Australia and Hawaii, annihilate our enemies' marine military force, and decimate our enemies' bases for counterattack ...

General Tomoyuki Yamashita also saw merit in the plan, later recalling:

With even Sydney and Brisbane in my hands, it would have been comparatively simple to subdue Australia. I would never visualise occupying it completely.

Colonel Takushiro Hattori spoke for the Army, however, when he refused to contemplate 'a reckless attack which would exceed the strength of Japan'.

Operation Ceylon

A devastating Japanese raid on Ceylon was supposed to be the prelude to an invasion, but more cautious counsels prevailed and British India was saved.

If Neville Chamberlain had thought Czechoslovakia a 'faraway country of which we know little', what on earth would he have made of the island of Ceylon? True, today's Sri Lanka was a possession of the British Empire but few in England were losing too much sleep about its fate. There was one exception, however, and he could hardly have been a more important one. In April, 1942, after the Japanese bombing of the island's capital, Colombo, Winston Churchill was coming as close as he ever got to panic. 'The most dangerous moment of the war,' he afterwards confided …

… And the one which caused me the greatest alarm, was when the Japanese Fleet was heading for Ceylon and the naval base there. The capture of Ceylon, the consequent control of the Indian Ocean, and the possibility at the same time of a German conquest of Egypt would have closed the ring and the future would have been black.

Easter Attack

On 5 April – Easter Sunday – the Japanese launched a surprise attack on Colombo from the air – much as they had done on

HMS *Cornwall* (pictured) and *Dorsetshire* sustained **48** hits between them in ten minutes.

Darwin, six weeks or so before. A flight of 125 planes – 'Val' dive bombers and 'Kate' attack-bombers, with support from Zero fighters – took off from aircraft carriers off the coast. Commander Mitsuo Fuchida led the flight; the First Fleet with its *Kido Butai* carrier battle-group (some 650km/ 400 miles to the south of Ceylon) was directed by Admiral Chuichi Nagumo.

Swooping down out of heavy cloud, the dive bombers began bombarding the city, though the docks were largely protected by a hail of anti-aircraft fire. British Hurricane fighters had some success in disrupting the attack, but a second wave arriving a few

minutes later was able to rain destruction on the city spread below.

Scattered … But Safe

The razing of Colombo had never been more than a subsidiary objective of an attack whose main aim had been the destruction of the British Eastern Fleet. Some serious hits were certainly scored: the cruisers HMS *Cornwall* and *Dorsetshire* were both sunk while the aircraft carrier HMS *Hermes* was set ablaze in a follow-up raid a few days later.

Britain's fleet, though, was substantially safe: at the first intimations of an impending raid, it had fled for the East African

TRANSCRIPT OF KEY PARAGRAPHS

On 16th February we were invited by the War Cabinet to prepare an appreciation of the situation in the Far East in the light of recent events.

2. Japan must realise that the defeat of Germany would very seriously prejudice her chances of ultimate victory.

4. Once Japan has effectively breached the Malayan Barrier, she has a clear run into the Indian Ocean, where we are dangerously weak in all respects. By attacks on Ceylon and India, Japan could raise overwhelming internal security problems in India and induce instability in Indian forces in all theatres of war. By the occupation of Ceylon, Japan would prevent us from reinforcing Burma and achieve a position suitable for building up a serious threat to our Indian Ocean communications. This would go far towards meeting both Japanese requirements, would help her offensive against Burma and provide relief to Germany by threatening India and the Middle East.

TO BE KEPT UNDER LOCK AND KEY. 12 Nom 28/2/62

It is requested that special care may be taken to ensure the secrecy of this document.

(THIS DOCUMENT IS THE PROPERTY OF HIS BRITANNIC MAJESTY'S GOVERNMENT).

102

S E C R E T.

W.P.(42)94.
(Also C.O.S.(42) 128)
21ST FEBRUARY, 1942.

WAR CABINET

COPY NO. 23

FAR EAST APPRECIATION.

Report by the Chiefs of Staff.

On 16th February we were invited by the War Cabinet to prepare an appreciation of the situation in the Far East in the light of recent events.

JAPANESE INTENTIONS.

2. Japan is pressing her offensive with the greatest vigour in order to take full advantage of her present superiority. Her immediate objects appear to be to complete her conquest of the Philippines, Sumatra and Java, and to exploit her invasion of Burma, which would threaten Chinese ability to continue fighting. She may also assault Port Darwin and Ceylon.

3. Japan must realise that the defeat of Germany would very seriously prejudice her chances of ultimate victory. Her strategy therefore is likely to be biased towards helping Germany insofar as that is compatible with her own requirements.

4. Once Japan has effectively breached the Malayan Barrier, she has a clear run into the Indian Ocean, where we are dangerously weak in all respects. By attacks on Ceylon and India, Japan could raise overwhelming internal security problems in India and induce instability in Indian forces in all theatres of war. By the occupation of Ceylon, Japan would prevent us from reinforcing Burma and achieve a position suitable for building up a serious threat to our Indian Ocean communications. This would go far towards meeting both Japanese requirements, would help her offensive against Burma and provide relief to Germany by threatening India and the Middle East.

5. To the east, New Caledonia, and Fiji are stepping stones to Australia and New Zealand. The conquest of these Islands would gravely compromise American ability to build up forces in those Dominions and to sieze advanced bases for naval action towards the A.B.D.A. area.

6. To sum up, in the near future we may expect to see:-

In the A.B.D.A. area.

(a) Java attacked by greatly superior forces.
(b) Port Darwin attacked.
(c) Seizure of advanced bases in the Andamans and Nicobars.

* W.M.(42) 21st Conclusions.

-1-

coast. Its dignity might now be in tatters, but it was physically intact, and in a position to fight another day. Devastating as it had been for Colombo, the raid had failed in its primary purpose. Now those who had conceived it had to submit to seeing their ambitious plans scaled down. It was Australia all over again: the Army refused to get involved in what its generals saw as a grandiose scheme that would overstretch their scant resources. They had to consolidate the gains they had already made.

Operation Madagascar

The Indian Ocean was already an unwelcoming place for Allied shipping. Had the Japanese succeeded in setting up submarine bases in Madagascar, things would almost certainly have been blacker yet.

Diego Suarez, now Antsiranana, at the northern tip of Madagascar, has been a naval base of some sort or another since at least the nineteenth century. A coaling station in the days of steam, the French protectorate had held a talismanic significance for the Japanese ever since the Russo-Japanese War of 1905. It had been here that Tsarist Russia's Second Pacific Squadron stopped to re-supply as it made its way to its destruction in the Straits of Tsushima, in a battle regarded as the most important naval engagement since Trafalgar.

A Strategic Outpost

Japan's interest in Madagascar in April 1942 was due to the vantage-point it gave over shipping in the Indian Ocean – especially now that the Royal Navy had been sent packing from Ceylon. Diego Suarez commanded comings and goings from all the ports of mainland East Africa – and any shipping following the Cape route between East and West. It made sense for any naval power hoping to establish dominance in the region to have a presence on this vital strategic island. Admiral Yamamoto saw it as offering the perfect base for submarines in particular.

No Trespassers

Strictly speaking, Japan had no business casting covetous eyes on Madagascar. The line of Longitude 70° East had been

TRANSCRIPT OF KEY PARAGRAPHS

Left: Operation IRONCLAD is of high importance to India because if Japanese by-pass Ceylon and establish themselves there with French connivance as they did in Indo-China, the whole of our communications with you and M.E would be imperilled if not cut.

Right: At this interview RIBBENTROP enquired whether Japan did not consider it necessary to occupy MADAGASCAR as a base for her strategy in the INDIAN Ocean. I replied that it was not a matter that I would know, whereupon RIBBENTROP said that if JAPAN did consider it necessary, Germany was prepared to give her full diplomatic support. But if VICHY were approached before the event, it would be at once passed on to BRITAIN and the UNITED STATES which would be unfortunate. It would be well therefore for JAPAN to present a fait accompli and as in the case of TIMOR, to take the line that she was occupying the island only so long as it was necessary during the war and after the war would respect FRANCE's sovereign rights.

MOST SECRET.

<u>TO BE KEPT UNDER LOCK AND KEY: NEVER TO BE REMOVED FROM THE OFFICE.</u>

<u>JAPAN AND MADAGASCAR: JAPANESE AMBASSADOR,</u>
<u>BERLIN, REPORTS VIEWS OF RIBBENTROP.</u>

No:　　102443

Date: 20th March, 1942.

From: Japanese Ambassador, BERLIN.

To:　Foreign Minister, TOKYO.

No: 378 Secret.

Date: 17th March, 1942.

My No.377. [Dept:Note: to follow].

At this interview RIBBENTROP enquired whether JAPAN did not consider it necessary to occupy MADAGASCAR as a base for her strategy in the INDIAN Ocean. I replied that it was not a matter that I would know, whereupon RIBBENTROP said that if JAPAN did consider it necessary, GERMANY was prepared to give her full diplomatic support. But if VICHY were approached before the event, it would be at once passed on to BRITAIN and the UNITED STATES which would be unfortunate. It would be well therefore for JAPAN to present a fait accompli and as in the case of TIMOR, to take the line that she was occupying the island only so long as it was necessary during the war and after the war would respect FRANCE's sovereign rights.

RIBBENTROP repeatedly said that, in view of the delicate condition of German-French relations, what he had said to me must be kept absolutely secret and I should, therefore, be grateful if Your Excellency would understand this message as for yourself only. I should also be grateful for information as to whether the Navy have any such intentions.

Director (4).
F.O.(3).
P.I.D.
Admiralty.
War Office (4).
India Office (2).
Colonial Office.
Air Ministry.　　Sir E.Bridges.
Major Morton.　　Dominions Office.

declared as the boundary between German and Japanese spheres of influence, while Madagascar was an imperial possession of Vichy France. Japanese plans for the island were doubly irregular, then. There was no need for the Japanese High Command to worry themselves unduly about France's feelings, perhaps, but Hitler was furious at the slight.

Rumour had it that he threatened to lend the British 20 divisions for the fight with Japan: the implication was that he was only half-joking at very most.

Axis Unease

The tensions over Madagascar highlight the instability of the Axis, especially the alliance between the Germans and the Japanese. If the Western Allies had their difficulties with the Soviet Union, the Axis too had its internal suspicions and divisions. Hitler was nothing if not a racist, and there are reasons to doubt that he ever regarded his relationship with the Japanese as a remotely equal one.

He certainly saw no reason to consult his Far Eastern ally about his key decisions. Sworn enemies of Russia since the war of 1905, over Manchuria, Japan struggled to keep up with Germany's relations with the Soviet Union. Appalled at the Nazi-Soviet Pact of 1939, it eventually managed to reconcile itself to the agreement to such an extent that it made its own non-aggression pact with the Soviets in April 1941. The ink on that was barely dry when, that very June, Hitler launched Operation Barbarossa. Japan chose to remain a bystander in that conflict.

This proprietorial attitude seems less than rational: it can hardly have mattered to him (or indeed to Churchill) which Axis power pounded away at British shipping in the Mozambique Channel. Yet, there is no doubt that the region was strategically crucial to the British. And not just for the Eastern Fleet in the Indian Ocean itself but as a back-door route for supplying the Eighth Army in North Africa. Hence the urgency with which, picking up whispers of Japanese intentions, Churchill launched a pre-emptive amphibious attack, Operation Ironclad; by November, Madagascar was a British base.

Amerika Bomber

Had this programme been brought to completion, it would have taken the war directly to the United States, but resources – and Hitler's patience – ran out too soon.

In July 1938 – more than one year before the war began and three before the United States became involved – Hermann Göring mused aloud about the need for an intercontinental bomber. The head of the *Reichsluftfahrtministerium* (Air Ministry) had always been something of a technocrat, taking an eager interest in the details of design and development, so it was not so surprising that he should have been intrigued by such a project. It was more unexpected from a diplomatic standpoint that he should have made his thinking public: the threat to the United States, though implicit, was unmistakable.

America's reluctance to involve itself in the hostilities prior to Pearl Harbor has been a subject of much debate, many historians criticizing the country for sitting on the fence. It's easy to forget that, as the Nazis saw it, the United States had done no such thing, but had made its support for Germany's enemies very clear.

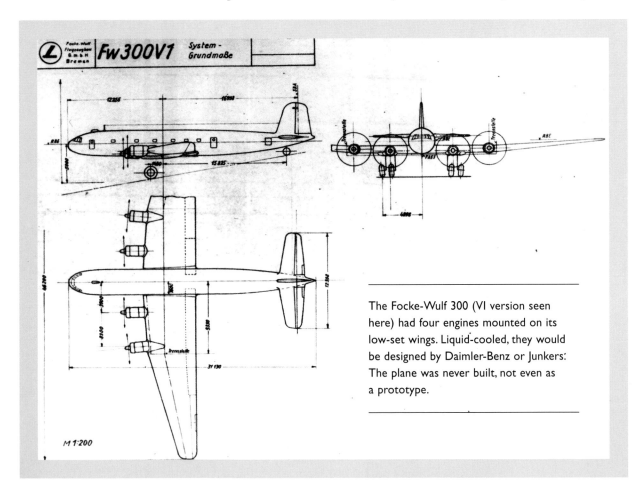

The Focke-Wulf 300 (VI version seen here) had four engines mounted on its low-set wings. Liquid-cooled, they would be designed by Daimler-Benz or Junkers. The plane was never built, not even as a prototype.

The British might mutter that strings were attached (in the form of territorial concessions, mainly island bases) when America agreed to supply the Royal Navy with 50 destroyers in September 1940, but as the Germans saw it 50 ships were 50 ships.

Atlantic Arena

It was certainly soon after the signing of the Destroyers for Bases Agreement that Göring got the long-range bomber project formally under way. And there was no beating about the bush when it came to naming what he announced was to be known as the *Amerika* bomber. Germany's five leading aviation manufacturers were asked by the *Reichsmarschall* to draw up plans for a plane capable of making the round trip from Germany to the United States and back, a distance of almost 11,000km (7000 miles). On the surface, at any rate, Germany had succeeded in opening up the Atlantic as an arena of war. Its U-boats were wreaking havoc among the convoys. By air, though, the ocean was off-limits, while in America itself people sat safely at home, spared the kind of pounding suffered by the people of Britain.

The *Amerika* would be a big beast – there was no way to avoid that. Along with the fuel for such an epic journey, it would have to be able to carry a payload of 6.5 tons or more – heavy bombs to make the trip worthwhile. New York was identified as the target destination but if, as Hitler hoped at the outset, the Portuguese dictator António de Oliveira Salazar were to make the Azores available for bases, a plane of this kind would be able to make forays far inland.

Aviation Attack

While Junkers, Heinkel, Messerschmidt, Focke-Wulf and Horten all got to work roughing out their blueprints for the *Amerika*, Göring's staff were busy

An *Amerika* bomber might easily have been a development of this Me 284.

Hermann Göring took his role seriously as head of the *Reichsluftfahrtministerium* (Air Ministry).

drawing up plans for its deployment. In the lengthy document they prepared for their chief's approval, one underlying assumption is clear. The project was intended to use air power to cancel out air power. Of the 19 likely US targets identified, most had some connection with the aviation industry: as well as aircraft and engine plants (including Pratt & Whitney, based in Connecticut; Wright Aeronautical, in New Jersey) there were aluminium processors, instrument makers and optics specialists. Factors to consider were not just the damage caused by long-range bombing raids – on industry, the military and general morale – but also the costly ramping-up of air defences America would feel obliged to undertake in response.

A Technical Challenge

The project was a major test of engineering ingenuity, and the different companies responded in different ways. Most, like Messerschmitt with the Me 264, Junkers with the Ju 390, and Heinkel with the He 277, came up with supersized versions of otherwise conventional aircraft. Appearances were deceptive, though: the exacting demands that were going to be made on airframes and engines required an enormous number of modifications – to engines especially, so that they could withstand the rigours of such long flights in such harsh conditions.

Careful calculations had to be made, and compromises reached, trading off speed and power against fuel efficiency – not just for economy's sake, but so that the aircraft would stand a chance of making it home after its trip.

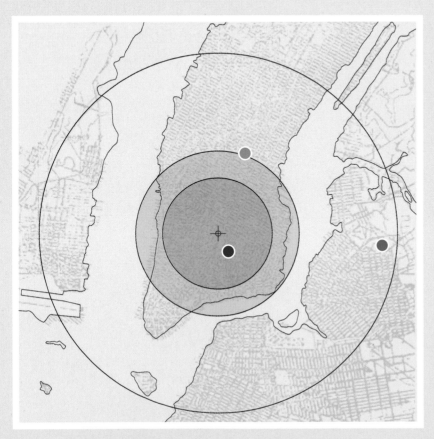

TARGET NYC

Manhattan was to be the target for the Nazis' *Amerika* attack: a nuclear bomb would have killed many thousands and severely disrupted US economic life, as well as dealing a devastating blow to morale. Around the epicentre, the destruction would have reached as far as mid-town, with significant damage done in Brooklyn and New Jersey. This map is based on a 1943 original, prepared by a *Luftwaffe* study team.

KEY

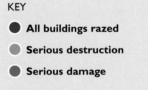

● **All buildings razed**

● **Serious destruction**

● **Serious damage**

Factor in the need to maximize capacity and lifting power, and the complexity became bewildering. Focke-Wulf ended up proposing two possible designs: the Fw 300, which had four wing-mounted engines and the Focke Wulf Ta 400, which was even larger and had six.

Branching Out
There was clear scope for lateral thinking. The maverick Horten brothers, Reimar and Walter, produced a chevron-shaped 'all-wing' aircraft, to be powered by early jet engines, and with something of the look of the Stealth Bomber flying today. It was indeed specially designed to slip undetected through radar fields, shielded not just by its shape but by its wooden construction, using a special glue that was high in carbon.

The brothers, both mavericks, were gratified by Göring's enthusiastic response to their design – but dismayed to find themselves asked to work with Junkers engineers. They insisted on adding extra tails and fins to enhance stability – at the expense, as the Hortens immediately recognized, of range.

Piggyback Plane
One suggestion was that a composite aircraft be constructed. Basically, one plane would ride piggyback upon another. A Heinkel He 177 long-range bomber would fly out as far as it could across the Atlantic, carrying a smaller Dornier Do 217 bomber on its back. Once it reached the

The Horten Ho IX was an advanced 'flying wing' design.

limit of its range, the He 177 would turn around, parting company with the Do 217. This would then continue to its target before – far out of reach of home now – ditching in the sea. Its crew would then be picked up by a waiting U-boat.

Out of Time, Out of Fuel
All these ideas fell foul of the *Führer*'s interference, and his limited attention-span; Hitler insisted on being involved, but was constantly distracted by more glamorous projects. And, as the hostilities wore on, mundane practicalities intervened to spoil the project – not least the outrageous requirements intercontinental flights were going to make in terms of fuel.

I never saw Hitler more beside himself as when, as if in a delirium, he was picturing to himself and us the downfall of New York in towers of flame.

Albert Speer, recollecting in his diary, 18 November 1947.

Project Z

Japan's equivalent to the *Amerika* bomber was born out of similar frustrations: how was the fight to be taken to their enemies?

The United States had been severely jolted by the Japanese attack on Pearl Harbor in 1941. From that time on, though, the element of surprise was gone: Americans threw themselves into a war effort which, by sheer scale and productivity, looked like overwhelming the Japanese in the long run. How were they to be put off their stride again?

Like the Germans, the Japanese concluded that they needed a long-range bomber capable of attacking targets in the continental United States. Such a weapon would also enable them to assist their German allies by attacking mines and industrial

Pearl Harbor had been a triumph – but the question was how to repeat it?

installations located in the Soviet Far East.

As the Germans had found, the technical challenges were daunting. But the Nakajima Corporation was not daunted.

Himself a naval engineer, founder Chikuhei Nakajima took personal charge, apparently revelling in the difficulties. So big a bomber would require six engines, he calculated. Its range would have to be at least 8450km (5250 miles), with a payload of 22 450kg (1000lb) bombs. Even at over 11,580m (38,000ft), out of reach of ground fire, the Z plane would be an obvious target for enemy fighters: it would need to have sufficient pace to outrun them. Nakajima acknowledged his doubts that the materials were available to allow such exacting specifications to be met, but he was irrepressible in his enthusiasm for the Project Z.

The Mitsubishi G4M 'Betty' was used to carry the Ohka flying bomb.

All at Sea

As the Pacific War intensified, indeed, he started to see the Z bomber as the secret weapon that would – pretty much by itself – bring about the defeat of the US fleet. So big a target, said his detractors, would surely be vulnerable to anti-aircraft fire from the surface? Especially when descending to the lower altitudes needed to stand a chance of hitting ships? No problem, Nakajima explained: the Z bomber would deal with any personnel attempting to shoot it down by making a preliminary strafing attack before its bombing run, using the machine guns mounted on its wings.

Of these, there were not two, not four, not 40, but *400*, set in rows and tiers, no more than 250mm (9.8in) apart. Since, said Nakajima, 'this 250mm distance is less than the size of a man's body, either standing or lying down', at least one bullet would be able to hit each man on the decks of enemy carriers or even on the enemy's anti-aircraft guns. With a formation of 15 Z planes, an area some 45m (150ft) wide and 10km (6 miles) long would be showered with bullets, catching at least 20 enemy ships, and up to 40.

We talk lightly of a 'hail of bullets' but enemy seamen, it appeared, were going to find out exactly what this would be like.

In the end, as time went on, the tide of battle turned and a mood of grim realism descended on the Japanese military establishment, Project Z seemed more and more a fantasy, Nakajima's folly.

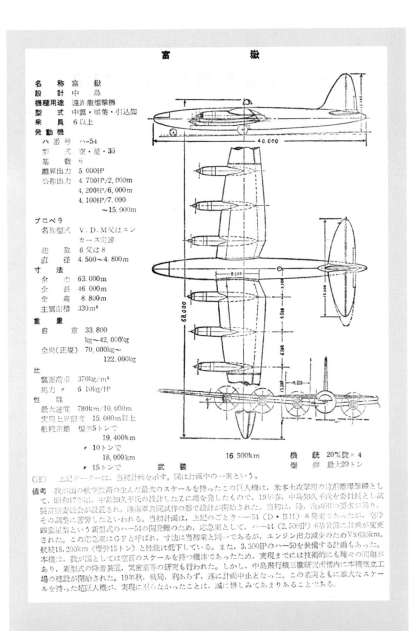

Nakajima's plans for his six-engined Z bomber went well beyond back-of-an-envelope jottings, even if at the same time they stopped some way short of a seriously developed, specifically worked-out blueprint. Ultimately, time ran out on an enormously (perhaps impossibly) ambitious project.

Operation Osprey

Ireland was again in the *Abwehr*'s sights, as German intelligence planned for the possibility of an invasion of the Free State by US forces stationed in the North.

Abwehr Chief Wilhelm Canaris had lost his patience with all things Irish even before the abandonment of Operation Whale, but the Emerald Isle's strategic possibilities still seemed too great to overlook. Granted, the distance was prohibitive, given the command of the Royal Navy at sea and the Royal Air Force in the air. Granted, too, deep uncertainty over the Free State government's sympathies and the unreliability (and sheer ineptness)

of the IRA. There the island sat, though: an unsinkable aircraft carrier in the eastern Atlantic; the perfect platform for attacks on the British mainland.

Lowered Expectations

By 1942, any invasion plans were on the back burner; even a renewal of the Blitz seemed unlikely, any time soon. So Hitler's concern, when he heard that several thousand US troops had just been stationed in Belfast, was that they were there with the object of invading the Free State and setting up bases there. This bothered him, not because it would thwart his own plans to invade Ireland as a stepping stone to British conquest, but because

Walter Schellenberg was to become the SS's head of foreign intelligence: Osprey was in capable hands.

US troops wait – ready for anything – on an Irish beach.

Sir John Maffey yesterday notified Mr De Valera that American troops were coming in. As he expected, he found the Prime Minister ... disconcerted and resentful.

Record by a member of the British High Commissioner's staff, January 1942.

the availability of support for Allied shipping from bases on the West Coast would immediately alter the balance in the Battle of the Atlantic, now at its height.

A Hundred Heroes

SS *Brigadeführer* Walter Schellenberg was given responsibility for Osprey. The plan was for crack commandos to be recruited as volunteers. Almost a hundred young men responded to the call. Already elite fighters, they were given extra training in everything from sabotage to language skills. The idea was that they would be infiltrated into Ireland to help make ready resistance, in case the Allied invasion came. Special attention was given to the use of the kind

of British-made weaponry likely to be available to Irish partisans who, it was expected, would be drawn from the regular Free State army as well as from the IRA.

Taking Charge

The logic underlying Osprey differs significantly from that behind either of its obvious predecessors, Operations Whale or Sea Eagle. The Germans expected to take direct charge of the resistance, rather than delegating it to the Irish themselves. Some Irish-born prisoners of war from the Friesack camp in Brandenburg were expected to accompany the expedition, but they were clearly to take a very secondary role. That this was the case perhaps

confirms the sense we have that the material produced by the programme had been disappointing. Friesack's graduates were Irishmen who had first joined the British and then gone over to the Germans – turncoats twice over, some would say. Without needing to be quite so censorious, we can still suspect that they were unlikely to show the extreme motivation and burning commitment to the cause that a high-risk operation like Osprey was likely to require. In the event, the Americans never did move into the Free State, so the operation never had to be implemented.

US troops train with a General Lee tank on Irish soil.

Operation Pastorius

As ineptly executed as it was audaciously conceived, this plan to take the war to the American home front was derailed before it could even get under way.

High drama or farce? It's hard to tell. On 13 June 1942, at the head of the beach at Amagansett, Long Island, Coastguard John C Cullen stumbled on some men in a furtive huddle in the dunes. Had he arrived a few minutes before, he would have seen the U-boat that had brought these would-be saboteurs to the United States, beached on a sandbank just 180m (200yd) from the shore. After a frantic struggle, its captain had managed to free his vessel just as the first commuter cars of the morning flashed past on Atlantic Avenue above.

Rumbled

As it was, Cullen had only to get his head around the fact that four men seemed to be changing out of German army uniforms and into all-American civilian clothes. This seems extraordinary, but the planners may have assumed that men in uniform, if caught before they had gone to earth, would have to be treated as prisoners of war.

Above: The prompt action of John Cullen (left) thwarted the saboteurs' plans.

Right: Wanted, Walter Kappe, of German Military Intelligence, the mastermind of Operation Pastorius.

WANTED

GERMAN SABOTEUR

Photo taken February 19, 1936

WALTER KAPPE, alias Walter Kappel

F.P.C. 16 M 28 W 00I
        M   8 W III

Cullen had no idea how to act. Stunned – and, in any case, outnumbered – he froze. When one of the men stuffed a wad of banknotes ($260) into his hand, an apparent bribe, he barely looked at the money before walking on. As his head cleared, he went back to the coastguard station and reported what he'd seen. By the time an armed patrol had reached the dunes, the Germans had disappeared, of course, catching an early train into New York. But their presence was known; their operation off to a dismal start.

Industrial Saboteurs

Named for Francis Daniel Pastorius, founder of America's first German settler community, Operation Pastorius had been masterminded by Lieutenant Walter Kappe of German Military Intelligence. An ambitious two-year programme of activities was planned. The focus was to be on sabotage attacks at hydroelectric schemes and associated aluminium plants. An HEP station near Niagara Falls had been selected; so too had smelters as far afield as Illinois and the Tennessee Valley and crucial locks at Louisville, Kentucky.

Kappe recruited agents from among the many who had responded to the summons (and generous grants) from the Ausland Institute calling German emigrants abroad to come back and help to build the Fatherland. Of the Pastorius team, Ernst Burger and Herbert Haupt were actually American citizens: the former had

even served in the National Guard. All the others had worked in the United States. In addition to a substantial supply of explosives (which were subsequently dug up among the Argansett dunes), they were given $175,000 funding for their campaign.

Hopes Dasched

Georg John Dasch would prove to be the weakest link. The man who had panicked at Argansett, trying to bribe Coastguard Cullen, lost his nerve completely and gave himself up less than a week later in Washington DC. Under interrogation, he quickly betrayed not only his Long Island comrades but another four agents who had been landed, this time undetected, from a second submarine on Ponte Vedra Beach, near Jacksonville in Florida.

> **You got a mother and father, haven't you? Wouldn't you like to see them again? ... Take this and have a good time. Forget what you've seen here.**
>
> *Georg Dasch tries to threaten, then to bribe, Coastguard John Cullen.*

A rogue's gallery of saboteurs, snapped by the authorities in New York City, 1942.

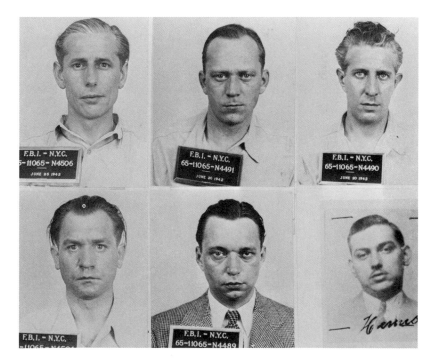

Operation Schamil

As the *Wehrmacht* advanced eastward in 1942, it was feared that the Soviets would destroy their oil refineries. Operation Schamil set out to prevent this happening.

A year into their Russian adventure, the Germans were making progress, though slower than expected, so spirited had been the Red Army's rearguard action – and so vast the arena across which they had to fight. The strategic plan for 1942's Summer campaign was given the codename Case Blue. In prosecuting the war against the Soviets, its aims, in the words of Hitler's *Führer* Directive No. 41, were to 'Cut them off, as far as is possible, from their most important centres of war industry.'

Caucasian Crux

For Army Group A, in the south, under the command of *Generalfeldmarschall* Wilhelm List, this meant occupying the strategically vital oilfields of the Caucasus. First, however, it meant finding a long and extremely arduous way across the southern plains of the Ukraine and on through the thick forests and the rugged mountains of the Caucasus itself. Hitler, slow to appreciate how difficult a theatre of war this was to perform in, was rapidly running out of patience with List.

The Germans had no fears at this point that the tide might turn against them, but it was already clear that they had lost the initiative to some extent. Especially down here in the south, where it was becoming clear that – even by Soviet standards – the infrastructure was going to be woefully inadequate; the roads and railways few, far between and in execrable condition.

It was one thing to carry all before them as they had till now,

The Caucasus' great oil refineries were in flames before the Germans arrived.

another to be doing so at the snail's pace it seemed they could soon expect to be making. Only now were the Germans beginning to grasp the implications of what their own maps told them. The landscape in the Caucasus was at best boneshakingly rugged; pockmarked with jagged peaks, it was lacerated by sharp escarpments and plunging ravines. Supposedly spearheading the advance, the First Panzer Army would, in fact, hold everyone else back as it inched along at an undignified crawl.

Pre-emptive Strike

No one was in any doubt that List and his army would win through and take the cities of Maikop, Grozny and Baku – but what would be left of their vital oil installations when they got there? The Soviets would obviously destroy them rather than allow them to fall into German hands – and, at this rate, they were going to have ample time.

This was clearly going to be a job for the Lehr-Regiment Brandenburg zBV 800, formed two years before specifically to carry out commando-style operations. Carried in by air, they could be dropped on to the essential sites by parachute, securing them before they could be destroyed.

In the event, the operation wasn't needed: Maikop, well to the west in Adygea, and lying in the gentler northern foothills of the Caucasus, was taken easily enough in Army Group A's advance. As for Grozny and Baku:

The Brandenburg zBV800 were an elite commando force.

it quickly became clear that the Germans weren't going to get near them. The Caucasian mountains proved as formidable a barrier as had been feared: the advance stalled and *Generalfeldmarschall* List was sacked.

Wilhelm List (left) was no miracle-worker. His invasion of the Caucasus quickly became bogged down.

We need the grain of the Ukraine. The industrial region of the Donets must work for us, instead of for Stalin. The Russian oil-supplies of the Caucasus must be cut off.

Hitler, August 1941.

Operation Bernhard

Having planned to bring the British economy to its knees, by flooding the nation with forgeries, the Nazis were forced to make do with minor 'dirty tricks'.

Bernhard Krüger conceived a bold and ingenious – but ultimately futile – scheme.

Operation Bernhard became known to the British public thanks to a 1981 TV series, *Private Schultz*. Significantly, this was a comedy rather than an action thriller. As scripted by Jack Pulman, the plot departed from its historical inspiration in many of its details – though it could hardly be said to have been any more improbable than Bernhard.

There really was a Bernhard: Bernhard Krüger, an SS *Sturmbannführer* with a background in the peacetime textile industry as an engineer.

From 1942, he combed the concentration camps of the Reich on Himmler's orders, snapping up those inmates who showed the talents needed to join his team of counterfeiters. Ultimately over

140-strong, they were based at Brandenburg's Sachsenhausen camp where, from 1939, they started acquiring not only the fantastically complex engraving skills required of the effective forger but others such as specialized paper-making (including authentic-looking watermarks) and printing.

Forging Ahead

Codebreaking skills were also key: Krüger wanted his forgeries to deceive not just small shopkeepers, bar-staff and taxi drivers but to take in bank cashiers – and, ideally, the financial authorities. For his mischief-making had an ambitious goal that went far beyond pulling

Sachsenhausen concentration camp provided Krüger's first recruits, and became the base for Operation Bernhard.

a fast one on unfortunate individuals. He had hopes of bringing the British economy crashing down. Deception of this nature, and on this sort of scale, meant producing an astonishingly high degree of visual verisimilitude and a convincing set of serial numbers as well.

By the middle of 1942, his team had been triumphantly successful in this, and over the next two-and-a-half years they turned out more than eight million notes, in denominations of £5, £10, £20 and £50, to a total 'value' of £132m. This was more than the Bank of England had in reserve and, indeed, is believed to have amounted to some 15 per cent of all the notes in circulation.

Pounds from Heaven

The original thinking had been that this money would literally be dumped on Britain from the sky. It would be dropped from bombers, and the planners assumed the passers-by who found it would spend it, causing chaos. By the time the money was available in sufficient quality and quantity, however, the means to get it to the target was no longer available. Germany had lost the Battle of Britain and, with its forces under such pressure on the Eastern Front, could not spare the fleets of bombers that would have been required. In the event, the money had to be used, comparatively sparingly, for funding special operations and making secret purchases on the black market – useful enough, but the merest pinpricks for the Allies

compared with the financial cataclysm that had been intended.

By the beginning of 1945, Krüger's team had turned their attentions to the US dollar. Things were shaping well when the war came to an end. A large supply of as yet undistributed notes fell into the hands of the Jewish underground in Palestine. They used these to help finance their campaign against the British.

Bernhard banknotes were masterpieces of the forger's art, fooling even the comparatively expert eye.

Operation Gertrude

Hitler's plan to take Turkey before its people could form a challenging alliance with the Azeris had to be abandoned in the face of Soviet gains.

'Who remembers the Armenians?' Hitler asked on 22 August 1939. Well he himself did, of course: their annihilation at the time of World War I had inspired him in his search for a Final Solution. Ironically, he was to remember the Armenians again in the summer of 1942. By this time, though, he had another end in view.

Onward, Armenia

Improbably enough, the genocidal maniac was bent on nation-building: Hitler planned a Greater Armenia in the Caucasus. This had for decades been the dream of Armenian irredentists who hoped to recover those areas lost since 1919. Significant minorities of Armenians now lived marooned in Georgia and – more important, from Germany's point of view – in Iran and Azerbaijan. Hitler was moved less by a desire to further the national aspirations of the Armenians than by a determination to frustrate those of the Turks.

The idea had taken hold in the early twentieth century that a new Pan-Turkic homeland should be created, extending from Istanbul through Armenia to Azerbaijan and Persia. 'Turan', as its promoters called it, had no historic precedent at all, though this sort of project was in the spirit of the times. Though linked by linguistic and cultural inheritance, the various Turkic peoples had drifted westward in waves as separate warbands, bound by only the loosest and the most opportunistic of alliances.

And to secure ownership and access to the rich oil reserves of Azerbaijan. Just as the fields of the Ukraine were to feed an expanding and ever-hungry Reich; the oilfields round Baku were going to keep the *blitzkrieg* fuelled.

All About Oil?

It would be wrong to say that, in the modern phrase, World War II was 'about oil'. Yet the demand for it did much to shape the way the war developed. Securing supplies was a top priority for a German war machine that relied upon petrol and higher-grade fuels for its vehicles and planes and on heavier crude for its factories and its ships. North Africa had a strategic significance beyond its oilfields, but Baku was regarded simply as an oil well for the Reich.

Germany's hold on North Africa's oil supplies already seemed insecure by the middle of 1942.

Its oil industry having developed through the 1930s, Baku was now a major prize.

It's a question of the possession of Baku, Field Marshal. Unless we get the Baku oil, the war is lost.
Hitler to Field Marshal Erich von Manstein, 1942.

Counting Chickens

The attack was scheduled to begin at the very end of 1942, and expected to be accomplished in about five weeks. Four infantry divisions would be brought from Denmark, where they were no longer needed, accompanied by an artillery brigade. The main attack would have to be concentrated in the north: a fleet of 27 ships providing support in the Aegean and Dodecanese.

Some troops would be brought from Kavala, northern Greece; others across the Black Sea from the Bulgarian coast. Turkey was to be almost encircled: two forces would strike northward from Syria (from Aleppo and Deir-ez-Zor); more would attack from Kirkuk, in northern Iraq, and from Yerevan in Armenia. And yet more men would come from Batumi, in Adjara, southwestern Georgia: bombers based here would then attack the Turkish army as it marched east to meet these threats.

A good plan, perhaps, but dependent on German dominance in the Caucasus to the north – and on the absence of distractions to the west. As it was, by the time for implementation came, the German attack had stalled at Stalingrad, the Red Army was pushing quickly south and Rommel had been defeated at the Second Battle of El Alamein.

Chapter Three
1943

The war was raging as ferociously as ever as 1943 began; but had there been the first glimmerings of light at the end of the Allied tunnel? It is easy to feel that way in hindsight; it was rather harder at the time.

The War rampaged on – as did Stalin, frantic for his 'Second Front'; so too did the dispute between the Americans and the British over whether to take the direct approach (a French invasion) or the indirect (through North Africa and southern Europe). And whilst the Western Allies had clearly seized the initiative in the Pacific (and, to a lesser extent, on the Asian mainland) they had a very long and bloody way to go.

Understandably, perhaps, proposed operations for the year betray a hankering after the left-field solution which would enable the fighting to be finessed, allow an end-run around months (even years?) of toil and misery. Schemes for the assassination of all the major war leaders – not to mention the abduction of Pope Pius XII – were all hatched in 1943. An aircraft carrier constructed out of ice; a tank too big and heavy to make the journey into battle: desperate times were bringing desperate measures.

The main men on the Axis side, Hitler and Mussolini were starting to feel the pressure. *Il Duce* in particular was living on borrowed time.

Operation Roundup

Quite how keen the Americans were to take the war to the Germans is clear from their plans for Operation Roundup – another proposal for an invasion of Normandy.

'Overpaid, over-sexed, over here,' said the more cynical members of the British public when America's GIs, airmen and sailors turned up in their midst. They might have added 'over-confident'. The Americans strode into the war in Europe with a self-belief that made a marked contrast to the jaded cynicism of their British allies. Their optimism is apparent in the eagerness – not to say insistence – with which they pursued the idea of a large-scale invasion of northern France.

The arguments in favour had been rehearsed throughout the spring and early summer months of 1942 when Operation Sledgehammer was discussed. That the British found the cons to be overwhelming was clear, so the Americans drew up a contingency plan. This too envisaged a large-scale landing and the establishment of a bridgehead in northern France. Why did this hold such an appeal for the Americans?

Looking Busy
Their first priority, in fact, was to be seen to be doing *something*.

Stalin's demands for a second front were as obstreperous now as they were understandable. 'The President had specifically ordered the United States Chiefs of Staff to launch some kind of ground offensive in the European zone in 1942,' Dwight D. Eisenhower was later to recall. Was there the faintest suggestion of office workers trying to 'look busy'? Certainly, that's the cynical interpretation of Roosevelt's call for action – for just about any action, of whatever sort, to placate the Soviets.

In fact, there was a sense in which it really *didn't* matter what the Western Allies did in 1942–3, as long as they did something. Anything they could do to take some of the pressure off the Soviets would be worthwhile. And however vague the President was being, the Chiefs had quickly narrowed the options down.

Examining the Options
According to Eisenhower, the Chiefs of Staff were asked by the President to consider possible strategies for the conduct of the war from the second half of 1942, and came up with three options:

The first was the direct reinforcement of the British armies in the Middle East by the Cape of Good Hope route, in an effort to destroy Rommel and his army

TRANSCRIPT OF KEY PARAGRAPHS

Copy of letter dated 30 October 1942 from General Eisenhower to General Ismay:

(a) There should be an immediate and searching review by the Combined Chiefs of Staff of the principal factors now applying to the world strategic situation, with the purpose of determining whether or not the 'Roundup' conception should be abandoned completely or whether it should be continued and pushed forward aggressively with an appropriate target date, possibly the spring of 1944.

(b) If decision is made to continue preparations for eventual 'Roundup', the question of the most effective method for carrying on this planning becomes highly important.

(c) My own suggestion is that an outline plan, including such major features as the general area and direction of attack, allocation of forces and resources, approximate timing and broad objectives, should be developed by Joint Planning Staffs.

C.O.S.(42) 370 (O).

1ST NOVEMBER, 1942.

WAR CABINET

CHIEFS OF STAFF COMMITTEE

OPERATION "ROUNDUP" – PLANNING

Copy of a letter dated 30th October, 1942,
from General Eisenhower to General Ismay.

*   *   *

Because of my impending departure from the United
Kingdom, I think it proper to present to the British Chiefs
of Staff the following views with respect to "Roundup" planni
which has been relegated, by the American Forces, to a positi
of secondary importance, during the last few months, due to
preoccupation in the "Torch" project.

(a) There should be an immediate and searching review by
the Combined Chiefs of Staff of the principal
factors now applying to the world strategic situation,
with the purpose of determining whether or not the
"Roundup" conception should be abandoned completely
or whether it should be continued and pushed forward
aggressively with an appropriate target date, possibly
the spring of 1944.

(b) If decision is made to continue preparations for a
eventual "Roundup", the question of the most effective
method for carrying on this planning becomes highly
important.

(c) My own suggestion is that an outline plan, including
such major features as the general area and direction
of attack, allocation of forces and resources,
approximate timing and broad objectives, should be
developed by Joint Planning Staffs and approved by the
Combined Chiefs of Staff.

(d) Operational planning under such a broad directive must,
for some months to come, be confined largely to
complete examination of resources, resulting in
appropriate recommendations to the Chiefs of Staff,

-1-

ly of the world strategic
keep abreast of the
uccessful execution of the
is work, in my opinion,
d, under the Chiefs of Staff,
e man. The system heretofore
o do this through a committee
Commanders-in-Chief is, in my
I have previously suggested
s of Combined Operations be
liminary work in this regard,
s staff not only comprises
al British services but
of the American Army. While
, divesting myself of all
erations of U.S. forces in the
ll direct General Hartle, who
se duties, to co-operate in
officers of suitable
Joint Planning Staff or to any
ch may be suggested as
her method of conducting this
ted by the Combined Chiefs of
ill be equally ready to
presentation. I do, however,
l that the method adopted be
ands of one man the duty of
the Combined Chiefs of Staff
lanning and who will
e instructions for
f such plans.

British Chiefs of Staff
tion was based upon
e to attack the Western
here the main German forces
an front and with the
rn Europe approximately
s existing in the summer
s the original
d merely a readiness to
nt that a crack in
ment an emergency

to the attention of the
early progress in
, which might possibly
a Russian collapse or
ted since it appears
of the United Kingdom,
tory level in the air, must be restored to a
troops. level by the transfer here of suitable American

*   *   *

(Sgd.) DWIGHT D. EISENHOWER.

Great George Street, S.W.1.

1st November, 1942.

-2-

and, by capturing Tripolitania (northwestern Libya), to gain secure control of the central Mediterranean.

The second was to prepare amphibious forces to seize northwest Africa with the idea of undertaking later operations eastward to catch Rommel in a giant vice and eventually open the entire Mediterranean for use by the United Nations.

The third was to undertake a limited operation on the northwest coast of France with a relatively small force but with objectives limited to the capture of an area that could be held against German attack and which would later form a bridgehead for use in

---

2

4. The Chief of Combined Operations has also submitted a note (Annex II) in which he shows that the Combined Operation training of all units of the Home Forces which are not employed in "Sledgehammer," and also of the United States forces arriving in this country, will come to a complete and immediate standstill as soon as we start mounting "Sledgehammer." The effect of this will be to postpone operation "Round-up" for two or three months.

5. At the War Cabinet meeting on the 11th June, the Prime Minister laid down, and the War Cabinet generally approved, that operations in 1942 should be governed by the following two principles:—

    (i) No substantial landing in France in 1942 unless we are going to stay: and

    (ii) No substantial landing in France unless the Germans are demoralised by failure against Russia.

It seems to us that the above conditions are unlikely to be fulfilled and that, therefore, the chances of launching operation "Sledgehammer" this year are remote.

6. It is true that there are certain military advantages in mounting "Sledgehammer," even though it is unlikely to be launched. In the first place, our preparations are bound to keep the Germans guessing. They may not force them to withdraw troops from their Eastern Front, but they are unlikely to weaken their Western Front, particularly in air forces. Secondly, the mounting of "Sledgehammer" will be a useful dress-rehearsal for "Round-up," especially for Commanders and Staffs.

7. There can be no doubt that the disadvantages mentioned in paragraphs 3 and 4 outweigh the advantages in paragraph 6. If we were free agents, we could not recommend that the operation should be mounted.

8. We have, however, given or subscribed to certain undertakings. In the first place, the following is an extract from the Aide-Mémoire which the Prime Minister handed to M. Molotov just before he returned to Russia:—

"We are making preparations for a landing on the Continent in August or September 1942. As already explained, the main limiting factor to the size of the landing force is the availability of special landing craft. Clearly, however, it would not further either the Russian cause or that of the Allies as a whole if, for the sake of action at any price, we embarked on some operation which ended in disaster and gave the enemy an opportunity for glorification at our discomfiture. It is impossible to say in advance whether the situation will be such as to make this operation feasible when the time comes. We can therefore give no promise in the matter, but, provided that it appears sound and sensible, we shall not hesitate to put our plans into effect."

If we do not make active and serious preparations for "Sledgehammer," the Russians are almost bound to know very soon that we are not fulfilling our promise that we would do so.

9. Secondly, the following are extracts from the conclusions of a meeting recently held in Washington between the President and the Prime Minister, and attended by General Marshall and the Chief of the Imperial General Staff:

    (i) Plans and preparations for the "Bolero" Operation in 1943 on as large a scale as possible are to be pushed forward with all speed and energy. It is, however, essential that the United States and Great Britain should be prepared to act offensively in 1942.

    (ii) Operations in France or the Low Countries in 1942 would, if successful, yield greater political and strategic gains than operations in any other theatre. Plans and preparations for the operations in this theatre are to be pressed forward with all possible speed, energy and ingenuity. The most resolute efforts must be made to overcome the obvious dangers and difficulties of the enterprise. If a sound and sensible plan can be contrived, we should not hesitate to give effect to it. If, on the other hand, detailed examination shows that, despite all efforts, success is improbable, we must be ready with an alternative.

TRANSCRIPT OF KEY PARAGRAPHS

The Chief of Combined Operations has also submitted a note in which he shows that the Combined Operation training of all units of the Home Forces which are not employed in 'Sledgehammer' and also of the United States forces arriving in this country, will come to a complete and immediate standstill as soon as we start mounting 'Sledgehammer'. The effect of this will be to postpone operation 'Roundup' for two or three months.

It is true that there are certain military advantages in mounting 'Sledgehammer', even though it is unlikely to be launched. In the first place, our preparations are bound to keep the Germans guessing. They may not force them to withdraw troops from their Eastern Front, but they are unlikely to weaken their Western Front, particularly in air forces. Secondly, the mounting of 'Sledgehammer' will be a useful dress-rehearsal for 'Roundup' especially for Commanders and Staffs.

Operation Torch was a success for Churchill's vision of victory. The Allies invaded North Africa in November 1942.

the large-scale invasion agreed upon as the ultimate objective.

Mixed Feelings

Britain was cautious, there's no doubt; nor, in the circumstances of 1942, is this wariness so difficult to understand. The Battle of Britain might have been won, but many communities had been left traumatized by weeks and months of bombing raids. And, for all the euphoria, no one seriously believed that the 'Few' of Fighter Command could go on to win the war unaided. They shrank from the idea of a full-scale invasion of France for much the same reasons as Hitler had finally thought better of a wholesale attack in the other direction: the logistics, given the likely resistance, were unthinkable. Hence their

reservations about Sledgehammer, and, when that was rejected, its American successor, Operation Roundup. This was similar to Sledgehammer in its conception, the crucial difference being that it accommodated British caution in being planned for execution almost 12 months later, in the early part of 1943 (perhaps May).

Their thinking was that the Axis should be attacked through what Winston Churchill called the 'soft underbelly' of Europe; and that it should be first bled weak by costly fighting in North Africa and the Mediterranean. The British leader was to get his way, of course: Operation Gymnast – subsequently renamed Torch – was undertaken that November. And Churchill's plan worked, it might be said: after a fierce

campaign in North Africa, the war was then carried via Sicily to the Italian mainland, and thence northward into the heart of the German homeland.

The Better Part of Valour

Rather than an all-out attack, the British Premier preferred to talk in terms of a 'ring', a 'noose' that the Allies placed around the German neck and which in the months to come would be progressively tightened. In vague, big-picture terms he looked forward to victory in the Battle of the Atlantic (still by no means certain, and at best a distant prospect) and the securing of air- and sea-power in the Mediterranean (barely begun), and then of a slow, inexorable closing-in which would finally win the war.

General Brooke (right) gets his point across to Churchill (left) and General Montgomery.

Slow and Steady

Churchill made a virtue of this methodical, slow-and-steady approach to the war. His Chief of Imperial General Staff (CIGS), General Alan Brooke, was more up-front about the element of nervousness underpinning it: he 'feared above all things a premature and unsuccessful return to the mainland of Europe', he told his biographer Sir Arthur Bryant:

I was quite clear in my own mind that the moment for the opening of a Western Front had not yet come and would not present itself during 1943. I felt that we must stick to my original policy for the conduct of the war … to begin the conquest of North Africa, so as to reopen the Mediterranean, restore a million tons of shipping by avoiding the Cape route; then eliminate Italy, bring in Turkey, threaten southern Europe, and then liberate France.

Significantly, though the liberation of France is mentioned, this comes at the very end of a long list. The British were in no hurry to dispatch another force across the Channel.

Precedents, Possibilities

Hindsight is 20/20, of course, and it has to be said that it does vindicate Churchill, but in the 1940s his contemporaries could argue that hindsight showed something else entirely. As First Lord of the Admiralty in 1914–15, Churchill had been the mastermind of the disastrous Dardanelles Campaign. An oblique attack on Germany and the Central Powers by means of a swipe at their Ottoman Turkish ally, this had ended in the futile carnage of Gallipoli. The virtues of taking the indirect approach (or, for that matter, of Churchill's 'military genius') were by no means obvious.

Certainly, the Americans were unconvinced. They favoured the direct approach. Their object was Berlin or Bust, and the sooner they set out, the better. And it is possible to argue that it was this approach that was vindicated by events, given that it was the invasion of Normandy which finally clinched victory in the West. What would have been the result if the invasion had been launched a year (or more) before?

Catastrophic failure, is one possible answer to that question. The D-Day landings were to constitute the greatest seaborne invasion history had ever seen – and they only narrowly succeeded. In 1943, the Germans had six infantry divisions and one panzer division ready to receive them, and more in waiting. In other words, success was not just a matter of landing troops, difficult and bloody as that proved to be; the invaders then had to find a way of breaking out against the formidable forces arrayed against them before they could even think of making progress towards Germany. And in 1943, despite victory in the Battle of Britain, the Western Allies did not yet have the degree of air superiority on which the invaders of 1944 were to depend.

Such discussion is academic, though. It was quickly becoming clear, as Eisenhower recalled, that the direct approach was absolutely out. There was no way around Britain's profound pessimism about the prospects for an all-out attack at this stage in the war:

No other course of action seemed feasible at the moment. The discussions were long and exhaustive. A major factor in all

American thinking of that time was a lively suspicion that the British contemplated the agreed-upon cross-Channel concept with distaste and with considerable mental reservations concerning the practicability of ever conducting a major invasion of northwest Europe.

Misgivings

'Ever' is a big word, of course. This 'major invasion' was eventually launched. By that time, things had swung – apparently irrevocably – in the Allies' favour. And America, paying the piper, called the tune.

There is evidence, however, that until a very late stage, the British continued to be reluctant to get on board. As late as October 1943, Alan Brooke reports receiving notes from Churchill during meetings of the General Staff urging him to 'swing the strategy back to the Mediterranean at the expense of the Channel'. He also makes it quite clear that he himself regarded preparations for Overlord as a sop to the Americans, one that was an unwelcome distraction from a 'soft underbelly' strategy that might have set the 'Balkans ablaze' and seen the whole war 'finished in 1943'.

There we have it, then: two contradictory strategies each called into question – and each apparently vindicated by events as they eventually unfolded. Such disagreements – or rather, the persuasive thinking that lie behind each – are what makes it so difficult to win a war.

A major factor in all American thinking of that time was a lively suspicion that the British contemplated the agreed-upon cross-Channel concept with distaste and with considerable mental reservations.

General Eisenhower, recalling Roundup, 1942.

D-Day demonstrated that the direct approach could work – albeit against a much-weakened Germany.

1.

THIS DOCUMENT IS THE PROPERTY OF HIS BRITANNIC MAJESTY'S GOVERNMENT

66

Printed for the War Cabinet. October 1942.

MOST SECRET.   Copy No. *14*

W.P. (42) 483.

October 24, 1942.

TO BE KEPT UNDER LOCK AND KEY.

It is requested that special care may be taken to
ensure the secrecy of this document.

WAR CABINET.

POLICY FOR THE CONDUCT OF THE WAR.

Memorandum by the Minister of Defence.

1. Pearl Harbour and the entry of the United States into the war on one
side, while Japan broke out upon us on the other, opened an entirely new phase
of the war. I proceeded with professional advisers to Washington in order to
concert future action with President Roosevelt. We were all agreed that the
overthrow of Hitler was the prime objective, both in magnitude and in time,
and that Japan must be held as far as possible until the defeat of Germany and
Italy enabled our whole force to be turned upon her.

2. At this time the President showed himself already deeply interested in
the plan for American intervention in French North Africa by landings at
Casablanca or Tangier. This operation was called "Gymnast." General
Auchinleck was then advancing towards Benghazi and Agedabia and we had the
hope that his operation, called "Crusader," would be followed by "Acrobat,"
namely the advance of our Desert Army to Tripoli. "Gymnast" was explored
at Washington but before any definite decision could be taken General
Auchinleck's forces were thrown back to the Gazala position. All prospects of
"Acrobat" were closed and "Gymnast" faded a good deal. However, both
the President and I continued to regard it as the main and most attractive form
of the first American impact upon the Western theatre of war.

[24533]

2.

2

3. In April 1942, General Marshall came over to England with a plan for
a mass invasion of the Continent by Anglo-American forces in April 1943. The
Defence Committee were in complete agreement with this conception of a great
campaign for the liberation of Europe. For this there were solid arguments.
The British Isles are the best assembly point for a great mass of American
troops and have already a considerable British Army. The Pas de Calais is the
only place where the whole power of the British Metropolitan Air Force, which
must in any case be located here with any American accessions, can be thrown
immediately and directly into the conflict. On the other hand, the enemy know
this, and have concentrated very strong air and ground forces in this area, and
fortified it with the utmost care. The tides and beaches are unfavourable, the ports
shallow and mined or destroyed. General Marshall's plan also contemplated a
landing from England into Northern France in 1942 while Germany was busy in
Russia. The shortage of landing craft in 1942 made this smaller operation
extremely doubtful. Nevertheless, we agreed with General Marshall that we
should proceed with plans for the seizing in 1942 of bridgeheads ("Sledgehammer") as a preliminary for 1943, and anyhow for a great assault on the
Continent in 1943. The name of the main operation is "Roundup," and the
administrative preparation, which is vast in extent, is called "Bolero."

4. It soon became apparent that the 1942 operation would have little
chances of success, unless the Germans were completely demoralised and virtually
in collapse, observing that it would have to be either an assault on the Pas de
Calais, where the enemy is strongest and conditions are most adverse, or,
alternatively, an opposed landing at some point outside air cover. Personally I
was sure that the newly raised United States formations, as well as our own
somewhat more matured forces, could not establish themselves on the French
coast, still less advance far inland, in the teeth of well-organised German
opposition.

5. Accordingly, I went to Washington in June 1942 and expressed these
doubts to the President and General Marshall. I also enlarged on the possibilities of "Gymnast" and pressed that it should be explored carefully and
conscientiously. In deference to the American reluctance to abandon
"Sledgehammer," it was agreed that further resolute efforts should be made to
overcome the obvious dangers and difficulties of the enterprise, and that, if a
sound and sensible plan could be contrived, we should not hesitate to give effect
to it. It was also agreed that, as an alternative for 1942, the "Gymnast" plan
should be completed in all details as soon as possible. In the above, I was guided
by the advice of our expert authorities, and sustained by the opinion of my
colleagues in the War Cabinet.

6. On my return to England our further studies convinced us that
"Sledgehammer" held out no prospects of success. Accordingly, General
Marshall and Admiral King came to London at our invitation towards the end
of July for the second London Conference. We all unitedly dissuaded them from
"Sledgehammer" in 1942 (about which they were beginning to feel uneasy).

TRANSCRIPT OF KEY PARAGRAPHS

Policy for the conduct of war from Winston Churchill 24 October, 1942

1. Pearl Harbour and the entry of the United States into the war on one side, while Japan broke out upon us on the other, opened an entirely new phase of the war. I proceeded with professional advisers to Washington in order to convert future actions with President Roosevelt. We were all agreed that the overthrow of Hitler was the prime objective, both in magnitude and in time, and that Japan must be held as far as possible until the defeat of Germany and Italy enable our whole force to be turned upon her.

2/3. On my return to England our further studies convince us that 'Sledgehammer' held out no prospects of success. Accordingly, General Marshall and Admiral King came to London at our invitation towards the end of July for the second London Conference. We all unitedly dissuaded them from 'Sledgehammer' in 1942 (about which they were beginning to feel uneasy) while urging that general preparation on a large scale for 'Roundup' should continue ... since then preparations have gone forward without ceasing, both for 'Gymnast' for the building up of 'Roundup'

6

3

while urging that general preparation on a large scale for "Roundup" should continue. As an alternative to "Sledgehammer," we begged them to throw their whole weight into an enlarged "Gymnast" as our 1942 operation. After long discussions, which are in my colleagues' memory, complete agreement was reached between all authorities, British and American, political and military. Since then preparations have gone forward without ceasing, both for "Gymnast," which was rechristened "Torch," and through "Bolero," for the building up of "Roundup," though at a much later date in 1943 than April.

7. The Russians meanwhile, completely ignorant of amphibious warfare and wilfully closing their eyes to the German strength on the French northern coast, continued to clamour for "a second front in Europe." On this we have protected ourselves by written declarations from all reproach of breach of faith. M. Molotov knew when he returned to Russia in June exactly how we stood about invading Northern France.

8. In order to convince our Russian ally that we had in no way broken faith to him, and to persuade him of the virtues of "Torch" (which now included action *inside* the Mediterranean), I went to Moscow in the middle of August where everything was plainly and even brutally explained. M. Stalin, while expressing dissatisfaction at the aid we were giving to Russia, was in my opinion convinced of what he called "the military correctness" of "Torch." So much for the past.

9. People say there ought to be a comprehensive plan of the war as a whole, and that all the United Nations ought to participate in it. There has always been on our part, since the United States entry, a perfectly clear view. I have never varied on the main points. We have at length got a large measure of agreement and co-operation from the United States. Everything is now moving forward into action. Our plan is in the first place "Torch," with its forerunner "Lightfoot." The success of these operations will dictate our main action in 1943. Not only shall we open a route under air protection through the Mediterranean, but we shall also be in a position to attack the under-belly of the Axis at whatever may be the softest point, *i.e.*, Sicily, Southern Italy or perhaps Sardinia: or again, if circumstances warrant, or as they may do, compel, the French Riviera or perhaps even, with Turkish aid, the Balkans. However this may turn out, and it is silly to try to peer too far ahead, our war from now on till the summer of 1943 will be waged in the Mediterranean theatre.

10. It will still be necessary to maintain a strong Army in Great Britain and to insist upon adequate United States reinforcements being assembled here. "Bolero" must continue at full blast, and we must persuade the Americans not to discard "Roundup," albeit much retarded. Thus we shall have in Great Britain ample troops to defend the Island against a German invasion and to pin down large forces on the northern coast of France. We shall also be ready to take advantage of a German collapse. In any case we should have a mass of troops in Great Britain ready to move to the Mediterranean theatre, or even possibly to the Arctic ("Jupiter").

4

11. All these matters have been sedulously thrashed out by the Chiefs of Staff, the Defence Committee and the War Cabinet, and I have heard of no difference in principle amongst them.

12. There preys upon us as the greatest danger to the United Nations, and particularly to our Island, the U-boat attack. The Navy call for greater assistance from the Air. I am proposing to my colleagues that we try for the present to obtain this extra assistance mainly from the United States, and that we encroach as little as possible upon our Bomber effort against Germany, which is of peculiar importance during these winter months. I have, on the contrary, asked for an increase in the Bomber effort, rising to 50 squadrons by the end of the year. Thereafter our bombing power will increase through the maturing of production. It may be that early in 1943 we shall have to damp down the Bomber offensive against Germany in order to meet the stress and peril of the U-boat war. I hope and trust not, but by then it will be possible at any rate to peg our bomber offensive at a higher level than at present. The issue is not one of principle, but of emphasis. At present, in spite of U-boat losses, the Bomber offensive should have first place in our air effort.

13. To sum up, our policy remains unaltered. Germany is the prime objective and Japan must be held. Our tasks are these :—

(1) To preserve the United Kingdom and our communications.
(2) "Lightfoot" and "Torch," and their exploitation.
(3) "Bolero," for a retarded but still paramount "Roundup."
(4) The Bomber offensive against Germany, minus any inroads that may have to be made upon it next year in order to meet the U-boat menace.
(5) Supplies to Russia by the Arctic route, with the possibility of "Jupiter" always borne in mind should the Russians offer a major contribution to it.
(6) The gathering of air and land forces south of Turkey and the Caspian, capable of either sustaining the Southern Russian flank and/or influencing Turkey, or, alternatively, if things go badly, defending Persia, Syria, Iraq and Palestine.
(7) Subject to prior claims, preparing for an attack on the Japanese communications via the Burma Road, by the recovery of Burma.

14. There are many minor but still important matters which should be mentioned in any complete review. But what is set down here is surely quite enough.

W. S. C.

October 24, 1942.

---

though at a much later date in 1943 than April.

4. To sum up, our policy remains unaltered. Germany is the prime objective and Japan must be held. Our tasks are these:
(1) To preserve the United Kingdom and our communications.
(2) 'Lightfoot' and 'Torch' and their exploitation.
(3) 'Bolero' for a retarded but still paramount Roundup.
(4) The bomber offensive against Germany, minus any inroads that may have to be made upon it next year in order to meet the U-boat menace.
(5) Supplies to Russia by the Arctic route, with the possibility of 'Jupiter' always borne in mind should the Russians offer a major contribution to it.
(6) The gathering of air and land forces south of Turkey and the Caspian, capable of either sustaining the Southern Russian flank and/or influencing Turkey, or alternatively, if things go badly, defending Persia, Syria, Iraq and Palestine.
(7) Subject to prior claims, preparing for an attack on the Japanese communications via the Burma Road, by the recovery of Burma.

There are many minor but still important matters which should be mentioned in any complete review. But what is set down here is surely quite enough.

Operation Constellation

The loss of the Channel Islands was a major blow – both strategically and psychologically. It became a point of honour to take them back.

Today the Channel Islands are famous as a tourist destination and tax haven – a place at one remove from the realities of normal life. As of June 1940, however, they found themselves very much in the front line as the first (and only) piece of British Commonwealth territory to fall into German hands. The British government having taken a tactical decision simply to write them off as indefensible, they were occupied without a shot being fired. Though many islanders had been evacuated in the preceding weeks, thousands were left behind: Jews were rounded up; many hundreds were deported. Reports of widespread collaboration appear to be exaggerated: though undoubtedly

6.   OPERATION 'CONSTELLATION'

C.O.S. (43) 66 (0).

THE COMMITTEE had before them a memorandum by the Chief of Combined Operations covering a Staff study of possible operations against the Channel Islands in 1943.

LORD LOUIS MOUNTBATTEN explained that in accordance with statements* made at Casablanca, he had, on return, proceeded to examine what operations against the Channel Islands could be carried out to synchronise with HUSKY, with the object of preventing the withdrawal from France of enemy forces to reinforce the Mediterranean. He hoped also to bring about an air battle.

He had come to the conclusion that the assault on Alderney would be the only operation possible with the limited resources of landing craft at his disposal after meeting the requirements for HUSKY.

*
Anfa 3rd Mtg., Min. 4 (b)

These Cabinet minutes state: 'Lord Louis Mountbatten explained that in accordance with statements made at Casablanca, he had, on return, proceeded to examine what operations against the Channel Islands could be carried out to synchronise with HUSKY, with the object of preventing the withdrawal from France of enemy forces to reinforce the Mediterranean. He hoped also to bring about an air battle.'

Britain had sacrificed the Channel Islands, but their occupation was still a blow.

there were cases, many men and women did their utmost to resist.

Digging In

Hitler saw the conquest of the islands as a propaganda coup, first and foremost. Their possession did not significantly advance his invasion plans, perched as they were just off the coast of France. As the launchpad for an attack on France, they were of enormous importance, though. By 1943, therefore, with the tide in the war apparently turning, it became of a matter of urgency for the British to get them back. And, by the same token, for the Germans to prevent them – hence the installation of a garrison up to 28,000 strong. Previously, in the course of 1941, an extensive and formidable system of concrete fortifications had been constructed around the coast. 'There is no doubt,' observed Vice-Admiral Lord Louis Mountbatten, 'that the enemy has fully appreciated the value of the Channel Islands and the potential threat those islands would offer if re-occupied by our forces.'

As drawn up by Mountbatten, Operation Constellation was the collective name for a number of separate operations centred on the individual islands of the group. Operations Condor, Concertina and Coverlet were designed for the retaking of Jersey, Alderney and Guernsey respectively.

A High Price

Desirable as this end might be, the securing of it promised to be costly – not just in men and military resources but in civilian lives. It was Mountbatten himself who noted:

Each island is a veritable fortress, the assault against which cannot be contemplated unless the defences are neutralised, or reduced to a very considerable extent by prior action.

The German positions would, in other words, have to be 'softened up' considerably by bombardment from sea and air before any landing from sea or air could be attempted. It was hard to see how this was to be done without obliterating much of these tiny

Once they were installed in the Channel Islands, the Germans dug in for the long haul.

islands' built-up areas. The idea was accordingly dismissed.

Overlooked by Overlord

The difficulties which discouraged Mountbatten in 1943 continued to apply in the months that followed. The Germans were dug in for the duration. And so the Allied attack on France, when it came in June 1944, bypassed the Channel Islands altogether, despite their clear strategic value as a stepping-stone. The Germans held out there, holding back a heavy siege. On the night of 8–9 March 1945, a small group even sallied forth and raided Granville on the mainland, sinking Allied shipping and returning with supplies.

Mountbatten felt his hands were tied: how to attack the Channel Islands but not their people?

Il Duce and the Dambusters

There are few blunter implements than a bomber squadron – yet that was the weapon Air Chief Marshall Sir Arthur Harris hoped to use to dispatch the Italian dictator Mussolini.

It was at the beginning of July 1943 that Anthony Eden sent a memo to Prime Minister Winston Churchill. He had, he reported, been approached by 'Bomber' Harris about the possibility of an aerial attack on Mussolini. A star turn since their exploits at the Ruhr dams that Spring, the Lancaster Bombers of 617 Squadron would approach across the Eternal City at rooftop height to make a precision attack on his

headquarters – and, 'in case the Duce is late that morning', on his home. Both buildings were 'unmistakeable', noted Britain's Foreign Secretary:

I suggest that if Mussolini were killed or even badly shaken, at the present time this might greatly increase our chance of knocking Italy out at an early date ...

Thumbs Down
Quite why Churchill didn't go for Harris's plan is far from clear. In some ways it seems just the kind of caper he would have liked. While no one had been more grown-up in sensing early on the gravity of the issues at stake in Hitler's rise, Churchill had held on to his boyish enthusiasm for

the sheer fun of war. Other things being equal, the more swashbuckling a strategy, the more it appealed to him, so the fact that he didn't give this one his approval does seem odd.

One possible problem may have been that Harris had hatched his scheme without sufficient regard to the views of the commanding officers and fliers who would have been responsible for putting his plan into execution. An impassioned advocate for the use of aerial bombardment in just about every area of warfare, he may have been getting ahead of himself – and his squadron's capabilities – here. It would probably be unfair to say that he was proposing the plan as a publicity stunt but, as his nickname suggests, Arthur Harris believed in bombing and wanted everyone else to. He was on a roll after the Dambuster raids, but was this too ambitious?

The available documentation stops tantalizingly short of revealing the attitude of the Royal Air Force, which may have concluded that the operation was not realistic. It was one thing to deprecate Italy's air defences, quite another to envisage sending a flight of large aircraft several miles across the country's capital at rooftop-height.

Mussolini still had a certain talismanic power in Italy, despite his defeats.

TRANSCRIPT OF KEY PARAGRAPHS

Harris has asked permission to try to bomb Mussolini in his office in Rome and to bomb his residence sumultaneously in case the Duce is late that morning.

The plan was made last year but was turned down because of the ban on bombing Rome at that time.

The attack would be made just above the roof tops and would give the only chance of destroying the two buildings without much other damage.

The Palazzo Venezia and the Villa Torlonia are unmistakeable and neither is within 1,500 yards of the Vatican City or the Vatican churches. Strict orders would be given against taking any action against anything in Rome except the two specified targets.

I suggest that if Mussolini were killed or even badly shaken at the present time this might greatly increase the chance of knocking Italy out at an early date and I therefore ask your permission to lay the operation on.

Rallying Round

The other obvious objection is to Eden's interpretation of the psychological effects of such an attack. It does certainly seem possible that Mussolini's death or injury might have dealt a severe blow to national morale in Italy. At the same time, however, it might equally well have served to stiffen resolve, outraging public opinion and producing an outpouring of patriotic sympathy for a leader currently loathed by many Italians.

And he was a leader whose authority was in any case slipping, now that the Allies had carried the day in the deserts of North Africa and were on the point of invading Italy from the south. A few weeks later, indeed, the question became academic: Mussolini was ousted in a coup of 25 July.

Project Habbakuk

A remarkable idea which, even today, sounds by turns beguilingly convincing and completely crazy is testimony to the ingenuity of wartime planning, if nothing else.

'Be utterly amazed,' said the Prophet Habakkuk (1: 5); 'for I am going to do something in your days that you would not believe, even if you were told.' Geoffrey Pyke was rusty in his recollection to the extent that he spelled the seer's name wrong, but his use of the quotation was spot-on. The maverick's maverick, Pyke was a journalist, a scientist of sorts, a speculator – and a man to whom the British establishment had learned to listen. But the idea he first floated in 1942 – to make an aircraft carrier of ice – was eccentric even by his standards.

Casting Cold Water
Yet, with the Azores off-limits, a radical scheme was needed if the Allies were to protect their Atlantic convoys beyond the reach of land-based aircraft, where U-boat wolf-packs were currently running riot. And the uses of ice had already been explored to some extent. Might huge rafts of it not be towed behind ships to give extra freight-carrying capacity, for example?

The Americans and Canadians were already experimenting with an ice-ship, on Patricia Lake, in the Rockies. This vessel's wooden frame was packed with ice-slabs to create a watertight hull. Along with driving engines, it had freon refrigeration units to chill the ice. It was, in short, a conventional-looking ship – only one that was made of ice. And, for what it's worth, it held together for the best part of an Alberta summer after the project had been abandoned.

The Sawdust Factor
Pyke was thinking along different lines. His Habbakuk 'aircraft carrier' would be a ship only in the loosest sense – little more than a floating platform. Pyke envisaged using not pure water-ice but a material to which he'd given his own name, pykrete. This wasn't his invention, but he'd seen the possibilities. It was a composite of water with sawdust

HABBAKUK HAZARDS

'Pykrete' apart, the construction of the Habbakuk aircraft carrier wasn't going to be so very extraordinary: plans show a boxy structure with a simple wooden frame. The Technical Committee asked to comment on the project did not dismiss the idea out of hand but did draw attention to potential difficulties. These ranged from performance problems to such basic challenges as that of finding a construction site that was cold enough but which would not itself get iced in.

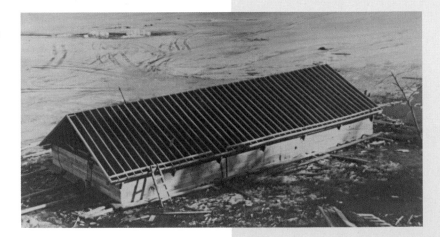

The completed Habbakuk model floats on a lake – but how well would it fare in more hostile surroundings?

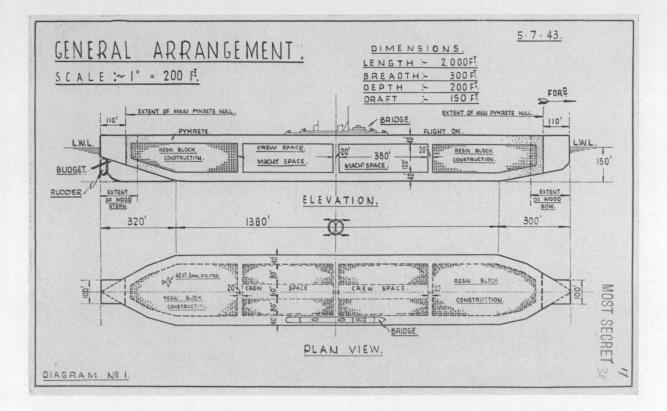

GENERAL ARRANGEMENT.

SCALE :~ 1" = 200 F.T

5.7.43.

DIMENSIONS.
LENGTH ~ 2,000 F.T
BREADTH ~ 300 F.T
DEPTH ~ 200 F.T
DRAFT ~ 150 F.T

FOR.D

EXTENT OF MAIN PYKRETE HULL.

BRIDGE.

FLIGHT DK.

EXTENT OF MAIN PYKRETE HULL.

110'

PYKRETE.

110'

L.W.L.

RESIN BLOCK CONSTRUCTION.

CREW SPACE
MACH.Y SPACE.

20'

380'

20'

RESIN BLOCK CONSTRUCTION.

L.W.L.

150'

BUDGET.

RUDDER.

EXTENT OF WOOD STERN.

MACH.Y SPACE.

20'

120'

40'

ELEVATION.

320'

1380'

300'

EXTENT OF WOOD BOW.

40 FT. SPAN FIGHTER.

RESIN BLOCK CONSTRUCTION.

20'

CREW
SPACE

CREW SPACE.

RESIN BLOCK
CONSTRUCTION.

20'

40'
80'
160'
80'
40'

100'

100'

BRIDGE.

PLAN VIEW.

DIAGRAM No 1.

MOST SECRET 311

17

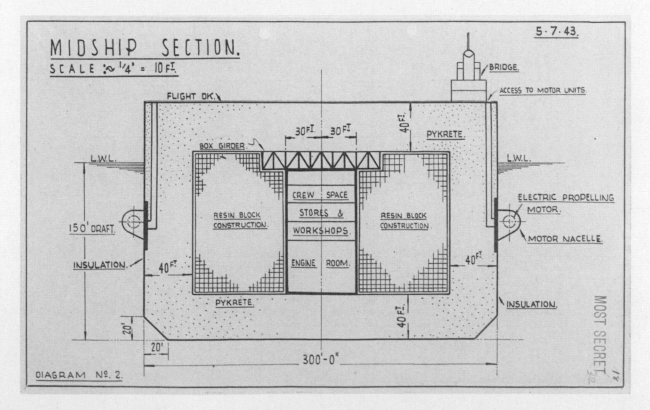

MIDSHIP SECTION.

SCALE :~ 1/4' = 10 F.T

5.7.43.

BRIDGE.

ACCESS TO MOTOR UNITS.

FLIGHT DK.

40 F.T

PYKRETE.

BOX GIRDER.

30 F.T

30 F.T

L.W.L.

L.W.L.

150' DRAFT.

RESIN BLOCK
CONSTRUCTION.

CREW SPACE
STORES &
WORKSHOPS.

ENGINE ROOM.

RESIN BLOCK
CONSTRUCTION.

ELECTRIC PROPELLING
MOTOR.

MOTOR NACELLE.

INSULATION.

40 FT.

40 FT.

INSULATION.

PYKRETE.

40 F.T

20'

20'

300'-0"

DIAGRAM No. 2.

MOST SECRET 312

18

279

HABBAKUK

REPORT OF THE MAIN (TECHNICAL) COMMITTEE.

As directed by the Prime Minister at his GEN.(43) 13/1ST MEETING on 10th June, 1943, the Main (Technical) Habbakuk Committee (listed below) have considered Item (i) of the two proposals which they were to study and wish to report as follows. Item (ii) will be covered by a further report.

COMMITTEE

R. Freeman	Chairman
K. C. Barnaby	Naval Design Advisor
J. D. Bernal	Scientific Research Advisor
D. A. Grant	Technical Co-ordinator
Marc Peter, Jr.	U.S.A. Technical Advisor
J. W. Rivett	Deputy Chairman

1. REQUIREMENTS.

Consideration has been given to the possible methods of producing a vessel to meet the following requirements:-

(a) The vessel must be delivered to its action station in early Spring of 1944.

(b) The length and breadth may be less than those formerly proposed. Subsequent instructions as to requirements have laid down provisionally a minimum length of 1,500 ft. and width of 250 ft.

A height of deck sufficient to ensure operation in weather conditions expected; this has been defined as not less than 22 ft.

(c) The vessel need not be self-propelled. Tugs may be used. A speed of 2 knots is sufficient.

(d) Long durability is not to be regarded as essential. It is more important to ensure rapidity of construction than high reliability.

Risk of damage, possibly critical, from extreme storms and successful enemy attack must be accepted.

2. SCHEMES CONSIDERED.

The following alternatives have been considered and rejected for the reasons stated.

(a) Vessel of Pure Ice.

The proved rate of construction does not ensure completion by the date required.

Evidence as to strength and uniformity of material do not justify confidence in the reliability of a large vessel in resisting wave action.

There is grave danger of critical cracking from an injury by a bomb.

Rate of melting in water and on the surface cannot be accurately assessed. This may be rapid and erratic, so jeopardising the stability of the ship.

20th June, 1943.

TRANSCRIPT OF KEY PARAGRAPHS

Report of the main technical committee (left and right)

The following alternatives have been considered and rejected for the reasons stated.
(a) Vessel of pure ice. There is grave danger of critical cracking from an injury by a bomb.

Rate of melting in water and on the surface cannot be accurately assessed. This may be rapid and erratic, so jeopardising the stability of the ship.

(b) Pykrete (pulp ice)
A vessel of this material with a wood skin is not impracticable but is subject to serious limitations. If made of ample strength to resist wave action, its depth would need to be of the order of 100ft. and construction within the time required cannot be promised. If made of reduced depth it would be subject to risk of damage in waves likely to be encountered. It would, therefore, probably have to be made at a site within a moderate distance for the final destination and where the site is not ice-bound in the early Spring.

H/1357
(5 pages)   280

2.   MOST SECRET

The least depth practicable below water level would be 100 ft. (giving only 10 ft. freeboard). Towing to site would be extremely hazardous and almost impracticable. Unless made in Russia the production site would be ice-bound until the late Spring and the vessel could not be delivered before June or July.

(b) Pykrete (Pulp Ice)

A vessel of this material with a wood skin is not impracticable but is subject to serious limitations. If made of ample strength to resist wave action, its depth would need to be of the order of 100 ft. and construction within the time required cannot be promised. If made of reduced depth it would be subject to risk of damage in waves likely to be encountered. It would, therefore, probably have to be made at a site within a moderate distance of the final destination and where the site is not ice-bound in the early Spring. Possible sites conforming to requirements will be extremely limited.

(c) Steel.

A steel vessel has not been investigated in detail because it is understood that the necessary material cannot be supplied. A rough estimate of the quantity of steel required is 50,000 tons. If this could be provided a steel vessel should be further considered.

(d) Concrete.

Construction in concrete necessitates the use of a bulk of material greatly in excess of that required for timber and not appreciably less costly per cubic foot. The structure could not be made in the time allowed and requires the use of a large tonnage of steel.

(e) Timber

A complete raft with freeboard of 22 ft., or a raft with less freeboard and a raised deck, require very much more timber than the type of vessel described below; neither type can be conveniently sub-divided for manufacture and assembly into numerous units, nor have they any advantages in reliability or resistance to enemy attack.

3. STRUCTURE RECOMMENDED.

A timber construction of the following type is considered practicable and recommended.

A vessel with a flight deck over 35 ft. above water level, supported on latticed timber girders which transfer the load to four main longitudinal floats.

These floats, each 25 ft. deep and 20 ft. wide, are about 20 ft. below water level to avoid wave action. This gives a draught of 45 ft.

To maintain floatation level and preserve stability there are two additional side floats at a higher level just dipping in still water. (Tank tests may, in fact, show that it is preferable to combine the outer floats on each side into single members).

The vessel is, in fact, a landing platform supported well above the water by floatation members which carry most of the weight below water level, with a capacity of four squadrons.

The deck area is 1,500 ft. x 250 ft.

Diagrammatic sketches are attached on the last page (5) of this report.

20th June, 1943.

frozen in. Since both these ingredients floated, a pykrete vessel would be unsinkable. The wood fibres bound the texture too, so that it did not shatter: bullets and shells simply bounced off. And because wood drastically reduces heat conductivity, a mass of pykrete melts more slowly than a similarly sized iceberg. Pyke planned to have refrigeration units on board, pumping refrigerant around the structure, to chill it.

On the Rocks

By the latter half of 1943, though, interest in Pyke's plan was melting away. His 'ship' needed less steel than a conventional carrier but still required a lot for the refrigeration-piping, and there was a severe shortage. In any case, President Salazar was now letting the Allies use the Azores, whilst new aircraft models carrying more fuel could take the fight to the Germans far out in the Atlantic.

Operation Handcuff

A British expedition to take the Greek island of Rhodes seemed fraught with danger. In the end the Germans got there first.

Greece had played its part in the war, first sending Italian invaders packing, then resisting staunchly the Germans who followed. Some historians suggest that this delayed the launch of Operation Barbarossa just long enough to enable the Soviet Union to achieve its ultimate success. Others object that Greece's war was no more than a sideshow, and Britain's commitment of forces a sentimental investment in the land of democracy. Either way, it was in vain: by April 1941, Greece was out of the war and Britain's commitment over – at a cost of 10,000 soldiers left behind as prisoners of war.

Out of the Picture ... Then In
The German occupation of Greece was often grim: thousands starved; thousands more were executed; others were killed by in-fighting between resistance groups. It was the same story in the islands, where the occupiers were predominantly Italians. Mussolini's men had slunk back in on the coattails of the Germans. As far as the narrative of the conflict is concerned, however, Greece and its islands had now disappeared into irrelevance, no longer a significant field of battle.

That changed abruptly in the middle of 1943 as it became clear that Italy was on the brink of surrender. Who was going to have the islands now? The southerly-lying Dodecanese archipelago was of especial interest given its strategic significance. Ownership offered the chance to control the passage of shipping throughout the Aegean and the eastern Mediterranean – and, always crucial for Britain, with its Asian empire, the approaches to Suez.

Rhodes Raid
Britain's Joint Planning Staff (JPS) was fired with enthusiasm for Operation Handcuff, the aim to lock the islands into the Allied sphere. Rhodes and Scarpanto were the two islands selected as the target for an attack. There were German forces on both, but these were small, and not expected to receive help from the defeated Italian garrisons. After a series of raids by heavy bombers, an amphibious attack would be made by British troops from Cyprus, with the USS *Kitty Hawk* offering logistical support.

Dwight's Doubts
The Americans were unsure. As ever, their goals were more direct. Eisenhower was already engrossed in his plans for Operations Avalanche and Buttress – the first Sicily landings – and much of his resources were committed. And, while the *Kitty Hawk* of the wartime era may literally have carried aircraft, she was not an aircraft carrier like the later vessels named after her. She would be vulnerable sailing, substantially unaccompanied, this far east. As for the British belief that the Italians would remain passive, this was not a safe assumption.

Finally, the moment passed and the Germans got the time they needed to cement their hold on the Dodecanese. Fortunately, this didn't make much difference in the long run.

Greek troops in buoyant mood prepare to depart for the Albanian front.

J.P.(43) 285 (FINAL)
14th AUGUST. 1943.

WAR CABINET

JOINT PLANNING STAFF

OPERATION "HANDCUFF"

Report by the Joint Planning Staff

As instructed+ we have examined the telegraphic summary* of a plan prepared by the Commanders-in-Chief, Middle East, for the capture of the islands of Rhodes and Scarpanto against German opposition only, the Italians being passive. This is a "set-piece" operation which the Commanders-in-Chief consider would, in the present state of the distribution of resources require six weeks to mount.

2. We consider the likelihood of mounting this operation during 1943 is remote for the following reasons:-

(a) While Italy is still in the war, the basic assumption that we shall meet German opposition only, the Italians being passive, is in itself unrealistic. Although it is possible that the Italian forces in Rhodes might give some previous sign of their intention not to assist the Germans in repelling an Allied assault, it would be difficult to be sure that they would live up to their intention.

(b) It is clear that so long as operation "Buttress" or "Avalanche" is being mounted, or undertaken, General Eisenhower cannot provide the necessary resources - mainly naval, air and landing craft - to make up Middle East requirements.

(c) Once Italy is out of the war the availability of resources for operation "Handcuff" will depend on the priority accorded at "Quadrant" to Mediterranean operations. If, as we, have previously recommended# priority is given to operations on the mainland of Italy, subsidiary action in the Balkans and the bombing of German industrial targets from Italy, it is probable that General Eisenhower will still be unable to afford the necessary resources for "Handcuff".

+ C.O.S. (43) 179th Meeting (O)
# C.O. 270
/ J.P.(43) 221

-1-

C.O.S. MEETING   MOST SECRET
17th AUGUST 1943.   ITEM 6

OPERATION "HANDCUFF"
(Ref. C.O.S.(43) 179th Meeting (O)
Minute 8.)

Report by Joint Planning Staff
J.P.(43) 285 (Final)

The J.P.S. consider, for various reasons, that the chances of mounting "HANDCUFF" this year are remote and they have therefore drafted a reply to the C's.-in-C. without regard to the air forces actually available.

2. The C's.-in-C. have stated their air requirements as 40 fighter and medium bomber squadrons plus 6 ship-borne S.E.F. squadrons and the use of a bomber force of 20 U.S. heavy bomber squadrons. This seems on the high side in view of the enemy opposition to be expected:- A maximum of 295 aircraft of which 100 are Italian and therefore likely to be ineffective if the hypothesis that the Italians may not fight at all is accepted. On the other hand, the distance from Cyprus to Rhodes (275 miles) would entail a heavy escort commitment and 9 squadrons plus the ship-borne fighters are earmarked for this purpose.

3. As regards paragraph 7 of the Paper and paragraph 2 of the draft telegram, although all the information here shows that the Kittyhawk cannot safely give cover at a range of 275 miles, I think it might be advisable to reword the last sentence of para. 2 of the telegram on the following lines:-

"On the other hand we doubt whether the Kittyhawk is capable of escorting medium bombers as far as Rhodes and Kos with any margin of safety and would like you to confirm that they can in fact do so."

4. I agree with the other points made in the paper and with the remainder of the telegram.

A.C.A.S.(P)
16.8.1943.

TRANSCRIPT OF KEY PARAGRAPHS

Left: Report by JPS:

We consider the likelihood of mounting this operation during 1943 is remote for the following reasons:

(a) Although it is possible that the Italian forces in Rhodes might give some previous sign of their intention not to assist the Germans in repelling an Allied assault, it would be difficult to be sure that they would live up to their intention.

(b) It is clear that so long as operation 'Buttress' or 'Avalanche' is being mounted, or undertaken, General Eisenhower cannot provide the necessary resources – mainly naval, air and landing craft – to make up Middle East requirements.

(c) Once Italy is out of the war the availability of resources for operation 'Handcuff' will depend on the priority accorded at 'Quadrant' to Mediterannean operations. If, as we have previously recommended, priority is given to operations on the mainland of Italy, subsidiary action in the Balkans and the bombing of German industrial targets from Italy, it is probably that General Eisenhower will still be unable to afford the necessary resources for 'Handcuff'.

Right: Response to report:
The J.P.S consider, for various reasons, that the chances of mounting 'Handcuff' this year are remote and they have therefore drafted a reply to the C's.-in-C without regard to the air forces actually available.

Operation Satin

A proposed American attack in Tunisia promised to make life extremely uncomfortable for Rommel's forces in the Desert, but there were considerable risks involved for the Allies too.

By the beginning of 1943, a little of the lustre had worn off Erwin Rommel: retreating westwards, the 'Desert Fox' had been run to earth in southern Tunisia. Though protected for now by the winter weather, he was all too well aware that lack of air support had left him at a grave disadvantage. He was far from giving up the fight, but he was wary of taking on Britain's battle-hardened Eighth Army, now advancing inexorably

Rommel's tactical genius could not prevail indefinitely against Allied might.

from the east; forays against the relatively newly arrived and inexperienced Americans appealed far more.

A Bold Stroke
This, as far as Britain's Alan Brooke was concerned, was exactly what was wrong with

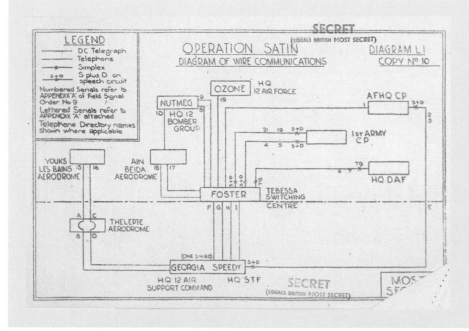

The Allies hoped that sheer organization would prove a match for Rommel's cavalier drive and dash. So indeed it might have done ... and ultimately did. Yet Operation Satin shows that a plan can be prosaic and still wildly unrealistic.

TRANSCRIPT OF
KEY PARAGRAPHS

Re: Air cargo transport
operation, Satin

1. In the process of
preparation for Satin
operation, supplies are
building approximately on
the prearranged schedule.
However, the period
available for consideration
of details has been short.
Exigiencies developed which
made it necessary to
transfer reponsibility
during the planning period.
Under these circumstances
it is anticipated that
emergency shortages can
develop. Depot stocks of
certain key technical
articles among which
emergency shortages
can develop are in the
Oran area.

2. It is anticipated that
demands will arise which
will require calls for
delivery of supplies by air
transport. It is presented
for consideration, therefore,
that tentative plans be set
up for cargo delivered by
air transport from Oran to
Tebessa. The services, to be
effective, should be
available on direct call by
the Commanding General,
Mediterranean Base Section
on request of Commanding
General, Satin Task Force.

Operation Satin, proposed by
General Eisenhower for execution
from 22 January. II Corps had
arrived in Africa just a couple of
months before on 8 November as
part of the Allies' Operation
Torch. Whilst recognizing that a
direct attack on Rommel was not
realistic, Eisenhower hoped his
force might turn up the pressure
by attacking important points on
his supply-line. To this end, he
wanted his 1st Armored Division
to sweep eastward across the
centre of the country from Gafsa
towards the Mediterranean, to the
ports of Sfax and Gabès or to the
vital airfield of Kairouan, which
was further inland.

There is no doubt that the
American Supreme Commander
had come up with an elegant
strategy. The Germans had been
worried about the possibility of

just such an operation. Not only would it make life difficult for Rommel in the south, but it would draw down German forces from the north – leaving Tunis itself open to direct assault by the British troops of General Kenneth A.N. Anderson's First Army.

A Tall Order

It was one thing to talk of disrupting German supply-lines, but how was Eisenhower's attack itself to be supplied? Speed would be of the essence, meaning that 1st Armored would have to travel light. Should all go well, this would hardly matter: there would be supplies and to spare in the bases they were about to take. Yet, should the raiders fail or should their progress even *slow* significantly for any reason, they would find themselves marooned, and ill-equipped to cope. Accordingly, the British were profoundly sceptical.

America's own General Lucian Truscott tried hard to be upbeat. It wasn't that Satin wouldn't work, he observed loyally; indeed, it would be 'logistically sound if everything is one hundred percent'. It was, he said, summing up, 'a knife edge proposition'.

Superceded

In the end, Eisenhower allowed himself to be persuaded that it was going to be an unnecessarily risky way of securing an end which it seemed was very soon going to be achieved in any case. Montgomery's Eighth Army and Anderson's First were converging quickly and in a matter of weeks would have cut off Rommel completely from the coast. It wasn't in fact to be quite that easy – Anderson was pushed back from Tunis by courageous defenders – but time was quickly running out for the Germans in North Africa.

A German Flak 88 gun awaits an Allied attack during the Desert War.

TRANSCRIPT OF KEY PARAGRAPHS

Re: Direction of Satin
9 January 1943

1. Recent conferences with reference to P/40 indicate a very close decision on the direction in which SATIN will move. Since it is felt that committee opinion generally leans toward the SFAX area, I submit this as a minority indication of my strong belief that SATIN should go to GABES.

2. The mission of Allied Forces in all Africa is destruction of Axis forces in this continent. All action must contribute to that end. Rommel and Nehring cannot be estimated separately. The enemy capabilities which will permit Rommel to join Nehring and assume an offensive attitude or escape through Sicily and Italy would likewise have a most unfortunate influence on that morale.

7. It should be remembered that Rommel has never failed to make use of a hole that has been left open to him. He will operate boldly and will live off the country or on our own supply depots if they are made available to him.

Sir
Rooks
1/11/43

ALLIED FORCE HEADQUARTERS

G-3 SECTION

9 January 1943.

MEMORANDUM TO: G-3.

SUBJECT   : Direction of SATIN.

1. Recent conferences with reference to P/40 indicate a very close decision on the direction in which SATIN will move. Since it is felt that committee opinion generally leans toward the SFAX area, I submit this as a minority indication of my strong belief that SATIN should go to GABES.

2. The mission of Allied Forces in all AFRICA is destruction of Axis forces in this continent. All action must contribute to that end. Rommel and Nehring cannot be estimated separately. The enemy is endeavoring his utmost to concentrate. That is his most dangerous capability.

3. The destruction of Rommel will have greater repercussions on the morale of Allied powers than will the immediate elimination of enemy forces in the TUNIS - BIZERTA bridgehead. The enemy capabilities which will permit Rommel to join Nehring and assume an offensive attitude or escape through SICILY and ITALY would likewise have a most unfortunate influence on that morale.

4. Montgomery has been pursuing Rommel with the utmost vigor. The only obstacle to annihilation of the Africa Corps has been the inability of Eighth Army to form and move an encircling force to hold the enemy until he can be destroyed. It is now in the power of the Allied Forces North Africa to furnish Montgomery with that encircling force. The Axis exit at GABES blocked will take from Rommel his maneuver room. Our seizure of SFAX on the other hand would permit Rommel to come closer to full supporting distance from the BIZERTA bridgehead but more dangerously will give him maneuver room as he comes through the GABES bottleneck.

5. It is felt that the risk of directing SATIN on GABES is not greater than it would be if it were directed on SFAX. Supply will be difficult initially. Succeeding operations should however make SFAX available to us. It is agreed that SFAX and GABES must be regarded together and operations against them should be in close succession but to let SFAX precede GABES gives time to Rommel.

6. The question of command will be of great importance and also a delicate inter-allied problem. As for ground forces it should be expected that the Eighth Army as it advances into the North African theater would come under control of AFHQ. A reasonable solution of the subordinate command in south TUNISIA would place Montgomery in operational control to include that force which closes the GABES bottleneck. Such an arrangement would be not only practical from a military point of view but would acknowledge the right of Montgomery to execute the "coup de grace" to Rommel. The seizure of the GABES area with the SATIN force would not necessitate the continued operation of the First Armored Division in that area. Its mobility and striking power make it effective in support of our operations in the SFAX - KAIROUAN area at a later but early period.

7. It should be remembered that Rommel has never failed to make use of a hole that has been left open to him. He will operate boldly and will live off the country or on our own supply depots if they are made available to him. If GABES is left open a reasonable capability on his part would be to join hands with Nehring, not through SFAX but around it, using our supplies where he found them.

8. It is strongly recommended that SATIN be directed on GABES.

W. G. Wyman

W. G. WYMAN,
Colonel, G.S.C.,
G-3 Planning.

Panamanian Possibilities

The idea of a surprise attack that would close the Panama Canal was audacious and enterprising. Too audacious and enterprising, it turned out.

Captain Chikao Yamamoto and Commander Yasuo Fujimori came up with the idea of attacking Panama in August 1943. The shock-value of the Pearl Harbor bombing long since spent, the Americans had now marshalled their immense military and industrial resources for the conflict and were making slow but steady progress in the Pacific.

A Second Pearl Harbor

Their supreme commander, Admiral Isoroku Yamamoto, needed to recover the initiative. The American public were still largely untouched by the war, and Yamamoto wanted to dent their confidence. A number of ideas for a 'second Pearl Harbor' had already been considered, including attacks on US coastal cities like San Francisco. He had also been developing a long-range submarine capacity that was designed to enable Japan to hit hard, and at enormous distance from her own shores.

The Panama Plan was to involve one of these submarines approaching the Pacific coast of Central America and then sending out a pair of *Seiran* seaplanes. This aircraft, specially designed, was capable both of dive-bombing and torpedo-launching. Ten would be needed to close the Canal, according to the planners. Flying at treetop level to escape detection, their pilots would travel across the Isthmus to Panama's Atlantic coast and attack the Gatun Lock: six precisely placed torpedos, plus about 3000kg (6600lb) of bombs, should do the trick. The closure of the Panama Canal might not be a crippling blow in military terms, given the size of the US fleet already present in the Pacific, but it would certainly be a shock to both the

Admiral Isoruku Yamamoto was anxious to recover the initiative he felt had long been lost.

American military establishment and the American public.

Revised Expectations

The months went by while everybody waited for the new submarines' delivery, and the pilots struggled to master the skills in dive-bombing needed to make the operation work. It is a

telling commentary on Japan's deteriorating prospects that what began as a routine out-and-home mission evolved almost imperceptibly into a *kamikaze* suicide attack before being abandoned in the fight to save the homeland.

A Submersible Aircraft Carrier

The brainchild of Admiral Isoroku Yamamoto, the concept of the *Sen-Toku* I-400-class submarine came to him in the aftermath of Pearl Harbor, 1941. That attack had made the fullest use of the advantage of surprise – how was that to be recaptured as the hostilities went on?

Yamamoto's audacious solution amounted to a submersible aircraft carrier: the *I-400* was the biggest submarine ever made. It would carry sufficient fuel to make a round-trip to any target, anywhere in the world. Along with its torpedos, it would carry deck-guns and a waterproof hangar. This would provide accommodation for at least two small *Seiran* seaplanes: catapult-launched, these had floats so they could land at sea and be winched

At 122m (400ft) in length, the *I-400* was the biggest submarine yet seen.

back aboard at mission's end. Each plane had range of 960km (600 miles) and could carry either an 800kg (1760lb) bomb or similarly-sized torpedo.

Not only was the *I-400* invisible above the surface, it was all but undetectable below. The hull was treated to suppress sound from inside and deflect sonar waves from without. This enabled it to steal up close to its target before surfacing to strike. Ultimately, of the 18 projected, only two came into service, and too late in the war to have any impact.

The loss of the water in Gatún Lake – and this is what I fear – would be a strategic calamity ... [and] more possible than I had believed.

US General Frank Andrews, September 1941.

Seen here in 1936, the Gatun Locks were an obvious choke-point for the Panama Canal.

Operation Culverin

Churchill's plan for recapturing a small area of Sumatra as a base for attacks on Japanese shipping had everything going for it – except for feasibility.

Aceh province occupies the northwestern tip of the island of Sumatra, Indonesia. The former Dutch colony had been taken by the Japanese in February 1942. They had swept through Indonesia at lightning speed, and though their progress had become progressively slower as the war went on, there was little to indicate by 1943 that their advance was being held.

Sumatran Stranglehold

Operation Culverin was first proposed at the Quebec Conference. (A culverin is a long, narrow-calibre cannon much used in the various conflicts of the seventeenth century.) The proposal came from Winston Churchill – a man much given to this sort of back-of-the-envelope strategic thinking. Whilst the reconquest of

Clockwise from front left: Roosevelt, Mackenzie King, Churchill, the Earl of Athlone.

TRANSCRIPT OF KEY PARAGRAPHS

Re: Order of Battle Culverin
9 Feb 1944

In order that organisation and final training of Army and Corps Tps can be carried out in good time before the operation is mounted, it will be necessary for those units, required from outside India, to complete Phase A of the Order of Battle, to assemble in India in sufficient time for this organisation and training to be completed.

In addition, Army HQ, the Second Corps HQ and the various L of C HQ must assemble in India early so as to begin planning.

6. It is requested, therefore, that you will examine the question of provision from your resources of Adm units necessary to maintain the personnel and vehicles shown in Appx, and state what, if any, units you can make available.

This HQ would then arrange for the balance of Adm units necessary to accompany the personnel shown in Appx A into India.

COPY.

IMMEDIATE

MOST SECRET

Subject:- ORDER OF BATTLE-
CULVERIN.

No. 65028/SD3
Adv HQ 11 Army Group SEA
New Delhi.   9 Feb. 44.

To:- Chief of the General
Staff (SD4), GHQ(I).

Ref our 65028/SD3 of 31 Jan 44 to HQ SEAC.

In order that organization and final training of Army and Corps Tps can be carried out in good time before the operation is mounted, it will be necessary for those units, required from outside INDIA, to complete Phase A of the Order of Battle, to assemble in INDIA in sufficient time for this organization and training to be completed.

In addition, Army HQ, the Second Corps HQ and the various L of C HQ must assemble in INDIA early so as to begin planning.

2.   Attached at Appx A is a summary of the personnel and vehicles, less adm units, which must, for these reasons, come into INDIA, giving dates by which each HQ or Group of Units should complete arrival.

3.   The dates shown in the Appx are based on the assumptions that
            (a) The operation is mounted on 1 Nov 44.
            (b) All movement of units in Phase A to ports of embarkation
                is completed by 1 Sep 44.

4.   The introduction of these HQ and units into INDIA, apart from the problem of accommodation, raises the question of provision of sufficient adm units to maintain them during the period they remain in INDIA.

5.   Adm planning now in hand at GHQ(I) may allow of provision for maintenance of the troops involved. On the other hand, it may be necessary for all adm units required to accompany these troops into INDIA.

6.   It is requested, therefore, that you will examine the question of provision from your resources of Adm units necessary to maintain the personnel and vehicles shown in Appx, and state what, if any, units you can make available.

This HQ would then arrange for the balance of Adm units necessary to accompany the personnel shown in Appx A into INDIA.

7.   It would be appreciated if your reply could reach this HQ by 1800 hrs on 11 Feb.

(Sd) I.S.O. Playfair,
General,
C-inC 11 Army Group SEA.

Copy To:- HQ. S.E.A.C.(2)
          EPS(BLUE)
          A/Q (PLANS)
          A
          Q(MAINT)

the archipelago as a whole was clearly going to have to wait, a limited strike at this part of Sumatra might be manageable, the Prime Minister argued. It would also provide the perfect base for Allied planes to persecute Japanese shipping through the Malacca Straits. This narrow stretch of water is the main sea-route between the Indian and Pacific Oceans. A choke-hold here could cause grave problems for the Japanese.

But, ever the chess-player, Churchill was thinking a step ahead. Not just about the control the Allies would gain over the

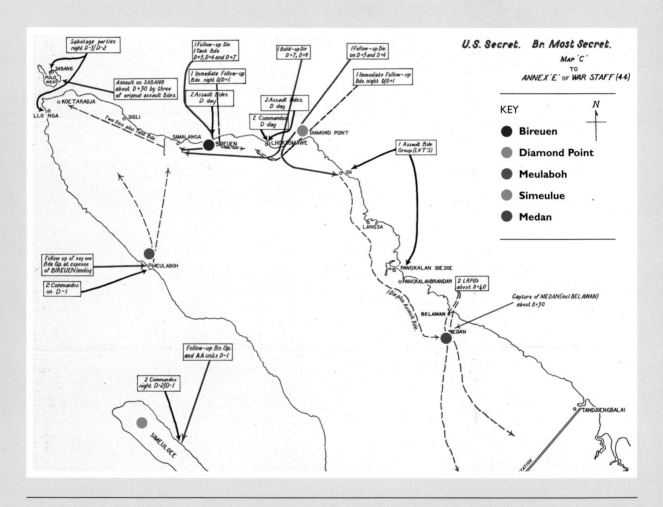

SUMATRAN SURPRISE

The bulk of Allied forces for Operation Culverin would land on Sumatra's northeastern coast, near Bireuen, and further to the east around Diamond Point – now Udjung Djamboaje – before pushing south. Possession of this coast would confer control of traffic in the Straits. But a subsidiary landing would take place on the southwestern side, at Meulaboh, whilst a small force would also have to secure Simeulue, an obvious application point for a potential counter-invasion.

The shelling of Sumatra did not take place till later in the war.

shipping lane but also about the efforts Japan would be compelled to make to get the territory back. By seizing northern Sumatra, he subsequently explained, 'we should be striking and seizing a point of our own against which the Japanese would have to beat themselves if they wished to avoid the severe drain that would be imposed on their shipping by our air action'.

Rejected, Revived, Re-Rejected
What can we say? Except that even the most elegant scheme may end up foundering on the rocks of practicality? Or be scuttled before

that, thanks to what may be over-defeatist thinking. Culverin was dropped – though not forgotten. It was revived in 1944, as the war was entering its final phase, when Lord Louis Mountbatten, as Supreme Commander of the Allies in Southeast Asia, was eager to take the fighting to the Japanese. Culverin was to be the first of a series of amphibious operations in the region, designed to put unprecedented pressure on the enemy. At sea, however, the Japanese seemed to be as strong as they had ever been: the time still didn't seem right for this sort of large-scale landing.

Lucrative as a successful CULVERIN might be, there appears much more to be gained by employing all the resources we now have available in an all-out drive into Burma.

General George Marshall puts the America view, 1943.

Operation Spark

Major General Henning von Tresckow had been disenchanted with Hitler since before the war.

Hitler and Mussolini view the damage after the later assassination attempt in 1944.

How differently might things have turned out had this particular spark only ignited? A number of German officers conspired seriously to assassinate their *Führer*.

It would take only one spark, said Henning von Tresckow, to set off an explosive reaction against Hitler, the 'arch-enemy of the world'. Led by their military, the German people would rise up against him. In hindsight, the image is an odd one: it's hard to see why any sort of spark should have been needed, with history's greatest-ever conflagration already raging. Still, it's easy enough to understand what the Major General meant.

As Chief of Staff of the Army Group Centre on the Eastern Front, he was perfectly placed to appreciate the depths of the crisis to which Hitler had brought his country – and to lobby leading soldiers and officials for some sort of action against the tyrant.

An Unpromising Start

Tresckow began by soliciting the support of General Günther Hans von Kluge and of General Field Marshal Fedor von Bock, key commanders on the Eastern Front. The former's opportunism had already become clear in the pace with which he'd climbed the career ladder; the latter's aristocratic disdain for the *arriviste* Hitler and his National Socialism was plain. And yet discretion seems to have been the better part of valour, as far as these two were concerned: however badly the war was going, neither was willing to take a stand. (Kluge in particular was to show

more enthusiasm for Claus Schenk Graf von Stauffenberg's July 1944 Bomb Plot – yet here too his faintheartedness was to let himself and others down.)

Discouraging as this was, Tresckow had better luck with *Generaloberst* Ludwig Beck – another product of the Prussian militarist tradition, and a longstanding (if diplomatic) critic of Hitler's. Tresckow's adjutant Lieutenant Fabian von Schlabrendorff and his intelliegence liaison officer Rudolf Christoph von Gersdorff were also recruited to a group that quickly hatched a conspiracy to assassinate the *Führer*.

A Catalogue of Cock-ups

Fate seems to have conspired against the conspirators. Cold air at altitude appears to have prevented a time bomb on Hitler's private plane from detonating on 13 March 1943. The explosive had been secreted in two Cointreau bottles, and was safely recovered later. A week later, a plan was made to blow up the *Führer* at a parade of captured Russian standards at a Berlin museum. Von Gersdorff volunteered to wear the explosives about his own person like a modern-day suicide bomber and set them off as he welcomed his leader to the exhibition. In the event, Hitler's handlers having juggled his schedule about as a routine security precaution, the time allocated for the event was cut short, and he was in and out of the exhibition in about two minutes. Von Gersdorff failed to

meet him, and instead faced the tricky challenge of divesting himself of his deadly costume.

Nine months later, the conspirators planned to place an explosive device at an exhibition of new winter uniforms, but the train carrying them was hit by a bomb during an Allied air raid the night before.

The 1944 bomb plot, though unsuccessful, did at least advertise to the outside world the existence of opposition inside Germany.

Operation Long Jump

'Operation Long Shot' more like it, perhaps, but the Nazis were quite serious in their plan to assassinate the 'Big Three' Allied leaders in Tehran.

Much has been made – and rightly so – of the success enjoyed by the Bletchley Park codebreakers in cracking the Enigma code. But this was just one episode in an ongoing code war, in which the victories were by no means all on the Allied side. German successes in the

Atlantic owed a great deal to their codebreakers' skill. They didn't just derive vital intelligence about ship deployment and convoy movements: it was via US naval intercepts that they found out about Eureka, the Allied leaders' conference in Tehran.

The conference had been called in response to Stalin's continuing demands for action by the Western Allies to relieve the pressure on his Soviet forces which – despite key victories – remained intense. The

The 'Big Three' were able to talk at the Tehran conference, untroubled by German conspiracies.

Allies for their part wanted the Soviet dictator's agreement to their strategies for the war and (now that it seemed to be swinging their way) to their longer-term plans for Europe.

Daring – or Desperate?
The Germans learned of the conference in mid-October. Here

was an opportunity to kill the biggest three birds with one special-operations stone! *Obersturmbannführer* Otto Skorzeny was asked to lead an assassination squad. A member of the Waffen SS, he was the man of the moment after masterminding a triumphant mission just weeks before. On 12 September, his raiding party had sprung the Italian dictator Mussolini from the captivity in which he had been placed by King Victor Emmanuel II after having been overthrown by his fellow Fascists.

The Gran Sasso Raid had involved agents on the ground working with a crack team of paratroop commanders who crash-landed gliders in the mountains around the castle in which *Il Duce* was being held. The attack at Tehran was anticipated to follow roughly the same procedure.

Among Friends

Getting German agents into Iran would not be difficult. The Iranian capital was full of refugees escaping the war in Europe. Since seizing power in 1923, moreover, the Shah had been trying to bring British and Soviet interference in his country to an end – and had found an ally in Hitler's Germany.

But others had been finding friends as well. Not least the great Soviet intelligence officer Nikolai Kuznetsov. Mingling with Germany's forces in the Ukraine, as *Oberleutnant* Paul Siebert, he had made a drinking buddy of SS *Sturmbannführer* Ulrich von Ortel. 'We will repeat the Abruzzi

jump!', Ortel had boasted in his cups, also offering to introduce his new companion to his old mate Skorzeny:

But it will be the Long Jump! We will eliminate Churchill and Stalin to turn the tide of the War! We will abduct Roosevelt to help our Führer *to come to terms with America!*

Kuznetsov had old friends too, of course, and the Soviet Embassy in Tehran was quick to hear his news. Their intelligence officers had already been hard at work identifying German agents (some 400 so far). It was easy for them to put two and two together and identify a group of German nationals newly arrived in the provincial city of Qum as Long Jump's advance party. The whole operation had to be called off.

In this, the Capital of our Ally, Iran, [we] have shaped and confirmed our common policy. We express our determination that our nations will work together in war and in the peace that will follow.

Declaration of the Three Powers, Tehran, 1 December 1943.

Mussolini's release at Gran Sasso had been a difficult operation, ably handled.

Operation Rabat

So murky is the question of the wartime role played by the Catholic Church that it's impossible to say with any certainty whether this operation was even planned.

The idea that the Nazis had schemed to abduct Pope Pius XII was first revealed by SS General Karl Wolff at his Nuremberg Trial in the immediate aftermath of the war. Not just the Pope, he insisted, but also the Curia – the topmost echelons of his administration – were to be seized.

Wolff amplified his own role in an interview he gave decades later to reporter Dan Kurzman of the *Washington Post*. Hitler, Wolff said, called him in for a meeting on 13 September 1943, when the Nazis were in the process of occupying Rome, ready to defend it against the advance of the Allies from the south. Before becoming Pontiff, Cardinal Eugenio Pacelli had been the Vatican's *Nuncio* (ambassador) in Germany. Hitler now spoke of the 'bitter contempt' that had existed between them ever since, and he now entrusted Wolff with a special mission:

I want you and your troops to occupy the Vatican City as soon as possible, secure its files and its art treasures and take the Pope and Curia to the north.

Cynics have dismissed as spin the story that the Nazis had had a plan for abducting Pius XII. They point out that there is no better way to retaliate the man known as Hitler's Pope than by suggesting that he himself became a target of the *Führer*. Certainly, it's a point pushed hard by Vatican-supporting media in recent years.

Reactionary

Pacelli had always been a conservative, authoritarian in his instincts and easy in his accommodation with Fascism in Italy. It is true that he held reservations about the political priorities of the far-right dictators then taking power across so much of Europe, but his greatest fear was of godless communism – and he was deeply suspicious of 'enlightened' liberalism.

It should also be remembered that the Church's attitude to the Nazis' racial agenda was more nuanced than many of its detractors tend to assume. Pacelli's predecessor Pius XI been so horrified by Hitler that he had reached the conclusion that the German dictator had been possessed by the Devil and made serious attempts to exorcize him at a distance. And yet, would it not have been simpler to speak out in clear condemnation? As for Pius XII, his assistance to anti-Nazi and Jewish groups is well-documented. Even so, a simple denunciation might have been worth much more: several eminent historians argue that if the Catholic Church in Germany had protested against the persecution

Nuncio Pacelli – later to be elected Pope Pius XII – leaves the Presidential Palace in Berlin in December 1929.

SS General Karl Wolff was a man of complex motives whose credibility must be in doubt.

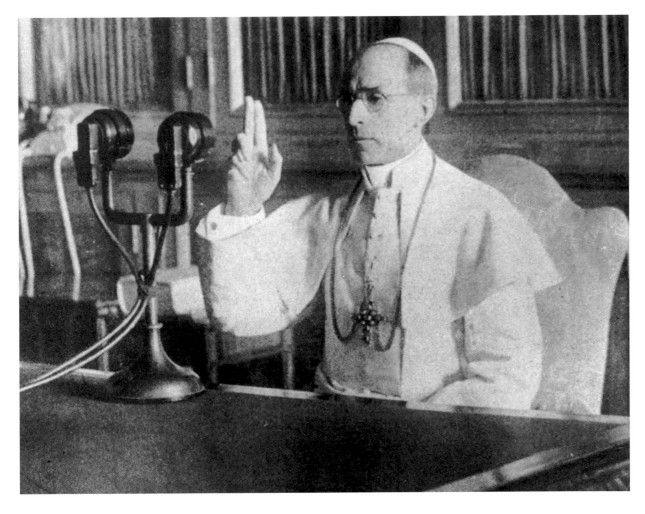

Pope Pius XII makes a radio broadcast from the Vatican. His message is a prayer for peace at Christmas, and an end to World War II.

of Jews, there could have been no Final Solution.

A Holy Hostage

But Pacelli's personal credentials aren't the essential point where the alleged abduction plot is concerned. Hitler's interest in the Pope was as a pawn:

I do not want him to fall into the hands of the Allies or to be under their political pressure and influence.

Was any such operation ever planned? Sceptics point out that there is little or no documentary evidence. Well, say their opponents, that's because it was all much too sensitive to be written down. So how reliable is Wolff? He claimed that he had disobeyed and even warned the Vatican of Hitler's intentions – but he first made the claims at his trial, when he had a clear interest in trying to make himself look good. The Vatican backs his claims – yet it too has an agenda. It could be that we're never going to know ...

The Pope is even ready to be deported to a concentration camp, but will do nothing against his conscience.

Italian Foreign Minister Count Galeazzo Ciano.

Operation Eisenhammer

A plan to smite the Soviets where it hurt with an 'iron hammer' had to be abandoned as inconvenient realities came crowding in.

'Communism is Soviet power plus the electrification of the whole country.' So said the Soviet Union's founder Vladimir Ilyich Lenin in 1920. The drive to turn on the power – a feature of successive five-year plans – was considered symbolic of the electrifying effects of communism on what had been a sleepy country, economically inert. First and foremost, though, it represented a real push towards modernization and an attempt to remake the nation as a twentieth-century industrial power. That modernization had been central to Soviet success during the 1930s – and it was still more crucial now, as the USSR strove frantically to hold things together while it waged war.

Hydroelectric schemes had been a mainstay for the Soviet economy since the 1930s.

Pulling the Plug
At the heart of the electrification programme had been the construction of a large and elaborate network of HEP schemes, drawing on the power of the mighty Volga and its tributaries. Three-quarters of the supply needed to keep vital defence industries running came from a few key installations. So why not take these out – and watch Soviet industry wind down (and very likely come shuddering to a halt)? That was certainly the question that Heinrich Steinmann asked. A senior Air Ministry official, he argued that a series of well-placed air strikes could quickly cut off Russia at the mains. And it would be very hard for the Soviets to get themselves reconnected given that they lacked the technology to build their own turbines. They had been compelled to import the ones they used, buying them on the open

The Soviets did not have the technology to build hydroelectric turbines of this type, which was built by Americans.

market at vast expense. Replacing them would be well-nigh impossible in this time of economic want and all-out war.

A Hammer Blow

Steinmann drew up his plan of attack in 1943. It was called *Eisenhammer* (Iron Hammer) in apparent reference to Vladimir Ilyich Ulyanov himself; the great revolutionary's codename had meant Iron Man. A concerted series of raids was envisaged, to be undertaken by Mistel long-range bombers, composite aircraft not unlike the He 177/Do 217 'piggyback planes' considered for the *Amerika* project. The Mistel was generally a Junkers Ju 88 bomber (an unmanned missile) , with a fighter bolted on above, to guide it into its attack.

These planes were already in development, designed to carry hugely heavy bombs (up to 1810kg/4000lb); but for Eisenhammer, still more specialized weapons would be needed. Steinmann wanted them to carry *summerballon* (summer balloon) bombs. Buoyed up by air-filled floats, these would be dropped upstream of the target installation and drift into position before detonating.

Irons in the Fire

A series of technical snags delayed development, however, and by the time the Mistels and the *summerballons* were both ready to be deployed, the Red Army was advancing at a rapid pace. A last-ditch gesture-attack in February 1945 had to be abandoned when most of the Mistel fleet was incinerated in an Allied air raid. Such Mistels as had survived were used in a hopeless attempt to destroy the Red Army's crossing-places on the Oder.

Would the German Luftwaffe not make a greater contribution to victory in the east by letting its bombers operate against the root of the Russian offensive strength ... instead of acting as artillery and dropping bombs in front of the infantry.

General Karl Koller, 9 November 1943.

An Allied air raid sent most of the Mistels up in flames in February 1945.

The (might-have-been) Mighty Maus

This gigantic tank would have been a terrifying sight on the battlefield – if the Germans could have got it there ...

Allied intelligence didn't mince its words: the Panzer VIII was 'an amazing vehicle'. Certainly, with a weight of 200 tonnes (196 UK tons; 220 US tons), this was the heaviest tank ever to be built. Hence, presumably, its nickname: *Maus* (mouse).

It's hard to resist the feeling that, at a time when he might have been more usefully occupied trying to win the war, Hitler was making a determined bid for the record books. Easy as it is to imagine Soviet faces paling as a line of these massive tanks advanced across the steppe, development didn't even start until the second half of 1942. By the time the project was seriously under way, the Germans had been turned at Stalingrad: the smash-and-grab assault was no longer the order of the day and the *Wehrmacht* was now forced into defensive mode.

Not that the *Maus* wasn't well-defended: with a hull-front almost 200mm (9in) thick, it would have resisted an Allied rocket or shell or bomb-burst. But with such a huge, high profile, it would have made a target that was easy to hit again. And again. And besides, it was peculiarly vulnerable to a hand-grenade – or even a Molotov cocktail – dropped into its proportionately oversized air-vents.

You also have to question the operational usefulness – whether in attack or defence situations – of a weapon that was bound to break every bridge it attempted to

An intense debate started and, except for me, all of those present found the 'Maus' magnificent.

Colonel General Heinz Guderian, in his postwar memoir.

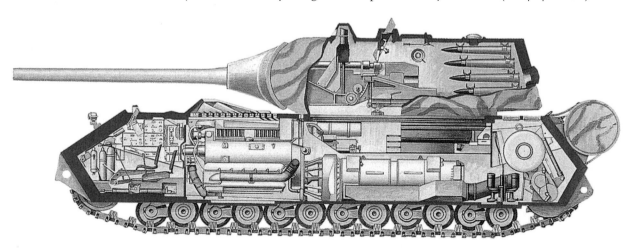

The *Maus* was set apart from other tanks by its awesome (even preposterous) scale.

cross. (In theory, this didn't matter: a sophisticated snorkel system gave the *Maus* an ability to ford rivers to a depth of 13.75m/ 45ft depth, though it was tested successfully to a depth only just over half of that.) Nor could it be transported by train unless the railway network was radically reinforced – not just bridges but culverts and sets of points.

And if the thought of facing an advancing *Maus* was certainly frightening, you would have plenty of time to think about how to respond, given that its top speed was just over 13km/h (8mph) – and this was achievable only in perfect conditions on the flat. The original idea had been for it to trundle along at almost twice that speed, but designers were unable to develop an engine

powerful enough to shift such a mass of metal that fast.

Indeed, to get so massive a weight to move at all was was a minor miracle of engineering in itself: an electrical transmission designed by Ferdinand Porsche was key. It used a diesel engine to drive a generator, and it was the power from this generator which drove the tank.

When considering the *Maus*, it is all too easy to recall the comment made by Frances' General Pierre Bosquet as he watched the Charge of the Light Brigade at Balaclava in 1854: 'C'est magnifique, mais ce n'est pas le guerre: c'est de la folie.' The *Maus* was indeed magnificent. But, given that it wasn't (in any functioning sense of the word) a tank, it too was madness.

Above: Auto-engineer Ferdinand Porsche watches as a the super-heavy prototype *Maus* is put through its paces.

Below: Porsche had designed a special electric transmission for the *Maus*. He is seen here at the first trial of the *Maus*.

Operation Velvet

A plan to help the Soviets by placing air squadrons in the Caucasus to protect the oilfields there came unstuck over Soviet suspicion of Western motives.

In recent years, scholars have debated whether *blitzkrieg* was an actual philosophy of warfare – a question that is unlikely to have troubled the peoples of France, the Netherlands or eastern Europe. Yet there's a real case for arguing that, rather than a set of principles, it was the ultimate improvisation: Hitler simply threw everything he had at his enemies. And as the leader of continental Europe's most important industrial power, he had a great deal of relatively sophisticated hardware (tanks, trucks, planes, ships, ammunition).

Oil Crisis

What he didn't have was certain vital war materials. Iron ore was one – hence his various operations in Scandinavia. Oil was the other obvious problem. Germany's military engine was powerful but a gas-guzzler. Access to the Middle East's oilfields had been a factor in his intervention in the North African Desert War towards the end of 1940. The Allies having broken through at the Second Battle of El Alamein, however, time seemed to be running out for this objective.

It isn't clear how much the Allies knew about Operation Gertrude, but it didn't take too

TRANSCRIPT OF KEY PARAGRAPHS

1. Letter from Stalin to Churchill:
The situation on our Caucasian front deteriorated somewhat as compared with October. The Germans succeeded in capturing the town Nalchik. They are approaching Vladikavkas where severe fighting is going on at present. Our difficulty here is our weakness in the fighter aircraft.

2. Air Marshall Drummond's alternative proposal: We are already some 500 Hurricans short of our Protocol agreement with the Russians. To make good this deficiency we would have to hold up supplies of Hurricanes to the Middle East and possibly to India. We could not, therefore, add a further 20 Hurricanes a month to the existing Russian allotment

3. Letter from Air Ministry to Britman, Washington: Drummond has now informed us that Soviet Government are not prepared to proceed with the original Anglo-American 'Velvet' project.

COPY. MOST SECRET   PRIME MINISTER'S
                     PERSONAL TELEGRAM
Personal and Secret.   Serial No. T.1470/2.

PREMIER STALIN TO PREMIER CHURCHILL.

1.   Your message received on the 5th November.

2..   My congratulations on the successful development of the military operations in Egypt. Let me express my confidence that now you will be able to completely annihilate the Rommel's gang and his Italian allies.

3.   We all here hope for the success of the Torch.

4.   Many thanks for your communication that you and President Roosevelt have decided to send in the near future to our Southern front the 20 British and American squadrons. A speedy arrival of these 20 squadrons would be a very valuable help.   The necessary consultation between the British, American and Soviet representatives on the preliminary arrangements could be best organised at first in Moscow and later in case of need direct in the Caucasus. I am already informed that the USA will send for this purpose the General E.E.Andler. I will await for your communication on who will be appointed to represent Great Britain.

5.   The situation on our Caucasian front deteriorated somewhat as compared with October. The Germans succeeded in capturing the town Nalchik. They are approaching Vladikavkas where severe fighting is going on at present. Our difficulty here is our weakness in the fighter aircraft.

6.   Let me express my gratitude for your congratulations in connection with the anniversary of the USSR.

KREMLIN. 8.11.1942.   STALIN.
Copies to:- P.S. to S. of S.
             C.A.S.
             V.C.A.S.
             A.C.A.S.(P)
             A.C.A.S.(O)
             A.C.A.S.(I)
             D.of Plans.

1.

much imagination that Hitler would have his eye on oil sources in the Caucasus. Especially because seizing the fields around Baku, would not just guarantee oil for Germany; it would also deny it to the Soviets.

A Helping Hand

A plan was hatched at the end of November 1943 during private discussions between Roosevelt, Churchill and Stalin at the Tehran Conference. The Soviet dictator responded favourably to the suggestion that Anglo-American Air Force fighter and bomber squadrons should be established at bases in the Caucasus. That way, they would be able to give much-needed air support should the Germans make a determined bid to take the Azeri oilfields. But other, more pressing concerns were occupying the leaders.

Suspicious Minds

Sketchy as it was, the idea for Operation Velvet scarcely warranted the name of 'plan'. In the weeks that followed, a team of Royal Air Force officers flew to Moscow to start putting flesh on these bare bones. They found their Soviet counterparts surprisingly guarded and lukewarm. Finally, the Soviet negotiators came out and said it: the Soviet Union would welcome aircraft but would much prefer to sort out pilots and support staff of its own; the Soviets did not want even friendly foreign personnel on its soil.

Why? Since the end of July, when the Germans' Operation Countdown had collapsed at Kursk, the Red Army had been on the offensive. Stalin could now feel some confidence that his Soviet forces had the initiative. And, it must be said, he possessed to an extraordinary degree that paranoid suspicion of outsiders which had long characterized the Soviet state.

2.

3.

Chapter Four
1944

A turning-point had been passed. At least, that was the way it was starting to seem for the Allies, who had the initiative now in Europe and were making slow but steady progress in the Pacific and the Far East.

In Churchill's terms, it was 'the beginning of the end'. The Axis was creaking badly. Italy had been out of the war since September 1943; Germany and Japan were very much on the defensive now. Both sides still sought magic solutions, Britain exploring ways of assassinating Hitler and bringing the Reich crashing down that way; Germany looking to kill Stalin in hopes that this would somehow stem the Russian tide.

Tempting as such solutions might have seemed, both sides had more realistic options, unpalatable as they might be to contemplate, given the costs and casualties to be expected. The Western Allies were already closing in on the enemy both in Europe and in Asia. Germany, for its part, had potentially situation-transforming weapons just starting to come on stream: the question was whether these could make an impact in the time remaining. And, from the Allied point of view, whether these secret weapons could be stopped and the momentum which had been established be maintained.

Hitler and his high command had much to discuss by 1944. Fortunately for the Allies, the *Führer* was not in the mood to take advice.

Operation Brimstone

The suggestion has been made that plans for an invasion of Sardinia were no more than a deception, but they were real – and might easily have worked.

'Where to now?', Allied commanders asked as victory in North Africa came to seem inevitable. Europe's 'soft underbelly' lay before them. In truth, it didn't seem half so soft now that invasion was possible as it had when but a distant hope.

Decisions, Decisions ...

The defeat of Rommel's Afrika Korps offered options – and the agony of choice. Unimaginable consequences – and untold lives – might be riding on their decision. Though Italy was indeed but a short hop away, its coasts were strongly guarded by the Germans; the main offshore islands were now bristling with pill-boxes and gun emplacements.

A significant school of thought among the Allied command argued for a 'left-hook' punch from Tunisia to Sardinia. This would give the attackers a vantage-point well to the north, from where to strike at Italy's industrial heartland in the north. Simultaneously, they could mount an assault on Corsica, from where it would be easy to attack the southern coast of France. Plans were drawn up for the US VI

TRANSCRIPT OF KEY PARAGRAPHS

1. Although this operation has not yet been approved by the Combined Chiefs of Staff it is considered that Force Commanders should be appointed and planning should start now, so that if the operation has to be undertaken, an agreed plan will be ready and time will not be lost.

2. It is not possible at present to detail the forces to be made available for this operation but it appears that:
a) The naval forces required can be made available from those which will be in the Mediterranean after Husky, provided that no other major operation is undertaken simultaneously.
b) The air forces required can be made available as soon as the situation in Husky allows them to be diverted from that operation.

Corps to attack Sardinia with the support of Britain's V Corps (1st and 4th or 56th Divisions). The US 82nd Airborne Division would be in reserve.

Sicily it is

In the end, though, it was decided that Sicily was the safer option: the sea crossing was likely to be less exposed. And if major hostilities in central Italy were going to be costly in lives, they would draw the German focus that much further away from the Allies' next target in Normandy.

Operation Husky accordingly went ahead: the landings on Sicily began on 9–10 July 1943 – so successfully that the Sardinian plan was dropped.

Sardinia Sidelined

The option of an attack on the island did, however, remain open. In fact, it was revived in the autumn of 1944, under the codename Operation Brimstone when it began to be feared that German fighters on Sardinia might even now thwart an advance that was making heavy weather of its advance into northern Italy in the face of fierce resistance. Plans were drawn up for an invasion to be mounted by Lieutenant-General Mark Clark's US Fifth Army. But as the moment for mounting the assault approached, it became clear that forces on the mainland were making progress. Since German forces in Sardinia were not going to be able to disrupt the Allied advance, they might just as well be left in impotent isolation.

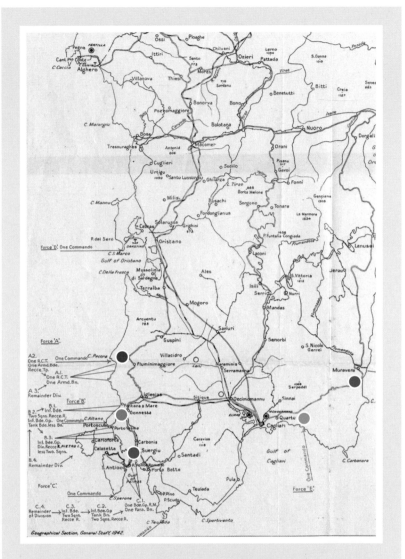

KEY

● Force 'A' attack
● Force 'B' attack
● Force 'C' attack
● Force 'E' attack
● Force 'F' attack

The Allies' 'most secret' map shows the main force of Brimstone's attack being concentrated in Sardinia's southwestern corner – where a line of sheltered bays faced Africa, practically inviting invasion. Subsidiary landings would be made further north – and 'round the back' along the island's eastern coast.

Operation Bulldozer

There's a sense of smoke and mirrors about this operation of 1944, a deceptive feint to begin with – and finally never carried out in any case.

Ian Fleming is famous as the creator of James Bond, though most are aware of his secret wartime work. Less well known are the contributions made by his elder brother in both the literary and the intelligence arenas. Peter's dazzling descriptions of his travels up the Amazon and across the

Central Asian steppes have a 'What ho!' Wodehousian humour that is irresistible. He also played a vital part in Britain's intelligence operations in the war. Fleming began by overseeing preparations to resist Operation Sealion. Then, as the threat of invasion receded, he was sent to south-east Asia, placed in charge of military deception operations there.

Cheering up Chiang

It was at about this time that the initial onrush of the Japanese was

held at Midway, but no one could have any illusions about the amount of fighting left to do. One imperative was to provide support for Chiang Kai-Shek and his Kuomintang troops, fighting a frantic rearguard action down by the Burmese border in Yunnan. Chiang was a difficult man to help, however, just about unending in his demands, and he considered the securing of the 'Burma Road' as key to China's survival. This land route (and the air-lane above it) allowed much-needed supplies to be carried from British India to China. For Chiang, though, the connection seemed to have a deeper psychological significance – his guarantee that his allies weren't going to cut him loose.

He seized on vague suggestions about diversionary attacks in southern Burma. Called on to lead his own forces on forays into northern Burma, he would agree only on condition that the Allies mounted major air-and-sea attacks in the south.

Akyab at Issue

Built on an island in the estuary of the Kaladan River, the seaport of Akyab (now Sittwe) was regarded as crucial; there was an important airfield there. Late in 1942, Earl Wavell's 14th Indian Division

Peter Fleming approached his work as spy and author with the same imagination and good humour.

advanced southwards as far as Akyab down the coast, but the Japanese stood firm and by the following April had pushed them back to where they'd started.

Deception and Disappointment

Chiang was enraged at the lack of action. When plans for an assault on the Andaman Islands were dropped, Fleming felt he had to offer an alternative. Hence Bulldozer, the plan he drew up in July 1943 for an amphibious assault on Akyab scheduled for spring 1944: the 36th Indian Division and 50th Parachute Brigade were to be involved. It

was to be one of his 'deceptive' operations, though, designed to persuade the Japanese that the Allies had a stronger presence in the south of Burma than they had thought; no more than a feint, as far as he was concerned.

The operation was supposed to take place, however. And so it was to general disappointment that, when the time approached, Bulldozer had to be stopped. The Japanese were on the march again, mounting a major offensive around Kohima and in Imphal, and all the available transport aircraft were needed to help contain them.

Left: Chinese Nationalist warlord Chiang Kai-Shek was a necessary – but immensely exacting – ally.

Below: Chinese troops in Burma help to keep open the vital corridor to British India.

Operation Transfigure

An imaginative attempt to spring the trap on a German Army already caught out by the Allied advance in Normandy ultimately turned out not to be needed.

By the end of July 1944, US forces had broken out from their beachhead on the coast of Normandy: Operation Cobra had been a complete success. As they pushed south- and eastward towards the heart of France, their course lay some way to the south of that of the Canadian and British divisions who (after several weeks of fierce fighting) had occupied the area around Caen.

Tanks Trapped

In the area between them, in what had become known as the Falaise Pocket, lay Germany's Seventh and Fifth Panzer Armies, under the command of Field Marshal

Right: Günther von Kluge found himself in an utterly impossible position in the summer of 1944.

Below: General Eisenhower rallies the men of 101st Airborne at Greenham Common, England, on 5 June 1944.

Günther von Kluge. While their comrades had been falling back, they were stuck here between the rock of the Allied advance and the hard place of Hitler's fury. The dictator had explicitly ordered Von Kluge not to retreat an inch but, on the contrary, to counter attack with all the speed he could.

The reality was that, if retreat was not permissible, advance was simply impossible – though Von Kluge did try, in the predictably disastrous Operation Lüttich. It merely drove home the fact that, with the pocket inexorably closing, Von Kluge would have to withdraw – and soon – if he was to have any chance of saving the bulk of his troops and tanks for future combat. It was this appreciation that led the Allied commanders to cast about for an action that would enable them to

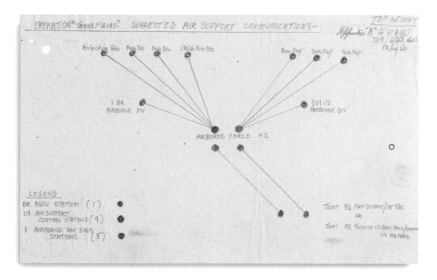

Left: Transfigure promised to be a complex and potentially fraught operation, involving personnel from three different countries. Communications were going to be vital: if their air-transporting and support went wrong, they could quite easily find themselves stranded in hostile territory.

Below: Operation Transfigure was planned to an extremely advanced stage and was even given the go-ahead, as this memo shows:
'The Supreme Commander has now ordered that executive action in connections with moves, etc., of American formations and units involved in Operation Transfigure will begin at once'.

cut off his retreat before he'd had the chance to make up his mind. Though the forces already on the ground were converging around him, they were doing so too slowly: why not drop an airborne army to his rear?

Airborne Answer

Hence Operation Transfigure. A First Allied Airborne Army was assembled, comprising the paratroops of the US 101st Airborne Division, Poland's 1st Independent Parachute Brigade, and Britain's 1st Airborne Division. It included too the not-quite-airborne troops of Britain's 52nd (Lowland) Division. These were regular infantrymen who, trained earlier in the war to travel light for mountain fighting, were well-adapted to being whisked about for rapid deployment by air. All were flown to airbases near the Normandy coast.

The plan was that they would be carried south on 13 August and dropped on and in the

vicinity of an airfield at Rambouillet. From here, they would fan out and take up positions on key roads leading south and east. An important

*Copy No. 11 also received (for GSO.1)
and destroyed. Sm. 11 Aug*

T O P   S E C R E T

Minutes of a meeting held in D Gp
CROYDON at 1030 hrs 10 Aug 44 to
consider the division of responsibilities
for adm and other matters for operation
TRANSFIGURE

21 AGp/1757/G(SD)

11 Aug 44.

Present :-

Lt-Col	L.F. Heard	HQ 21 Army Gp (G(SD)) (Chairman)
Col	C.H. Bonesteele (US)	G-3 HQ 12 US Army Gp
Col	W.L. Baneger (US)	G-4 HQ 12 US Army Gp
Capt	M.J. Rodlinger (US)	G-3 HQ 12 US Army Gp
Lt-Col	G.H.N. Wilson	HQ Airborne Tps A
Maj	N.J.L. Field	HQ Airborne Tps G
Col	O.B.S. Poole	Q(Plans) HQ 21 Army Gp
Lt-Col	P.R. Drew	Q(M) HQ 21 Army Gp
Lt-Col	A.V. Britten	G(Plans) HQ 21 Army Gp
Lt-Col	C.F. Byers	G(SD) HQ 21 Army Gp
Lt-Col	I.J. Milne	G(Air) HQ 21 Army Gp
Lt-Col	R.H. Reynolds	E HQ 21 Army Gp
Lt-Col	J.D. Hill	Rep SO in C HQ 21 Army Gp
Lt-Col	G.P. Sanders	P & PW HQ 21 Army Gp
Lt-Col	H. Bleecker	LAC HQ 21 Army Gp
Maj	R.B.O. Hyatt	G(Ops) HQ 21 Army Gp
Maj	P. Talbot-Smith	RA HQ 21 Army Gp
Maj	I.J. Slay (US)	E(Airfds) HQ 21 Army Gp
Maj	D. Booth	E(Airfds) HQ 21 Army Gp
Maj	G.C. Meares	G(SD) HQ 21 Army Gp (Secretary)

1.   The Chairman explained that although this discussion was going to be based on this specific operation similar conditions might arise at any time and it was therefore necessary to clarify the various channels of communication.

In this particular instance a British Comd was going to operate in the US Zone and would have under comd British/European Allied and US Forces, and although the whole was operating under a US Comd there were certain peculiar domestic British subjects, e.g. appointments of offrs, the channels of communication for which required clarification.   Although the period of the operation was initially a short one, there might well be quite a long period when Airborne Tps would function in a normal ground role during which period many more points, such as trg, would have to be dealt with.

2.   The various points were then discussed and the decisions arrived at are shown in Appx A att.

Major GS
(Secretary)

G(SD) Main HQ
21 Army Gp
FW

Copy to: 12 US Army Gp (G-3 Sec and G-4 Sec)
HQ Airborne Tps (2)
HQ 21 Army Gp - G(Ops)
                        G(Plans)
                        G(Air)
                        A(Adv Sec)
                        A(Rear)
                        Q(Plans)
                        Q(M)

Q(Maint)
Q(AE)
E(Main)(2)
SO in C
RA
LAC

P & PW
Civil Affairs

*Recd
7815
11 Aug.*

TRANSCRIPT OF KEY PARAGRAPHS

Left:
Minutes from a meeting held 10 Aug 1944 to consider the division of responsibilities for operation for adm and other matters for operation Transfigure:

The Chairman explained that although this discussion was going to be based on this specific operation similar conditions might arise at any time and it was therefore necessary to clarify the various channels of communication.

Although the period of the operation was initially a short one, there might well be quite a long period when Airborne Tps would function in a normal ground role during which period many more points, such as trg, would have to be dealt with.

Right:
Operation Transfigure cancelled.

section of Germany's army in the West would be surrounded.

Transfigure Transcended
Eisenhower was at first an enthusiast for Transfigure. He is said to have believed that it would very likely bring an end to the war in Europe. But, with George S. Patton in command as of 1 August, Cobra had shifted up a gear and was now sweeping eastward across the countryside at an extraordinary rate. It soon became clear that the planned airborne assault would not be needed, since Patton's advance had left the hole in the pocket all but sealed. As things turned out, closing it up brought an important victory but didn't quite end the war. With that conclusion clearly in sight, though, no one really minded.

Operation Foxley

Life imitated art in this extravagantly ambitious plan to assassinate Hitler; unfortunately, fiction obstinately refused to be reproduced as fact.

Geoffrey Household's novel *Rogue Male* was walking off the bookshop shelves in 1939. Quite understandably: this intensely imagined story of a solitary hunter who must escape after trying to assassinate a dictator in his mountain lair is a thrilling read. Unputdownable, even. Indeed, officials of the Special Operations Executive (SOE) still seem to have had it in their hands and to have been buying into its founding premises with complete conviction when they drew up their plans for Operation Foxley in 1944.

Licensed Mavericks

A certain amount of anarchic extravagance was expected of – even essential to – the SOE, founded by Churchill in 1940 as the 'Ministry of Ungentlemanly Warfare'. Staff were encouraged to think the unthinkable – anything which might help 'set Europe ablaze'. Off-the-wall ideas were positively prized.

It has to be said, however, that a more conventional approach to Operation Foxley might not have come amiss. Early attempts to come up with a plan to bomb one of the *Führer*'s trains had to be dropped given the impossibility of establishing a clear itinerary or

schedule. Between the demands of running a country and conducting a major war – not to mention the elaborate precautions of extreme paranoia – Hitler was completely unpredictable in his movements.

Hitler at Home

A lesson might have been learned from this when the focus turned to the Berghof – Hitler's Alpine retreat, where it was now decided to hunt him down. Excited by the

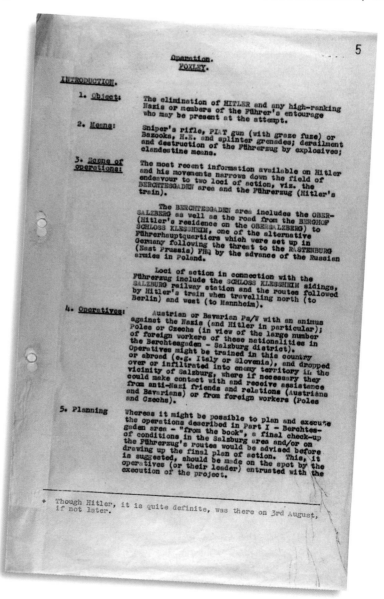

TRANSCRIPT OF KEY PARAGRAPHS

Object: The elimination of Hitler and any high-ranking Nazis or members of the Führer's entourage who may be present at the attempt.

Means: Sniper's rifle, PIAT gun (with graze fuse) or Bazooka, H.E. and splinter grenades; derailment and destruction of the Führerzug by explosives; clandestine means.

Scene of operations: The most recent information available on Hitler and his movements narrows down the field of endeavour to two loci of action, viz, the Berchtesgaden area and the Fuhrerzug (Hitler's train).

Planning: Whereas it might be possible to plan and execute the operations described in Part I – Berchtesgaden area – "from the book", a final check-up of conditions in the Salzburg area and/or on the Fuhrerzug's routes would be advised before drawing up the final plan of action. This, it is suggested, should be made on the spot by the operatives (or their leader) entrusted with the executions of the project.

Berchtesgaden gave Adolf Hitler a quiet refuge – and a fittingly dramatic photo-backdrop.

admitted coup of discovering that they now held in one of their POW camps a member of the *Führer*'s personal bodyguard who was in communicative mood, the SOE drew up an extensive dossier describing the Berghof's domestic and security arrangements and Hitler's routines when he was there.

As far as it went, he was a creature of habit: tantalizingly so, given that he apparently took a solitary walk each day around exactly the same woodland route. To make things even easier for his assassins, a Nazi flag flew above the Berghof complex whenever the *Führer* was in residence, advertising his availability to his would-be killers.

Fantasy Fiction

From a novelist's point of view, perhaps, this offered a plausible possibility; in the real world, it wasn't quite so convincing. A team of assassins might well have to lie low in local woods for weeks – even months – on end before the busy dictator found a moment for a little 'me time'. The chances of their evading detection all that time were next to non-existent. It didn't matter how much detail they were able to assemble about everything from the *Führer*'s favourite foods to his bedtime reading: if they couldn't guess when he was coming to the Berghof, their chances of success were slim.

Even so, when the plan was finally renounced, the SOE weren't swayed by such mundane considerations but by rather more speculative ones. Would Hitler's assassination, far from causing collapse, prompt a German resurgence as the people rallied at his martyr's death – perhaps under a leader who was more realistic and more effective? In truth, it might be said, they need not have worried ...

Operation Zeppelin

The Nazis' plan to assassinate Stalin was meticulously planned and might even have succeeded had it not been for a chance remark and a remarkably quick-witted guard.

In the autumn of 1944, the Germans prepared a careful conspiracy to attack and kill Stalin, their chosen assassin a Soviet prisoner of war. Pyotr Shilo, native of Chernigov, northern Ukraine, came from a family of Kulaks – those independent farmers who had become Stalin's special enemies in the 1930s. But he had also got himself into trouble for embezzlement, and it has been suggested that this gave him his main grudge against the state.

Cloak and Dagger

The Germans trusted Shilo enough to turn him loose in Russia under an assumed identity, the irony of which he will presumably have enjoyed. He was, his papers informed any interested party, one Major Tavrin of SMERSH (the Communist counter-intelligence agency) and he was a Hero of the Soviet Union, no less. With him would be his wife – quite genuinely, for although the two had been total strangers up till now, they had

been hastily married to strengthen their partnership.

'Major Tavrin' was armed with a special grenade launcher fastened to his forearm under a discreetly-widened sleeve; he also carried a handgun whose bullets had been given envenomed tips. Equipped with a range of official-looking documents and rubber stamps, the Tavrins were given over 400,000 roubles. Having been landed just outside Moscow, they were to make their way into the city on a motorbike they took with them for the purpose. They would then bluff their way into the very heart

> **Not a moment passes without our enemies trying to seize some little chink through which they crawl and do harm to us.**
>
> *Joseph Stalin*

Stalin, with Molotov, prepares to take the salute at the military march-past in Red Square.

of the Kremlin and assassinate the dictator in his den.

The Tavrins took off from a Latvian airfield on the night of 5 September on board an Arado 232B transport plane belonging to *Kampfgeschwader* (KG) 200, the special-operations wing of the *Luftwaffe*. Soviet intelligence was already aware that something was afoot, though unsure what exactly: they had received a tip-off from the Riga tailor commissioned to customize a coat with one widened sleeve.

Soviet SNAFU

The Soviets may have been lying in wait, but it was an organizational mix-up that led an alert though ill-informed battery on the ground to fire at the plane. It scored a hit, forcing the Arado to come down well to the west of where it should have landed. The pilot landed safely but, as he did

so, a wing swung round and struck a tree; an engine burst into flames, attracting the attention of Soviet forces in the vicinity. (Even so, while some of the crew were captured, a couple managed to make it back to German lines.)

Unguarded Comment

Major and Mrs Tavrin, meanwhile, had gone speeding off to Moscow on their motorbike, just as planned. Their papers did the trick at all the checkpoints that they passed. All seemed well, until the Major made a chance remark about their having ridden all through the night, which raised the suspicions of a sentry: if that were true, he realized, they two would surely have been damp from a rainstorm some hours before. The couple were quickly arrested, the assassination foiled. Operation Zeppelin was over before it had barely begun.

An Arado A2 232 brought Major and Mrs Tavrin and their motorbike deep into Belarus.

Project Danny

What seemed a likely strategy for dealing with the VI menace was unable to be put into effect because the US Army forgot who it was fighting.

One wartime operation that went ahead – and all too effectively – was the launch of the V1 flying bomb (*Vergeltungswaffe* means 'retaliatory weapon'). In Britain they became known as 'doodlebugs', from the buzzing sound they made – and which was typically the last thing their victims (almost 10,000 people in southeastern England) heard before they died. Powered by early jet engines, this invention

Had it started earlier, the 'Second Blitz' brought by the VI might have changed the outcome of the war.

More than a hundred VIs a day hit London through the late summer of 1944.

of Wernher von Braun was really what in the postwar period we have come to call a cruise missile. Since its range was limited, the V1 was dispatched from bases in northern France.

Britain vs the V1
Not surprisingly, Allied air attacks were repeatedly made in an

attempt to destroy these sites (attempts had been made since 1942, indeed, when the development of a mysterious secret weapon had been no more than the vaguest of rumours). But – again not surprisingly – these were formidably well dug-in. The first V1 landed on London (not coincidentally) just one week

after D-Day, on 13 June 1944, setting the proverbial cat among the pigeons. Just when things had started swinging the Allies' way in Western Europe, here was a new weapon against which they had no credible defence. The authorities had reason to be worried: their helplessness was only too clear to a London population that had succeeded in keeping its nerve through the horrors of the Blitz but was now feeling a high level of consternation. The V1 attacks, Hitler had calculated, 'will make the British willing to make peace'. He was exaggerating, of course – but by how much?

What the British did first, of course, was redouble their efforts to break out from the Normandy landing-zone. Right now they were stalled – and braced for a counter-attack – west of Caen. But with morale on the home front ebbing fast, and fears of what the V1 might do next, the pressure was on to find an answer.

Tim to the Rescue?

Hence Project Danny, a plan to deploy carrier-capable F4U Corsairs of the US Marine Corps, armed with an advanced weapon of America's own. The Tiny Tim air-to-ground rocket was dropped like a bomb, falling free for several seconds before a trailing lanyard snapped, triggering ignition, so that it fired only when it was at a safe distance from the launching aircraft. Flying at over 885km/h (550mph), it was accurate only to

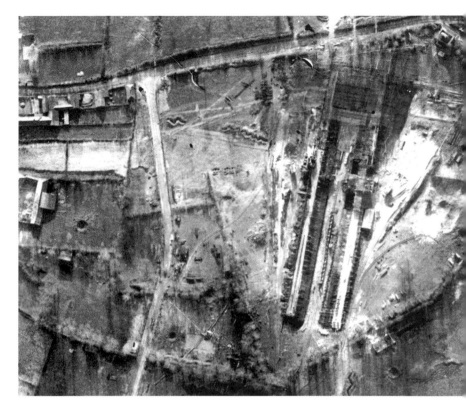

a range of just less than a mile, but this was quite good enough for close-range attacks on enemy shipping, the purpose for which the weapon had been designed. But it had been found to be effective too against defensive earthworks and concrete fortifications, and it was these bunker-busting abilities which would be called on now.

And it might have worked at that. Who knows? Good old-fashioned inter-service rivalry intervened, Army chiefs refusing to take part in what was going to have to be a joint operation with the Marine Corps. Fortunately, the breakout from Normandy was soon completed and the French V1 bases overrun.

The V1 sites were a target for relentless Allied air attacks from 1942.

That's the end of this briefing. As long as I'm in charge there'll never be a Marine in Europe.

General Marshall

Plan Z

War came too early for the Nazi *Kriegsmarine*, a 10-year programme of rebuilding having barely been begun when the hostilities started in 1939.

Defeated in the field of war, then crushed at the conference table: no wonder Germans resented the 'agreement' they'd been coerced into at Versailles. Under its terms, the nation blamed for the war just

Type XXIs are built in Bremen. The U-boats' success drew resources from the conventional *Kriegsmarine*.

past was to be militarily emasculated, weak and helpless: the Weimar Republic would be completely at the mercy of other states. The *Lufstreitkräfte* of Baron von Richthofen and Max Immelmann had been disbanded and was not to be re-formed. The army had been savagely cut down to size. And what had so recently been a major naval power was to be allowed only six small battleships, a few cruisers and destroyers and assorted patrol boats; any submarine capability was banned outright.

Overturning the Treaty

When Hitler came to power in March 1933, with the explicit intention of restoring German prestige in the world, the intention of tearing up this treaty was, at the very least, implicit. The reality was, though, that Germany had already been hard at work for some years trying to find ways round the limitations placed on it by the Versailles Treaty. Quite how unpopular these conditions were in Germany is clear from the fact that even the Weimar governments whose effeteness

The *Scharnhorst* was sunk off Norway's North Cape in 1943.

Hitler had so despised had made strenuous efforts to circumvent their spirit. A concerted effort had been made to maximize performance, so that relatively small vessels could 'punch above their weight'. Some dazzlingly imaginative innovations had been introduced, enhancing armour and engines, so that ships would be better armed than faster adversaries, and faster than better-armed ones.

The Anglo-German Naval Agreement of 1935 bowed to the inevitability of the Nazi's rearmament programme whilst at the same time trying to put limits on it. The agreement allowed Germany to increase the size of its navy as long as its total tonnage did not rise above 35 per cent of the Royal Navy's. This was reached by Britain without reference to its supposed French and Italian allies, which caused resentment at the time. In

hindsight, this seems of a piece with the appeasement policy of the years that followed.

A Rival to the Royal Navy

It certainly shows that, given an inch, Hitler was sure to take a mile. For it was now that he started considering a far more ambitious maritime masterplan. Formally decreed on 27 January 1937, Plan Z represented a decade-long programme of expansion. The new model Nazi navy would have far more than 35 per cent of the tonnage of the British fleet; if it didn't match it completely, ton for ton, that was because the *Führer* recognized that this was not achievable in the immediate term. His aim instead was to match the British not in absolute tonnage or numbers but

Admiral Dönitz's stock soared as commander of the U-boats. He became the *Führer*'s appointed successor.

in effectiveness, building himself a fleet of fast service-vessels and U-boats.

It was still going to be formidable by normal standards, comprising:

- four aircraft carriers, two of them displacing 33,500 tons;
- six battleships, of anything up to 110,000 tons;
- three battle cruisers (approximately 35,000 tons);
- 12 smaller 'P-class' cruisers and two other heavy cruisers;
- six light cruisers approximately 10,000 tons);
- six large destroyers.

In addition, the *Kriegsmarine* was going to have a large force of U-Boats (around 250 in all).

Safety in Numbers

The Germans went for quantity rather than for sheer size: the Royal Navy was still going to be far bigger, both in overall tonnage and average, ship-for-ship. This

If Germany is to gain a secure position as a world power, as the Führer wishes, then … it will require secure naval routes and communications and guaranteed access to the high seas.

German Naval report, 1938.

Right: In the fight for the *Führer's* attention, Admiral Raeder came a poor second to Göring and his *Luftwaffe*.

Below: Fanfare greeted the *Bismarck's* 1939 launch, but the battle to build the navy was already lost.

was a conscious decision: Britain's Navy was going to be a non-negotiable element in any conflict, and Germany's ships were going to have to run the gauntlet every time they ventured beyond the Baltic Sea. It made sense not to have too many maritime eggs in too few baskets – hence the decision to have more, if smaller, ships. There was also an appreciation that, as the smaller navy, the *Kriegsmarine* would be cast in the raider's role: speed and manoeuvrability were going to be more crucial than weight would be.

Losing Interest

So what happened? Plan Z wasn't cancelled as such, it was just all rather slow in getting started and, at the same time, rapidly overtaken by events. For all the

Führer's fighting talk, Germany didn't have the capacity to back it up with action: the country didn't have enough shipyards, and the ones it did have were not big or well-equipped enough. And then, once again, there was the problem of Hitler's attention-span: he had no understanding of or sympathy with the Navy. One warship seems to have been pretty much like another as far as he was concerned, and the (actually often brilliant) innovations his naval designers were introducing weren't exciting enough to hold his interest. Göring's *Luftwaffe* was consistently prioritized (in so far as the *Führer* could be consistent in anything); the capable but quietly spoken naval chief Grand Admiral Erich Raeder did not have the skill in handling Hitler that his air force rival did.

And then, of course, there was the fact that Hitler wasn't prepared to wait the 10 years originally allowed for the scheme to come to

fruition. Germany's all-new fleet hadn't been supposed to be ready until the end of 1945. And even that schedule was not being met: of the ships commissioned in 1935, not a single one was ready when hostilities started.

Making Do

The Germans did have three pre-Plan Z 'pocket battleships' (heavy cruisers): the *Admiral Graf Spee*, the *Admiral Scheer* and the *Deutschland*. They also had two other battlecruisers the *Gneisenau* and the *Scharnhorst*. Of the Plan Z package, two battleships – the *Bismarck* and *Tirpitz* – were approaching completion by 1939; the former was commissioned in 1940; the latter in 1941. Also well under way was the aircraft carrier the *Graf Zeppelin* – but, though launched in 1938, it was never to be completed.

Early Reverses

So the loss of the *Graf Spee* off Montevideo in 1939 loomed disproportionately large; as did losses off Norway. The *Kriegsmarine* found itself depleted at an early stage of the war.

   Germany's U-boats fared better, thanks in part to Admiral Karl Dönitz's genius, and to the Allies' tardiness in getting a workable convoy system going. Hitler quickly decided to tear up Plan Z, scrap those ships on their way to being completed and go all out to build up the U-boat fleet.

The *Graf Spee*'s loss in December 1939 was a serious setback in Germany's naval war.

High-Pressure Propulsion: the V-3

This super-weapon promised to be a beautifully deadly bit of engineering, but another engineer found a way to prevent its deployment.

A cannon is a simple device: a blast in the breech provides energy for a projectile that hurtles out of a cylindrical barrel, which determines its direction. But what if a sequence of explosions each added its extra impetus to the moving shell so that, by the time it left the barrel, it was travelling at a far faster speed? Such a system, suggested August Cönders, an engineer with Röchling Iron and Steel, would allow the construction of a 'supergun' that might easily have London within its range.

The V3 was to be placed at fortified sites near the Channel coast of France.

To the untrained eye, the V3 looked more like an oil installation than a weapon.

Jumping the Gun

The idea wasn't new: America's Azel S. Lyman and James Richard Haskell had designed a 'multicharge gun' in 1885. But the engineering required had been too far ahead of their time. To accommodate the necessary series of timed explosions, the barrel had to be too long to stand unsupported. Lyman and Haskell built an earthen ramp for their giant cannon, so that it looked more like a length of pipeline than a gun. The subsidiary charges were set in side-chambers at angles to the barrel so that the energy they produced was directed inward. The timing had to be

right to the tenth of a second to maximize the cumulative thrust.

That was the easy bit, however: the problem was containing the blast from the first discharge so that it didn't just race the projectile up the barrel and set the secondary charges off early. The whole sequence was supposed to be only a split-second long, and the margin of error infinitesimal. The American engineers were forced to admit defeat.

Hitler's High Pressure

Cönders felt confident he could solve these problems. His *Hochdruckpumpe*, or high-pressure pump (HDP), looked much like the Lyman-Haskell Multicharge Gun, except that solid-fuel rockets were used in the side-chambers. A reduced-scale prototype (20mm calibre) worked well. Hitler, enthused, called on Cönders to push ahead: he envisaged a line of 50 full-sized (100mm) guns pumping high-explosive shells at London. These were to be lined up in protected positions just inland of the Channel coast at Mimoyecques.

Unfortunately, Cönders' full-sized prototype at Magdeburg proved disappointing, so Hitler summoned Germany's leading armaments companies to help. They refined the dartlike 1.8m (6ft) shells, producing much more

encouraging results: several shells were lobbed over 88km (54 miles); one landed 93km (57 miles) away – though when a further shot was fired, the barrel burst, which was not so good.

Things were moving in the right direction, though: it was only a matter of time before Cönders' cannon was firing. In vain, the Allies now pounded the reinforced bunkers built at Mimoyecques by the Nazis.

The Pump Turned Off

A fellow engineer foiled him: Barnes 'Bouncing Bomb' Wallis. His 'Tallboy' was dropped by the same 617 Squadron that had used his Upkeep bombs against the Ruhr dams. Reaching supersonic speed before driving into the earth to a depth of 20m (65ft) and exploding, it was a match for the concrete bunkers of the Mimoyecques works. The V3 would have no safe home.

TRANSCRIPT OF KEY PARAGRAPHS

From: Spanish Minister, Angora
To: Minister for Foreign Affairs, Madrid

Mr Earle, the personal delegate of the President of the United States, tells me that he has received instructions to be ready to undertake a journey to Germany, without details as to the place or method of getting there. It is his wish to go to America for a thorough exchange of views.

He informed me that the anti-Russian party in the United States grows daily, and that the President himself bears in the mind the Soviet danger.

The informer, who a month in advance, told him (Earle) about the V.1. raids, now assures him that V.3, aimed at America, will come into operation before the of this month.

V2 Intercontinental

The V2 that so traumatized London might have done the same for New York and Washington had plans for a Nazi Intercontinental Ballistic Missile (ICBM) been fulfilled.

For a few terrifying months in 1944 and 1945, London was at the mercy of a wonder-weapon. Where the V1 had powered itself for its entire journey, the V2 was shot high into the air (up to 193km/120 miles high) before falling back to earth. Some 3000

were launched in total, from 9 September 1944; Paris, Brussels and Antwerp were also targeted.

Unlike the V1 'doodlebug', the V2 came without warning, as far as civilians on the ground were concerned; nothing was heard, since it descended at up to four times the speed of sound. On the other hand, given that it hit the ground at 4000km/h (2500mph), it had generally buried itself deep in the earth by the time its warhead detonated. The designers had not yet found a way to make

For [Wernher von Braun] and his team, this was not the development of a weapon but a step forward into the future of technology.

Albert Speer.

Plans for the Intercontinental V2 were well advanced. Several different shapes were tested in wind-tunnels.

The V2 very clearly anticipated the space rockets of the postwar era.

it explode in the air above the target. Even so, it killed thousands of people.

An Intercontinental Capacity
Yet how much more formidable it would be if it could be deployed against the United States. This would, of course, call for a far greater range than that of the A4 version currently in use. Theoretical discussions did take place about the possibility of mounting a V2 atop a massive booster rocket: this 'A10' might have had a range of more than 4000km (2500 miles). For the moment, though, this was just so much scientific chat. Far more practical at this stage was the proposal to launch from a submarine somewhere off America's east coast.

There was no insurmountable problem. Rather, the project

suffered from a lack of focus – easy as it is to make this point in hindsight. A rocket launcher on a U-boat's deck had been used successfully as early as 1942: rockets could be fired from the surface or up to 12m (40ft) beneath. But since the uses of this capacity weren't yet apparent – or, at least, did not justify the limitations set on the submarine's all-round performance – the

experiments weren't taken any further. Not till a year later were they revived with the advent of the V2. But the rocket itself was a distraction – and a drain; it was guzzling up available funding; little was left for the mundane business of launching technology.

Misfiring Missile
Operation Prufstand XII, as it was called, faced serious technical difficulties, moreover. There was no way that a rocket 14m (46ft) long and 1.65m (5ft 5in) in diameter could be carried inside a U-boat. Instead, it would have to be pulled behind in a watertight housing, unfuelled for safety; only once in position could it be mounted on its desktop launcher and loaded up with the ethanol, water and liquid oxygen which, when mixed, would provide the explosive thrust required for firing.

In the end, the V2 ran out of time. Though mobile launchers were developed to replace the static sites destroyed by the Allies, the project couldn't be sustained logistically as Germany's infrastructure collapsed in the last months of the war.

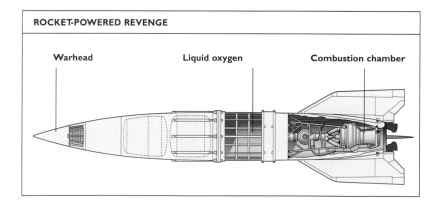

ROCKET-POWERED REVENGE

Warhead   Liquid oxygen   Combustion chamber

Chapter Five
1945

Few people now believed that Germany or Japan could prevent an Allied victory – unfortunately, they were in the German and Japanese high commands. As the war went on, its ferocity unabated, both sides prepared for a battle to the death.

As the war approached its end, all caution was thrown to the winds – and, indeed, all sanity, it sometimes seemed. For, while Hitler put the finishing touches to his plans for a Nazi Götterdämmerung, Churchill was apparently coming to believe that the World War had gone so well that he should start another one – with the Soviet Union – without delay.

On the ground, meanwhile, the Red Army was carving its relentless way through Eastern Europe, while the Western Allies were racing for the Rhine. In the wider Pacific, the war was largely won, despite last-ditch Japanese heroics on Iwo Jima and Okinawa. Plans were already taking shape for what promised to be a hellish struggle for the Japanese homeland. The inferno had come early for its people, in months of air raids, but bitter resistance was anticipated none the less. No one felt remotely upbeat about 'Operation Downfall'. First, however, an enormous and elaborately-organized logistical effort would be required.

A B-29 bomber unleashes a cluster of incendiary devices upon the waterfront of Kobe, Japan. Allied air supremacy was such by now that overwhelming pressure could be brought to bear – on the Axis war machine, on infrastructure and civilians.

Operation Unthinkable

'Unthinkable' it may have been, but Churchill had thought it through. His plan to roll over the Soviets was dismissed out of hand by the Chiefs of Staff.

'Poor Neville Chamberlain believed he could trust Hitler. He was wrong. But I don't think I'm wrong about Stalin.' Winston Churchill's comments after the Yalta Conference of February, 1945, are revealing – and not just for their early use of the Hitler–Stalin comparison. The greatest statesman of his age had – his greatest admirers would have admitted – an ego of equivalent stature. He'd been right about the Nazi threat – years before it had commonly recognized; he'd been right about the conduct of the war. He'd been right in his assessment of the mood of the British people and of how morale should be maintained. He was not accustomed to the role of being wrong.

Troubling Times

That he already suspected he might be is, of course, implicit in his remark: why else say it if he had no doubts? One thing is for certain: as the war tore towards its conclusion, Western leaders were already looking beyond, and coldly considering the conflict that was to come. They had never sought the Soviet Union as an ally; had indeed rejected Stalin's overtures during the 1930s; and

Might these victorious Allied troops have had it all to do again against the Soviets?

their co-operation had been uneasy – and often signally ill-tempered – when it came.

Already, before the war was won, the Western Allies were growing nervous about the strength of the Soviet presence in Eastern Europe. Red Army forces in the region were three times the size of the British and American forces in the West. And they gave the clear impression that they were there to stay.

Yada Yada Yalta

Convened as the war entered what promised to be its final phase, the Yalta Conference called Franklin D Roosevelt and Winston Churchill together to a Tsarist Summer palace on the Crimean coast. There, removed from all the

tumult and the stress of war, they could talk through their plans for the postwar settlement.

The victorious Allied powers (Britain, America, France and the Soviet Union) were to have their different zones of occupation in Germany as a whole and in Berlin. The Soviet leader also gave his commitment that, within 90 days of victory in Europe, his Far Eastern forces would move against the Japanese.

Crucial to the discussions were the destinies of the conquered countries. Free elections were to be held to consult the democratic will, it was agreed. Poland was more specifically considered. Stalin was anxious to expand its territory as a buffer against a potentially rejuvenated Germany. His forces

Joseph Stalin and Winston Churchill: behind the bluff smiles there was the deepest of suspicion.

had already established a pro-Soviet provisional government (the Polish Committee of National Liberation) at Lublin. It was vital, the Western Allies insisted, that this 'be reorganized on a broader democratic basis with the inclusion of democratic leaders from Poland and from Poles abroad'. To this end, 'free and unfettered elections' must be held.

Stalin agreed that these would be held 'as soon as possible', and the 'Big Three' leaders were able to pose for their concluding photos wreathed in smiles. However warm the words,

though, the actual commitments made were few and had been vaguely formulated: a great deal was now going to depend on Soviet goodwill.

TOP SECRET

OFFICE OF THE MINISTER OF DEFENCE

PRIME MINISTER

In the attached report on Operation 'UNTHINKABLE', the Chiefs of Staff have set out the bare facts, which they can elaborate in discussion with you, if you so desire. They felt that the less was put on paper on this subject the better.

H. L. Ismay

8th June, 1945

In a letter to the Prime Minister regarding Operation Unthinkable, General Ismay suggests that 'the less was put on paper on this subject the better'.

From Iron Heel to Iron Curtain

'That Churchill is capable of anything,' Stalin complained to Marshall Zhukov – though whether even the Red Tsar in his paranoia could have guessed what was in the British Prime Minister's mind must be in doubt. What little trust Churchill had placed in him at the time of Yalta ebbed quickly in the following weeks. The Red Army was camped out in Eastern Europe, with all the appearance of an immovable force – and none of the appearance of a democratizing one.

'Terrible things have happened,' Churchill told his Foreign Secretary, Anthony Eden, in April 1945, in a private letter which at the same time had the ringing rhetoric of a public speech:

A tide of Russian domination is sweeping forward … After it is over, the territories under Russian

Final

22nd May, 1945.

WAR CABINET

JOINT PLANNING STAFF

OPERATION "UNTHINKABLE"

Report by the Joint Planning Staff.

We have examined Operation UNTHINKABLE. As instructed, we have taken the following assumptions on whi[ch] to base our examination:-

(a) The undertaking has the full support of public opinion in both the British Empire and the United States and consequently, the morale of British and American troops continues high.

(b) Great Britain and the United States have full assistance from the Polish armed forces and can count upon the use of German manpower and what remains of German industrial capacity.

(c) No credit is taken for assistance from the forces of other Western Powers, although any bases in their territory, or other facilities which may be required, are made available.

(d) Russia allies herself with Japan.

(e) The date for the opening of hostilities is 1st July, 1945.

(f) Redeployment and release schemes continue till 1st July and then stop.

Owing to the special need for secrecy, the normal staffs [of] Service Ministries have not been consulted.

OBJECT

2.   The overall or political object is to impose upon Russia the will of the United States and British Empire.

Even though "the will" of these two countries may b[e] defined as no more than a square deal for Poland, that does not necessarily limit the military commitment. A quick success might induce the Russians to submit to our will at least for the time being; but it might not. That is for the Russians to decide. If they want total war, they are in a position to have it.

-1-

TRANSCRIPT OF KEY PARAGRAPHS

Report by the Joint Planning Staff.

We have examined Operation Unthinkable. As instructed, we have taken the following assumption on what to base our examination:-

(a) The undertaking has the full support of public opinion in both the British Empire and the United States and consequently, the morale of British and American troops continues high.

(d) The date for the opening of hostilities is 1st July, 1945

Object: The overall or political object is to impose upon Russia the will of the United States and British Empire.

Even though "the will" of these two countries may be defined as no more than a square deal for Poland, that does not necessarily limit the military commitment. A quick success might induce the Russians to submit to our will at least for the time being; but it might not. That is for the Russians to decide. If they want total war, they are in a position to have it.

The Red Army was surging westward at an alarming rate.

control will include the Baltic provinces, all of eastern Germany, all Czechoslovakia, a large part of Austria, the whole of Yugoslavia, Hungary, Romania and Bulgaria. This constitutes one of the most melancholy events in the history of Europe, and one to which there is no parallel.

The speech in which he coined the phrase the 'Iron Curtain' was still almost a year away, but the thinking behind it was already in place – as, in fairness, was the Soviet domination it described.

But Churchill had a further fear: that, rather than helping Britain and the United States to sort out Japan, the Soviets would make an alliance with the Japanese against the West. A victory that now appeared inevitable might quickly crumble if Britain and America found themselves with a fight on these

two fronts. Not content to wring his hands or simply sit and wait till this disaster happened, Churchill asked the British Armed Forces' Joint Planning Staff to come up with a plan.

All to Do Again

The language of government documents tends to err on the side of austerity and understatement. No one could say that about the paper which was put before Churchill's War Cabinet on 22 May 1945. The great British public had barely had the chance to shake off its V.E. Day hangover and the government was being asked to respond to a report entitled 'Russia: Threat to Western Civilization'. The Chiefs' aim, they said, had been to draw up a feasible plan 'to impose upon Russia the will of the United States and the British Empire':

Even though 'the will' of these two countries may be defined as no more than a square deal for Poland, that does not necessarily limit the military commitment. A quick success might induce the Russians to submit to our will at least for the time being; but it might not. That is for the Russians to decide. If they want total war, they are in a position to have it.

That was just it, of course. For all the fighting talk, the Soviets really were in a position to have a total war, with an overwhelming presence on the ground in Europe.

New-Found Friends

Churchill had an answer to that: 100,000 Poles already fighting for the Western Allies would gladly give their all to defend their homeland. Especially because the Soviets were rounding up those who'd resisted the Germans and shipping them eastward – to an uncertain fate. In addition, Churchill insouciantly said, there were those hundreds of thousands of German soldiers whose surrender his forces had just taken. They'd be happy to have another crack at the Soviets, he reasoned. He'd already ordered Field Marshal Montgomery to take special care to keep their captured weapons and ammunition safe so that they could be restored to them if needed with immediate effect.

Not surprisingly, perhaps, the Joint Planning Staff were unconvinced that British Tommies – exhausted as they were – would be willing to stand shoulder-to-shoulder with the *Wehrmacht* in an entirely new chapter of the war. It wasn't that they trusted the Soviets; Churchill's gloomy view was being borne out only too demonstrably, week by week. But there really didn't seem to be anything the West could do.

Ismay has a word in Churchill's ear at the Cairo Conference, 1943.

G. R.

TOP SECRET

DRAFT

<u>GENERAL ISMAY</u>
<u>C.O.S. COMMITTEE</u>

I have read the Chiefs of Staff note on "UNTHINKABLE"
dated 8th June, which shows Russian preponderance of 2-1 on
land.

2.   If the Americans withdraw to their zone and move the
bulk of their forces back to the United States and to the
Pacific, the Russians have the power to advance to the North
Sea and the Atlantic. Pray have a study made of how then we
could defend our Island, assuming that France and the Low
Countries were powerless to resist the Russian advance to the
sea. What Naval forces should we need and where would they
be based? What would be the strength of the Army required,
and how should it be disposed? How much Air Force would be
needed and where would the main air-fields be located?
Possession of airfields in Denmark would give us great
advantage and keep open the sea passage to the Baltic where
the Navy could operate. The possession of bridgeheads in
the Low Countries or France should also be considered.

3.   By retaining the codeword "UNTHINKABLE" the Staffs
will realise that this remains a precautionary study of what,
I hope, is still a ~~highly improbable event~~.
                    purer hypothetical contingency.

Aktion 24

Like a cornered rat, Germany was determined to go down fighting – only desperation can explain the concept behind Aktion 24.

In the dying weeks of the war, the mood of Germany's defenders passed from resolute to frantic. They would fight with everything they had to keep back the Soviets. Their country's honour was at stake. But it wasn't just that which gave them a jolt of adrenaline to enable them to crank up a now-decrepit military machine another gear. The Germans knew all too well the swathe of atrocity they had cut through western Russia in the

course of their invasion – and they knew all too well the revenge the Red Army was exacting even now in eastern Prussia.

A Desperate Plight
Rape, torture and indiscriminate killing was the order of the day. The figures tell the story: 33 per cent of the German soldiers killed in the war lost their lives in the last four and a half months: 450,000 in January, 1945; 295,000 in February; 284,000 in March and 281,000 in April. Some two million women were raped – many repeatedly. The German psyche as a whole was being violated.

This background has to be

Soviet troops cross a German bridge: the Nazis were quite desperate to stop the Reds' advance.

borne in mind when the plan for Aktion 24 comes to be considered because otherwise it simply makes no sense. In ordinary circumstances – even the ordinary circumstances of a country in the throes of a total war – it's hard to see how the Germans could ever have thought of carrying out the action.

A Suicidal Strategy
The strategic thinking behind the plan was rational enough: the railway bridges at Thorn, Warsaw, Deblin and Dunjawec would be needed by the Red Army to bring

in supplies to support their advance on Berlin. These crossings had to be cut at any cost.

Briefly, the idea was that specially adapted Dornier Do 24 flying boats would be loaded up with explosives and crash-dived into key bridges over the River Weichsel (Vistula). Four planes were actually taken in to the workshops to be refitted for this mission. The Do 24 was favoured because of its carrying capacity: huge amounts of high explosive could be crammed on board.

Fall Guys

To this extent, Aktion 24 could be seen as a Japanese-style *kamikaze* operation, but there was a twist to the German version as envisaged here. Skilled pilots were beyond price in the current situation: even

for so important an aim, no single one could be spared – let alone four. Instead, the decision was taken that experienced fliers would take the planes to the attack zones and land them safely some way upstream, before climbing into rubber dinghies and rowing to the shore. (How they were to make it home in territory already swarming with Soviet troops was never explained.)

The planes would then be left in the hands of special *Sebstopfer* (self-sacrificing) pilots who had learned just enough to take off and fly into the piers of the bridges. Whether the Soviets would have let any of the planes get that far must again be doubted. It didn't matter: the customized planes were destroyed in air raids before any attacks could be carried out.

Facing reality was ten times worse than just hearing about it. Throughout the night, we huddled together in mortal fear.

Dorothea von Schwanenfluegel recalls the Soviet advance of 1945.

The Germans were ready to write off their remaining Do 24s in suicidal last-ditch actions.

National Redoubt

Documents recently released by the British authorities reveal the consternation felt at an apparent Nazi resolve to make a heroic last stand at a secret Alpine stronghold.

By the end of 1944, the writing was on the wall for Germany's war of conquest, for Adolf Hitler and his Nazi project. Caught between the rock of the Western Allies' advance and the even-harder place of the Red Army's rampage, the only thing left to do was to go down fighting. If there was little appetite on the Western side for a negotiated peace, there was on the part of the Soviet Union no desire for anything but revenge. Millions had died; many more millions of Soviet citizens had suffered in what had been not just an anti-communist crusade but an anti-Slavic race war.

For ordinary Germans, the outlook was dismal: once the spree of rape and casual killing was over, they had years of subjection, hardship and humiliation ahead. For their Nazi rulers, though, the future promised public humiliation; torture; endless imprisonment or death; slave labour in Siberia ignominy – and that was it. With nothing to hope for by surrender and nothing to lose by standing and fighting to the last, a crazy resolve to resist to the death made perfect sense.

Going Down Fighting

The outlook for the Allies could hardly have been more different: from their point of view, the war

Slow to acknowledge the reality of defeat, Hitler was determined to go down fighting.

was all but won. And today we know it was – which gives their victory an aura of inevitability. At the time, they certainly didn't see things that way. Instead, they were haunted by the possibility that, holding triumph in their hands, they might let it go.

Hence the fear that the Nazis were preparing to hole up in an Alpine redoubt, from which they would sally forth to conduct an ongoing guerrilla war. With a complex of fortifications, camps, caves and underground workings

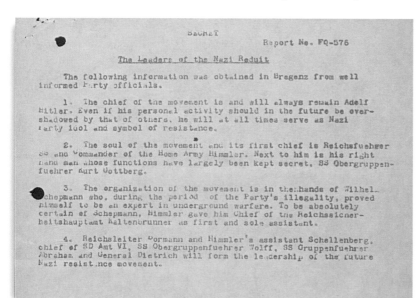

The importance of Adolf Hitler was summarized in this report:
'1. The chief of movement is and will always remain Adolf Hitler. Even if his personal activity in the future be over-shadowed by that of others, he will at all times serve as Nazi Party idol and symbol of resistance.'

TRANSCRIPT OF KEY PARAGRAPHS

Country: Germay/Austria
Subject: Evacuation movement of Bavarian localities.
Date of Report: 28 March 1945
Source: Cezanne/French Intelligence
Place of Origin Switzerland

1. Thousands of Nazi party officials have recently arrived in the Bavarian localities of Tölz, Fresing and Landshut. They come from the east, west and north of Germany. It is probably, in Source's opinion, that these localities will become important Party centers in case the Party withdraws in Alpine "redoubt".

2. At the same time considerable quantities of foods have been transported from Northern Italy through the Brenner pass to Tölz, as well as to Villach through Lienz and Spittal, in Austria.

3. Railway repair workshops are being moved from Steinsmanger (Hungary) to Ling-Steyr and Innsbruck (Austria).

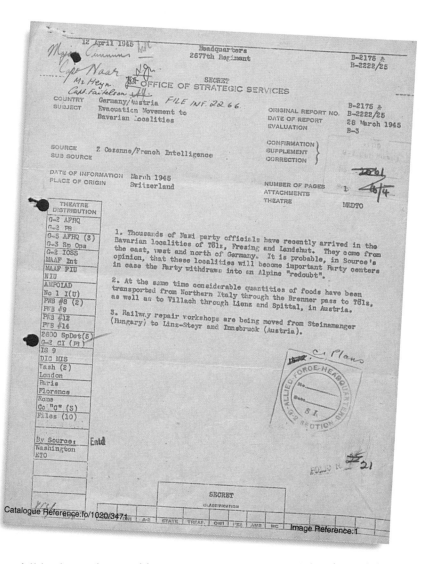

Catalogue Reference:fo/1020/3471   Image Reference:1

to fall back on, they could conduct a campaign of terror in occupied Germany and beyond. The Alps was a natural fortress – one aspect that had appealed to Hitler when he had his holiday residence built up here at the Berghof, at Obersalzberg, outside Berchtesgaden. While no one thought the Nazis could directly take on and defeat the Allies from such a stronghold, they could coordinate fierce resistance for years to come. A briefing of the Office of Strategic Services (OSS), circulated on 15 March 1945, is clear in its assumption that resolute resistance would be continued from a redoubt.

Redoubtable Rhetoric

The philosophy, familiar from that of the Swiss, had been hinted at in the defiant speeches of several Nazi leaders, not least the propaganda minister Joseph

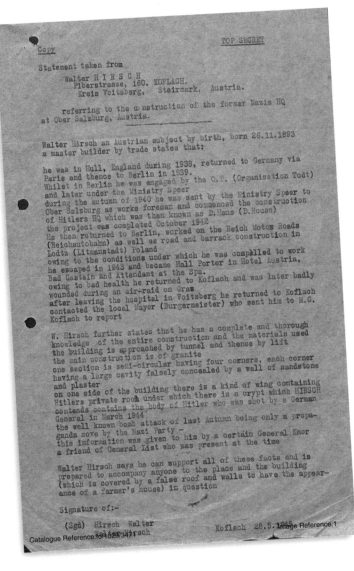

Copy   TOP SECRET

Statement taken from
      Walter H I R S C H.
      Piberstrasse, 160. KOFLACH.
      Kreis Voitsberg,   Steirmark,   Austria.

      referring to the construction of the former Nazis HQ
at Ober Salzburg, Austria.
      ─────────────────

Walter Hirsch an Austrian subject by birth, born 26.11.1893
a master builder by trade states that:

he was in Hull, England during 1938, returned to Germany via
Paris and thence to Berlin in 1939.
Whilst in Berlin he was engaged by the O.T. (Organisation Todt)
and later under the Ministry Speer
during the autumn of 1940 he was sent by the Ministry Speer to
Ober Salzburg as works foreman and commenced the construction
of Hitlers HQ which was then known as D.Haus (D.House)
the project was completed October 1942
He then returned to Berlin, worked on the Reich Motor Roads
(Reichsautobahn) as well as road and barrack construction in
Lodtz (Litzmanstadt) Poland
owing to the conditions under which he was compelled to work
he escaped in 1943 and became Hall Porter in Hotel Austria,
Bad Gastein and Attendant at the Spa.
owing to bad health he returned to Koflach and was later badly
wounded during an air-raid on Graz
after leaving the hospital in Voitsberg he returned to Koflach
contacted the local Mayor (Burgermeister) who sent him to M.G.
Koflach to report

W. Hirsch further states that he has a complete and thorough
knowledge of the entire construction and the materials used
the building is approached by tunnel and thence by lift
the main construction is of granite
one section is semi-circular having four corners, each corner
having a large cavity falsely concealed by a wall of sandstone
and plaster
on one side of the building there is a kind of wing containing
Hitlers private room under which there is a crypt which HIRSCH
contends contains the body of Hitler who was shot by a German
General in March 1944
the well known bomb attack of last Autumn being only a propaganda move by the Nazi Party
this information was given to him by a certain General Knor
a friend of General List who was present at the time

Walter Hirsch says he can support all of these facts and is
prepared to accompany anyone to the place and the building
(which is covered by a false roof and walls to have the appearance of a farmer's house) in question

Signature of:-

   (Sgd) Hirsch Walter
Catalogue Reference:WO/208/3471   Koflach 28.5.1945 Image Reference:1

Goebbels. Far from preparing the way for a rational capitulation, the language of the Nazis was getting more intemperate. 'Rarely in history has a brave people struggling for its life faced such terrible tests …', wrote Goebbels:

We are bearing a heavy fate because we are fighting for a good cause, and are called to bravely endure the battle to achieve greatness.

Was this more than rousing rhetoric, cynically deployed? The Allies were not disposed to take any chances. The 15 March report does seem surprisingly vague and general in its terms. Hitler was Nazi's 'idol', it informs the reader; he 'is and will always remain' the movement's leader; Himmler, meanwhile, was the movement's 'soul'. A sceptic might say that the writer of the report was in danger

TRANSCRIPT OF KEY PARAGRAPHS

Statement taken from Walther Hirsch, Austria referring to the construction of the former Nazis HQ at Ober Salzburg Austria.

Walter Hirsch an Austrian subject by birth, born 26.11.1893 a master builder by trade states that:

during the autumn of 1940 he was sent by the Ministry Speer to Ober Salzburg as works foreman and commenced the construction of Hitler's HQ which was then known as D.Haus.
The project was completed October 1942
W. Hirsh further states that he has a complete and thorough knowledge of the entire construction and the materials used. The building is approached by tunnel and thence by lift.
… on one side of the building there is a kind of wing containing Hitler's private room under which there is a crypt which Hirsch contends contains the body of Hitler who was shot by a German General in March 1944.
Hirsh says he can support all of these facts and is prepared to accompany anyone to the place.

of listening too uncritically to the Nazis' mood-music. Rightly or wrongly, though, Allied Intelligence believed that the Nazis continued to believe. There may have been a fair few fellow-travellers and opportunists in years gone by, but to a surviving hard-core they attributed a certain evil integrity.

Hard Evidence?

And the OSS were not basing their ideas on big-talking bravado alone. Another report of 28 March describes what is said to be an observed influx of personnel and supplies into Alpine Bavaria. And, in successive reports (they come thick and fast from this point on) the evidence accumulates.

Accuracy is hard to come by, of course: one report, dated 27 April, suggests that sufficient provisions have been laid in to keep 25,000 men for a year; another – dated three weeks earlier – claims that there are enough supplies to sustain anything up to 60,000 men for two full years.

By now, Allied intelligence agencies had established an impressive presence on the ground in the general area and also conducted meticulous surveys from the air. A lengthy report compiled from photographic evidence goes through the Alpine region with a fine-toothed comb, identifying abandoned quarries and cave-complexes that showed signs of recent activity and which may have been developed along with more obvious construction work. Sixty-nine different sites

are recorded in the Austrian Alps alone. Wire-fenced camps with four, six, 35 huts; six-storey buildings; other items such as small sheds, or even piles of 'stores in open', are listed, as is any sign of roadbuilding, earth-moving or excavation – even 'spoil and tracks'.

Redoubt Doubts

Such detail is persuasive – until one reflects upon the inherent improbability of there being any significant area of Germany or Austria that didn't have groups of huts or construction work in progress. Some historians have suggested that such work as there was on this 'National Redoubt' was no more than an elaborate decoy, designed to distract the West from the preparations the leadership was making to hold onto Berlin.

This sort of speculation would seem to be trumped by the evidence supplied to the Allies by

Walter Hirsch in late May 1945. A master-builder, Hirsch claimed that he had actually helped to build a bunker complex at Obersalzberg. Does the fact that his (admirably specific) testimony includes the insistence that Hitler's body had been placed in a crypt beneath his private room in the complex – and had done since his assassination by a German general in 1944 – add credence to his claims or take it away? The more 'evidence' we have, it seems, the harder it is to know whether the 'National Redoubt' was an unfulfilled operation for a last-ditch defence of Germany or a successful (but still unavailing) decoy plan.

The Alpine landscape was effectively inventorized by Allied intelligence. Everything down to small sheds and piles of stores was recorded. Despite such 'evidence', many historians doubt whether the Redoubt was ever for real; some even suggest that it was a deliberate deception on the Germans' part.

ITEM NO.	GSGS 4416 SHEET NO. & MAP REF.	ITEM	LOCATION	DESCRIPTION	NEW SINCE	PHOTOS
						CONFIDENTIAL
Sheet Z-4						
16	Z-4/414507	Probable storage.	LEVIS.	2 large store sheds beside railway.	15 Feb 45	S460/1060 5413-4 13 Mar 45
17	Z-4/415509	Probable storage.	LEVIS.	Store shed 340 x 100 ft approx.	15 Feb 45	S460/1060 5412-3 13 Mar 45
18	Z-4/418512	M.T. Depot.	FELDKIRCH.	One medium, one small shed.	9 Apr 45	S460/1140 3386-7 15 Apr 45
19	Z-4/445707	Hutted camp.	South-eastern INNSBRUCK.	7 medium huts.	2 Apr 45	S460/1140 4243-4 15 Apr 45
20	Z-4/445716	Probable storage.	INNSBRUCK.	1 large camouflaged building.	2 Apr 45	S460/1140 4242-3 15 Apr 45
21	Z-4/451551	Hutted camp.	ROSENHELL.	2 medium, 3 small huts.	2 Apr 45	S460/1140 3404-5 15 Apr 45
22	Z-4/467593	Hutted camp.	Northern limits of FRAXERN.	8 medium huts.	++	682/1059 4288-9 2 Apr 45
23	Z-4/492769	Hutted camp under construction.	North-western LAUTERACH.	6 medium hut foundations, 1 small.	2 Apr 45	S460/1140 4159-61 15 Apr 45
24	Z-4/515696	Probable workers' camp.	DORNBIRN.	12 small one-storeyed buildings.	2 Apr 45	S460/1140 3093-4 15 Apr 45

● Initial cover, but activity indicates recent construction.

que Reference:fo/1020/3471   Image Reference:1

Operation Downfall

Only the advent of the atom bomb prevented the execution of an invasion plan that would have brought about the climactic battle of the war.

Everyone knows how World War II ended: the dropping of the bombs at Hiroshima and Nagasaki marked the inauguration of the Nuclear Age. It's easy to forget how fortunate it was (though 'opportune' might be a better word) that the Manhattan Project paid off so spectacularly when it did. The war might well have turned out otherwise.

Indeed, as far as the commanders in the field (and even senior staff) were concerned, this was going to be a conventional struggle to the bitter end. It wasn't just that, for secrecy's stake, they had to go through the motions of making plans without reference to the power of the atom bomb. So secret was this project that it wasn't revealed even to top commanders: the atom bomb didn't exist, as far as they were aware. So when they prepared their plans for the final fight against Japan, they did so in grim earnest: this really was the way it was going to be, they thought.

Under Siege
There was no doubt now that the tide had at long last turned and

Japan's wood-built cities – including Toyko above were all but razed by terrifying firestorms.

was now running in the Allies' favour, but they were a long and bloody way from victory – that much was clear. The Japanese could not be expected to give an inch. They would not just be fighting for their lives now but for their wives and families – and for a homeland they held sacred. The Allies' objective had to be to create so much disruption that – regardless of courage or desperation – resistance in the field could not be sustained.

Sporadic air-raids had been launched against Japan throughout the war but, in the second half of 1944, a sustained campaign of bombing had begun. This gathered momentum as the Americans gained new bases in the recaptured Pacific Islands and by the beginning of 1945, Japan was under siege.

The attack came from the sea as well as from the air: Operation Starvation got under way in March. The plan, though ambitious, was simple in its logic. Japan's coastal waters were to be so heavily mined that the country would be cut off from the sea. If the codename didn't beat about the bush, neither did Admiral Chester Nimitz, Commander in Chief of America's Pacific Fleet and overall Commander of Allied Forces in the Pacific. More than 12,000 mines were laid – some by submarines, but most dropped from 160 specially adapted B-29 Superfortresses.

Unspectacular, discreet – and inevitably overshadowed by subsequent events – the operation was one of the great unsung

successes of the war. In all, some 670 ships were sunk or damaged – more than 1,250,000 tons. Traffic in most of the main shipping lanes had to be suspended; Japan's ports were left unusable. It had been one of the unsung successes of the war.

Firestorm

The Superfortresses were busy bombing too: by now, such havoc had been played with Japanese air-defences that they could ply back and forth from airfields in the Pacific Islands during daylight hours and at low altitude by darkness. The Japanese joked grimly that these raids were as regular as the mail. This, General LeMay appreciated, had become a campaign against national morale, which meant that – like it or not – it was a campaign against civilians. Japan's rugged, thickly forested interior was relatively inhospitable. Its people had

Fleet Admiral Nimitz would have played a central role had Operation Downfall gone ahead.

Killing Japanese didn't bother me very much at that time. It was getting the war over that bothered me.

Curtis Le May, recalling his feelings about the firebombing of Japan.

COUNTDOWN TO DEFEAT

20 October 1944 US troops land in Philippines.

23–26 October Naval Battle of Leyte, Philippines. Japanese use *kamikaze* tactics for the first – but are still defeated.

22 January 1945 Allies reopen 'Burma Road', allowing supplies to reach Kuomintang in China.

9–10 February Tokyo Firestorm – caused by US bombing – kills 100,000 and makes a million homeless.

19 February American forces land on Iwo Jima.

26 March First US troops land on Okinawa; main body follow on 1 April.

29 May Great Yokohama Air Raid – 30 per cent of the city destroyed (and 8000 killed).

21 June Okinawa captured.

16 July 'Trinity' – first ever nuclear test conducted successfully at Alamogordo, New Mexico.

6 August – 'Little Boy' explodes over Hiroshima.

9 August – 'Fat Man' falls on Nagasaki.

15 August – Emperor Hirohito offers Japan's capitulation. General MacArthur will take his formal surrender on 27 September.

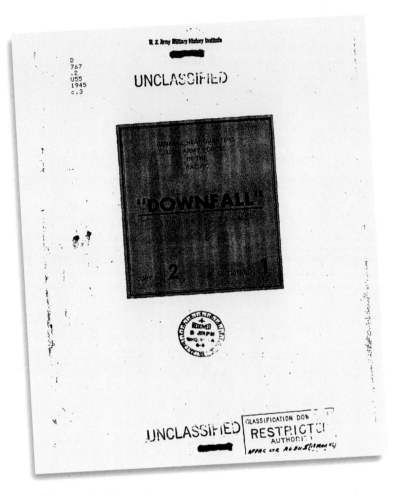

The front cover of the highly extensive Strategic Plan for Operation Downfall, the proposed Allied invasion plan.

historically crowded into urban centres along the coasts. These were predominantly timber-built: fire had always been a problem; why not make it the main instrument of his attack? The destructive potential of the firestorm had already been established in Hamburg, in 1943. LeMay resolved to make it happen here.

Time to Commit

However brutal the softening up, the Allies were going to have to commit themselves at some point to an invasion and occupation of Japan if the war were ever to be brought to a conclusion. What promised to be the greatest amphibious operation ever was devised. The plans for Downfall were first – and somewhat tentatively – proposed at the beginning of February 1945, at the so-called Argonaut Conference of the Combined Chiefs of Staff in Malta. They were set in motion at a meeting of 25 May. As President of only a few weeks' standing, Harry S Truman was present with the Joint Chiefs of Staff, and on the agenda was the invasion of Japan.

For the first time, this didn't seem premature. The battle of Okinawa, despite having taken two months already, and with several weeks of fighting and heavy casualties still to come, was clearly drawing to its close. The tide had defintely turned: the Japanese were fighting furiously, but with the heroism of despair rather than the confident courage of before. Once the Americans had made themselves masters of Okinawa, and the rest of the Ryukyu island group, Japan would be left without its last Pacific outpost. 'All' that remained would be the fight for the home islands.

Accordingly, it was agreed that an invasion force be led by General Douglas MacArthur, CINCAFPAC (Commander in Chief Army Forces Pacific) with support provided by Admiral Nimitz CINCPAC (Commander in Chief, Pacific Fleet).

In a Nutshell
General Douglas MacArthur, the man entrusted with the task of executing the operation, summed up the situation – and the logic behind Downfall – succinctly:

Troops would have mustered in the Marianas, the Philippines and Hawaii, for the last great push against the Japanese homeland. Operation Downfall would have involved a million men.

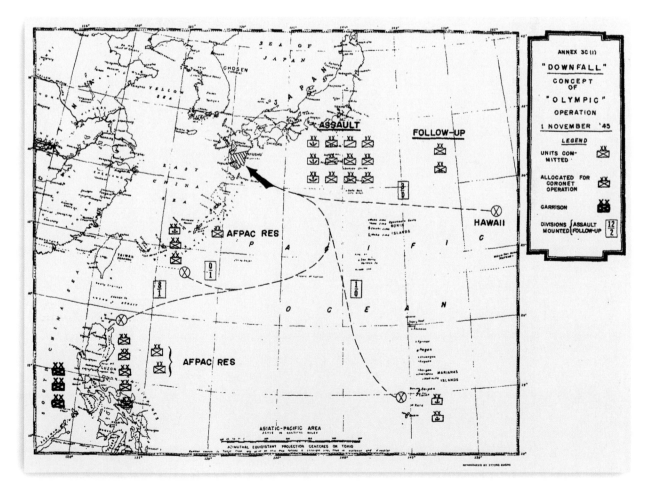

The Japanese fleet has been reduced to practical impotency. The Japanese air force has been reduced to a line of action which involves unco-ordinated, suicidal attacks against our forces, employing all types of planes, including trainers. Its attrition is heavy and its power for sustained action is diminishing rapidly. Those conditions will be accentuated after the establishment of our air forces in the Ryukyus. With the increase in the tempo of very long range attacks, the enemy's ability to provide replacement planes will diminish and the Japanese potentiality will decline at an increasing rate. It is believed that the development of air bases in the Ryukyus will, in conjunction with carrier-based planes, give us sufficient air power to support landings on Kyushu and that the establishment of our air forces there will ensure complete air supremacy over Honshu.

An Invasion Plan

Japan is an archipelago, of course, with Kyushu its southernmost island and the Ryukyu Islands extending in a chain to the south. The Allied plan would carry to its conclusion the 'island-hopping' strategy followed till now, using the Ryukyu group as the jumping-off point for the final assault.

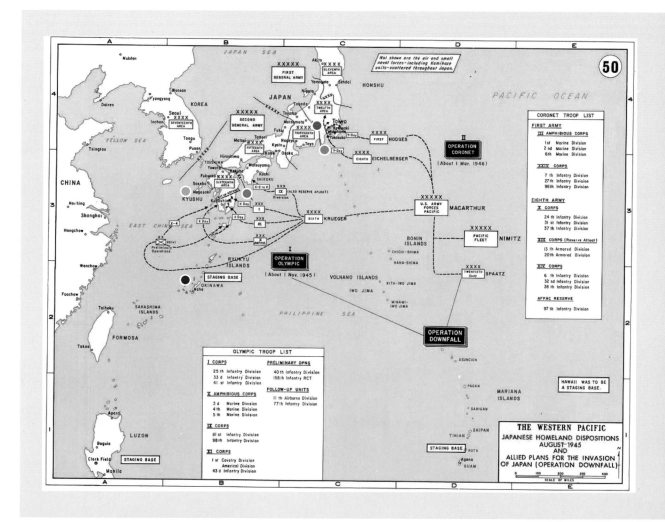

Scheduled to begin on 1 November, Operation Olympic was to come at Kyushu from the south, securing a base from which air and sea attacks on main population centres could be maintained and intensified. If this failed to bring about complete surrender, a second phase, Operation Coronet, would follow. Beginning on 1 March 1946, this would involve a large-scale direct attack on Honshu's central Kanto

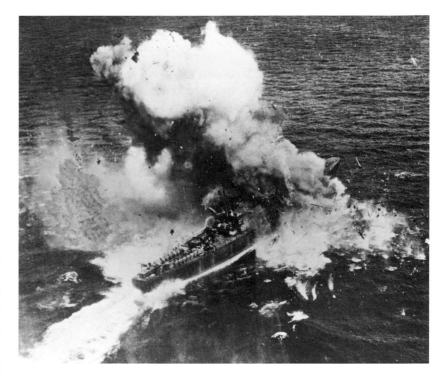

Firmly on the offensive now, the Allies were destroying the Imperial Japanese Navy ship by ship.

IN FOR THE KILL

One last 'hop' was to take American airborne and infantry forces from the Ryukyu Islands to Kyushu, while the Pacific Fleet fanned out around the southerly island to land Marines, bring in supplies and lend support. The focus was to move further north for Coronet four months later.

KEY

- 🔴 **Ryukyu Islands**
- ⚪ **Kyushu**
- 🔵 **Limit of bridgehead**
- ⚪ **Tokyo Bay**
- 🔴 **Kanto Plain**

Plain, including Tokyo. There were tactical reasons for the two-phase plan, but the principal concern was logistical.

Though the war in Europe was expected to have been over for some weeks by the time Olympic was launched, there was much work still to be done. And the challenges of shipping so many troops and so much equipment all the way to the Far East meant that it would be well into 1946 before serious reinforcements could be made available.

The Perfect Base

The most southerly of Japan's main islands, Kyushu might have been designed to favour the Allies: it had open bays and natural harbours – perfect for the initial landing, and as anchorages for warships in the campaign to come. Protected by hills to the north, it had wide open plains where airfields could be quickly built: the Americans envisaged bringing in no fewer than 3000 planes. Of course, Kyushu wasn't an empty landscape awaiting occupation. On the contrary, it was strongly fortified. The Americans knew from intelligence intercepts that the Japanese suspected they would take this line of attack and were consequently moving in troops and improving fortifications.

A Staggering Scale

Southern Kyushu was first to be softened up with attacks by planes from carriers offshore and from airfields on recaptured islands like Guam, Tinian and Saipan (Marianas) and from offshore islands of the Japanese archipelago like Okinawa. The amphibious attack itself would be backed by 1900 planes from no fewer than 32 US and British carriers off the coast; 2700 further planes would make runs in from Okinawa. Three or four different landing sites would be chosen to provide a multi-pronged offensive: 14 divisions (more than 400,000 troops) were to be involved. Some 1300 transport ships and landing-craft were going to be required.

An enormous undertaking, then. By comparison, the previous year's Normandy landings had involved five Allied divisions and a further three airborne. Coronet was going to require 25 further divisions –

020

~~RESTRICTED~~   UNCLASSIFIED

GENERAL HEADQUARTERS
UNITED STATES ARMY FORCES IN THE PACIFIC

"DOWNFALL"

Strategic Plan

for

Operations in the Japanese Archipelago

28 May 1945

1. The attached Strategic Plan constitutes the basis for directives for operations to force the unconditional surrender of JAPAN by seizure of vital objectives in the Japanese Archipelago.

2. Pending the issue of directives based thereon, the Plan is circulated to senior Commanders and Staff Sections of United States Army Forces in the Pacific and to the Commander-in-Chief, United States Pacific Fleet, as a general guide covering the larger phases of allocation of means and of coordination in order to facilitate planning and implementation, both operational and logistic. It is not designed to restrict executing agencies in detailed development of their final plans of operations.

3. The Plan is being forwarded to the Commanding General, Twentieth Air Force, for his information and guidance.

4. Directives and Staff Studies covering the several operations to be conducted will be issued by Headquarters concerned at appropriate times.

For the Commander-in-Chief:

R. K. SUTHERLAND
Lieutenant General, United States Army,
Chief of Staff.

UNCLASSIFIED

~~RESTRICTED~~

TRANSCRIPT OF KEY PARAGRAPHS

Left:
1. The attached strategic Plan constitutes the basis for directives for operations to force the unconditional surrender of Japan by seizure of vital objectives in the Japanese Archipelago.

Right:
This plan is formulated to directives contained in JCS 1259/4 3 April 1945 and JCS radiogram WX, 26 May 1945. It covers operations of United States Army and Naval Forces in the Pacific to force the unconditional surrender of Japan by invasion of the Japanese Archipelago
The following over-all objective for the operations is assigned by the Joint Chiefs of Staff:

"To force the unconditional surrender of Japan by:
(1) Lowering Japanese ability and will to resist by establishing sea and air blockades, conducting intensive air bombardments and destroying Japanese air and naval strength.
(2) Invading and seizing objectives in the industrial heart of Japan.

GENERAL HEADQUARTERS
UNITED STATES ARMY FORCES IN THE PACIFIC

"DOWNFALL"

Strategic Plan

for

Operations in the Japanese Archipelago

28 May. 1945

1. *DIRECTIVE.*

a. This Plan is formulated pursuant to directives contained in JCS 1259/4, 3 April 1945 and JCS radiogram WX 87938, 26 May 1945. It covers operations of United States Army and Naval Forces in the PACIFIC to force the unconditional surrender of JAPAN by invasion of the Japanese Archipelago.

b. The following over-all objective for the operations is assigned by the Joint Chiefs of Staff:

"To force the unconditional surrender of JAPAN by:

(1) Lowering Japanese ability and will to resist by establishing sea and air blockades, conducting intensive air bombardments and destroying Japanese air and naval strength.

(2) Invading and seizing objectives in the industrial heart of JAPAN."

c. The following basic command relationships are established by the Joint Chiefs of Staff:

(1) Command of all United States Army resources in the PACIFIC (less the Twentieth Air Force, Alaskan Department and Southeast Pacific) is vested in the Commander-in-Chief, United States Army Forces in the Pacific.

(2) Command of all United States Naval resources in the PACIFIC (less Southeast Pacific) is vested in the Commander-in-Chief, United States Pacific Fleet.

(3) The Twentieth Air Force, for the present, continues operations under the direct control of the Joint Chiefs of Staff to support the accomplishment of the over-all objective.

(4) The Commander-in-Chief, United States Army Forces in the Pacific is charged with making plans and preparations for the campaign in JAPAN. He cooperates with the Commander-in-Chief, United States Pacific Fleet in the plans and preparations for the naval and amphibious phases of the invasion of JAPAN.

(5) The Commander-in-Chief, United States Pacific Fleet is charged with making plans and preparations for the naval and amphibious phases of the invasion of JAPAN. He cooperates with the Commander-in-Chief, United States Army Forces in the Pacific on the plans and preparations for the campaign in JAPAN.

(6) The Commanding General, Twentieth Air Force cooperates with the Commander-in-Chief, United States Army Forces in the Pacific and with the Commander-in-Chief, United States Pacific Fleet in the preparation of plans connected with the invasion of JAPAN.

(7) The Commander-in-Chief, United States Army Forces in the Pacific is charged with the primary responsibility for the conduct of the operation

—1—

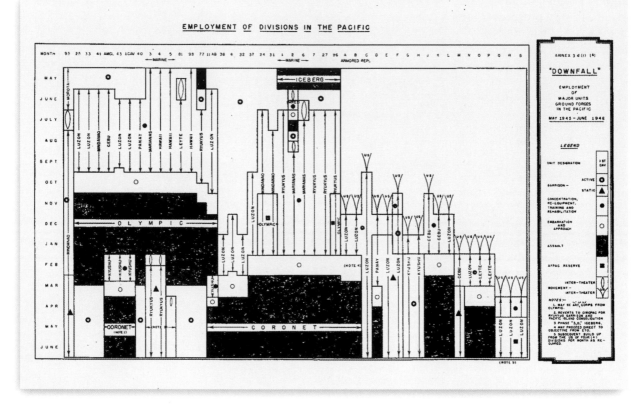

With such a long lead-time, it was possible for Operation Downfall to be planned in great detail. The deployments required were worked out in all but exhaustive detail to avoid any unforeseen complications.

Kyushu-based and carrier-based fighters, properly coordinated, should be capable of furnishing adequate fighter support for CORONET.

From the Joint Planners' assessment of Kyushu's viability as the operation's bridgehead.

almost half a million men, with another 610,000 tons of supplies. Though the planners don't seem to have got into that sort of detail, both operations were going to call for naval back-up on a massive scale: hundreds of warships were likely to be involved. MacArthur, buoyant as he was in his view about the prospects for success, had conceded that 'Logistic considerations present the most difficult problem.'

Having established themselves securely – and got their 686,000 tons of equipment and supplies ashore – these armies would promptly begin pushing north. Halfway up the island, an upland

ridge running east–west provided a natural barrier of sorts. Here they would take up their positions to guard against any Japanese counter-attack. This was to be their frontier for the time being.

Whatever it Takes
For Coronet in particular, the tone, crisply military to start with, seems to lose conviction as the plan unfolds. It ends up calling for 'such operations ... as may be necessary to terminate organized resistance in the Japanese archipelago'. Some degree of vagueness was unavoidable, to be fair. There was no reasonable expectation of Japanese surrender to round

things off neatly: on the contrary, there was every prospect that the enemy would fight on to the death. The Allies fully expected to win now, but could not predict with any confidence when they would do so. Instead, at some unspecified – and perhaps imperceptible – point, the balance of the conflict would tip and all-out assault become something more like a process of mopping up. This final phase might go on for months or even years.

Japan too was preparing to do whatever it might take – to postpone the inevitable, at least. The country was in a parlous state: Operation Starvation was working – almost literally: people were estimated to be receiving about a third of their daily nutritional requirements; rice was rationed to tiny amounts, and fish just about unknown. Industry too had been starved – of raw materials – severely compromising the country's ability to go on waging war; the writing was all too clearly on the wall.

A Last Stand

While some spoke in ringing tones of the way the millions would be mobilized to fight the foreigners with bamboo spears, most shook their heads sadly at such rhetoric. Unfortunately for them, the deluded ones were among the military elite – still very much in power in Japan. All set for a heroic last stand, they stepped up their preparations: army, navy and air force planes; trainers and reconnaissance aircraft – anything that would fly

– were adapted for use as flying bombs for *kamikaze* pilots. By July, 8000 had been made available, with a further 2500 promised for September. Japan would at least go down in a blaze of glory.

Into this desperate – and increasingly unreal – atmosphere, 'Little Boy' fell, a bolt from the blue; no more expected by most Americans than it had been by the Japanese. It was Japan that bore the impact, of course, as two cities were wholly flattened. More than 130,000 people were killed, and hundreds of thousands more received the radiation doses that

were to eat away at them over the years that followed. Advocates of the atom bomb say that it saved lives – especially American ones. As far as it goes, that claim can hardly be denied, however debatable the ethical concerns. Operation Downfall had come within an ace of going forward: it's impossible to imagine how so difficult an assault on such a scale could have been carried out without commensurate casualties.

The atom bombs at Hiroshima and (seen here) Nagasaki rendered Downfall an irrelevance.

BIBLIOGRAPHY

Allen, Louis, *Burma: The Longest War, 1941–45* (New York: St Martin's Press, 1985).

Allen, Thomas B. and Polmar, Norman, *Codename Downfall: The Secret Plan to Invade Japan* (London: Headline, 1995).

Ambrose, Stephen E., *The Supreme Commander: The War Years of Dwight D. Eisenhower* (New York: Doubleday, 1970).

Beevor, Antony, *D-Day: The Battle for Normandy* (London: Viking, 2009).

Bradley, John H., Griess, Thomas E. and Dice, Jack W., *The Second World War: Asia and the Pacific* (Garden City Park, NY: Square One, 2002).

Breuer, William B., *Secret Weapons of World War II* (New York: Wiley, 2000).

Chant, Christopher, *The Encyclopedia of Codenames of World War II* (London: Routledge & Kegan Paul, 1985).

Churchill, Winston S., *The Second World War, Volume I: The Gathering Storm* (London: Penguin Classics, 2005).

———, *The Second World War, Volume II: Their Finest Hour* (London: Penguin Classics, 2005).

———, *The Second World War, Volume III: The Grand Alliance* (London: Penguin Classics, 2005).

———, *The Second World War, Volume IV: The Hinge of Fate* (London: Penguin Classics, 2005).

———, *The Second World War, Volume V: Closing the Ring* (London: Penguin Classics, 2005).

———, *The Second World War, Volume VI: Triumph and Tragedy* (London: Penguin Classics, 2005).

Duffy, James P., *Target America: Hitler's Plan to Attack the United States* (Westport, CT: Greenwood, 2004).

Eisenhower, Dwight D., *Crusade in Europe* (London: Heinemann, 1948).

Este, Carlo d', *Warlord: Churchill at War, 1874–1945* (London: Allen Lane, 2009).

Evans, Martin Marix, *Invasion: Operation Sea Lion, 1940* (Harlow: Longman, 2004).

Evans, Richard J., *The Third Reich at War: How the Nazis Led Germany from Conquest to Disaster* (London: Allen Lane, 2008).

Fisk, Robert, *In Time of War: Ireland, Ulster and the Price of Neutrality, 1939–45* (London: Deutsch, 1983).

Fleming, Peter, *Operation Sea Lion: An Account of the German Preparations and the British Counter-Measures* (New York: Simon & Schuster, 1957).

Gilmour, John, *Sweden, the Swastika and Stalin: The Swedish Experience in the Second World War* (Edinburgh: Edinburgh University Press, 2010).

Girvin, Brian, *The Emergency: Neutral Ireland 1939–45* (Basingstoke: Macmillan, 2006).

Gray, Tony, *The Lost Years: Emergency in Ireland, 1939–45* (London: Little, Brown, 1997).

Grunden, Walter E., *Secret Weapons and World War II: Japan in the Shadow of Big Science* (Lawrence, KS: University of Kansas Press, 2005).

Hastings, Max, *Finest Years: Churchill as Warlord, 1940–45* (London: HarperPress, 2009).

———, *Overlord: D-Day and the Battle for Normandy* (New York: Simon & Schuster, 1984).

Hogg, Ian V., *German Secret Weapons of the Second World War* (Barnsley: Greenhill, 1998).

Holmes, Richard, *Churchill's Bunker: The Secret Headquarters at the Heart of Britain's Victory* (London: Profile, 2009).

Kershaw, Ian, *Hitler, 1936–45: Nemesis* (London: Allen Lane, 2000)

Kershaw, Robert, *War Without Garlands: Operation Barbarossa 1941–1942* (London: Ian Allan, 2008).

Kimball, Warren, *Forged in War: Churchill, Roosevelt and the Second World War* (London: HarperCollins, 1997).

Marston, Daniel, *The Pacific War Companion: From Pearl Harbor to Hiroshima* (Oxford: Osprey, 2007).

Nalty, Bernard C., *War in the Pacific: Pearl Harbor to Tokyo Bay* (Norman, OK: University of Oklahoma Press, 1999).

Overy, Richard, *1939: Countdown to War* (London: Allen Lane, 2009).r

Rankin, Nicholas, *Churchill's Wizards: The British Genius for Deception 1914–1945* (London: Faber, 2008).

Roberts, Andrew, *The Storm of War: A New History of the Second World War* (London: Allen Lane, 2009).

Sakaida, Henry, Nila, Gary and Takaki, Koji, *I-400: Japan's Secret Air Strike Submarine – Objective*

Panama Canal (Crowborough, E. Sussex: Hikoki, 2005).

Stevens, Andrew, *The Secret History of World War II: The Wartime Cables and Correspondence Between Stalin, Roosevelt and Churchill* (Old Saybrook, CT: Konecky and Konecky, 2008).

Webster, Donovan, *The Burma Road: The Epic History of the China-Burma-India Theater in World War II* (New York: Farrar Straus Giroux, 2003).

Wills, Clair, *That Neutral Island: A Cultural History of Ireland During the Second World War* (London: Faber, 2007).

INDEX

PICTURE CREDITS

SPANISH MINISTER, ANGORA, REPORTS MR. EARLE'S

APPOINTMENT TO GERMANY.

No: 139197

Date: 9th December, 1944.

From: Spanish Minister, ANGORA.

To: Minister for Foreign Affairs, MADRID.

No: 315-6.

Date: 5th December, 1944.

[Cable: I B].

Mr. EARLE, the personal delegate of the President of the UNITED STATES, tells me that he has received instructions to be ready to undertake a journey to GERMANY, without details as to the place or method of getting there. It is his wish to go to AMERICA first for a thorough exchange of views.

He informed me that the anti-Russian party in the UNITED STATES grows daily, and that the President himself bears in mind the Soviet danger even if ---- necessities of the war force him to temporize and not dispense with help that is so valuable for the moment. A French doctor who knows de GAULLE personally said that this progressive ---- [? was due to him].

The informer who, a month in advance, told him [EARLE] about the V.1. raids, now assures him that V.3 aimed at AMERICA will come into operation